Omar!

Omar!

My Life On and Off the Field

Omar Vizquel
with Bob Dyer

GRAY & COMPANY, PUBLISHERS
CLEVELAND

GRAY & COMPANY, PUBLISHERS
1588 E. 40th St.
Cleveland, Ohio 44103
www.grayco.com

Library of Congress Cataloging-in-Publication Data
Vizquel, Omar.
Omar! / Omar Vizquel with Bob Dyer.
p. cm.
1. Vizquel, Omar. 2. Baseball players—United States—
Biography. I.
Dyer, Bob. II. Title.
GV865.V59 A3 2002
796.357'092—dc21 2002001278

ISBN 1-886228-55-8 hc
ISBN 1-886228-59-0 sc

Printed in the United States of America

10 9 8 7 6 5 4 3 2

To my mom, whose love and dedication for her kids made us what we are. To my dad, who practiced baseball with us even when he came home from work exhausted. To my sister, Gabriela, whose smile and love for kids makes me remember how beautiful life is every day. To my brother, Carlos, who has always been next to me, on the field and off, my best double-play partner ever. To my wife, Nicole, who stuck with me through the hard times, who gave me the best gift I ever got—my son—and whose understanding of life and appreciation for another culture is part of her beauty. And to my son, Nico, who is the brightest light in my life and the reason I understand, finally, why my parents took such great care of me when I was young.

— O.V.

To my late mother, Jane, who passed along her love of language and ideas. To my father, Big Al, who taught me the importance of doing things right. To my brother, Bill, the Comeback Kid. To my older daughter, Carrie, my beautiful ball of fire, and my younger daughter, Kimmie, my sensitive, inquisitive gem. And to my wonderful wife, Becky, who has ridden right beside me on the roller coaster for nearly a quarter-century, hardly ever barfing on my shoes.

— B.D.

Contents

"Baseball is a dance of the heart and the spirit. The best players have that dance inside of them."

—Brian Souers, Akron Aeros batboy

(*Akron Beacon Journal,* July 2, 1997)

Omar!

Game Seven

THE MOST IMPORTANT ASSET for a major league baseball player is not speed or size or strength. It's mental toughness.

I pride myself on being strong between the ears. At this level of competition, 80 percent of the game is psychological. Unless you have absolute faith in your ability, it doesn't matter how fast you can run or how hard you can throw.

That's why I was worried when I went to the mound in the ninth inning of Game Seven of the 1997 World Series.

Jose Mesa, our ace relief pitcher, had come in to try to protect a one-run lead. All we had to do was get three outs and we'd win the ultimate title. The eyes of the world were focused on every move we made. Unfortunately, Jose's own eyes were vacant. Completely empty. Nobody home. You could almost see right through him.

Jose's first pitch bounced five feet in front of the plate. And, as every Cleveland Indians fan knows, things got worse from there.

I can still remember everything about that day. After all, fewer than 1,000 people in the history of baseball have ever played in the seventh game of a World Series. Bob Feller never did. Lou Boudreau never did. Mark McGwire never did. Neither have Barry Bonds, Sammy Sosa, or Ken Griffey, Jr. Including the spectacular Yankees-Diamondbacks match-up of 2001, the Series has gone the distance only 34 times in 97 seasons.

Every little kid who ever put on a baseball glove has fantasized about playing in the seventh game of a World Series. That dream only gets more intense when you get to the big leagues.

Some suggested that winning a World Series against the Florida Marlins would have cheapened the dream. After all, the Marlins had only been in existence for five years. Their owners had gone out and bought most of their top players. The franchise didn't have the rich tradition of the Dodgers or Cardinals or Braves, according to the argument.

Baloney. Any team that makes it to the World Series is a powerhouse. Just to get there, you have to win consistently for seven months. Then you must win a short, intense division series, followed by a longer, more intense league championship series. So I didn't care who we played. I just wanted that championship ring. I wanted it so badly, in fact, that I would have surrendered several years of my life to get it. Seriously.

I still would.

The only thing that took the edge off the Series for me, from a purely personal perspective, was that all the hitting overshadowed the defense. In the first five games, the winning team scored 7, 6, 14, 10, and 8 runs. The third game, which we won 14-11, was the second-highest-scoring game in World Series history. With all that bashing going on, good defensive plays were overlooked. And, if I do say so myself, I played great defense in that Series. I have all the games on videotape, and I still watch them.

Except for that deadly ninth inning, the '97 Series was absolutely awesome, both on and off the field.

The first two games and the last two were in Florida, and we had a great time. We stayed at the Sheraton Bal Harbour resort, about halfway between Miami and Fort Lauderdale, right on the Atlantic Ocean. It had a 10-acre swimming pool that wound around through tropical gardens. There was a huge slide, too. I don't get too excited about fancy hotels anymore, because the team stays in nice places all the time. But this was special. This was like being on a vacation with all of my teammates.

Between the first two games, we had a day off. Our manager,

Mike Hargrove, warned us to stay inside, to take it easy and not risk a freak injury. He told us, "Don't beat yourself up in the sun. Don't be riding jet skis." So, naturally, we all went to the beach, caught some rays, and rode jet skis.

During the regular season, wives were permitted to travel with the team only on a couple of designated road trips. But during the playoffs, wives and fiancees were welcomed. That made the post-season even more festive. My wife, Nicole, was there, along with our son, Nico. My mom and dad came, too, and everybody had a blast.

The wives loved the place for another reason: right across the street was a big collection of upscale stores like Gucci, Cartier, and Versace. Ballplayers' wives are pretty good at shopping.

As the Series moved forward, though, the mood got more and more serious. By the morning of Game Seven, nobody even dreamed of going jetskiing. We barely even left the hotel.

Things had been going so well throughout the month of October that our dream seemed to be right there waiting for us, one short bus ride away in the humid Florida night. We had been living a charmed life.

In the Division Series against the Yankees, we were a mere four outs away from being eliminated, then charged back to tie Game Four on Sandy Alomar's homer and win it on my infield single.

We worked more miracles in another heart-stopping series against Baltimore. That series included the best *bad* play I ever made. After splitting the first two games in Baltimore, we returned to Cleveland and staged a five-hour marathon. In the bottom of the 12th, with the score tied, I was at the plate with Marquis Grissom on third. The count went to two balls and one strike. I looked down to third-base coach Jeff Newman, who gave me the signal for a suicide squeeze. I had been warned in the dugout that we might try to squeeze home the winning run, so I wasn't entirely shocked. But, believe me, my heart was pumping.

They don't call it a "suicide squeeze" for nothing. You either put your bat on the ball or you die, because your coaches and your teammates will kill you—especially the defenseless guy charging in from third.

Well, I committed suicide. Missed the pitch completely. Randy Myers threw a good slider low in the strike zone, and I just couldn't get any wood on it. Fortunately, the Orioles' catcher, Lenny Webster, made an even worse play. He couldn't catch the ball. It wasn't a tough pitch to handle; he simply got excited and muffed it. The ball rolled just far enough away that Grissom was able to score. And I lived to play another day.

After a full month of incredible moments like that, we believed we were on the brink of our greatest moment ever. One thing was certain: Game Seven would be the biggest pressure-cooker any of us had ever jumped into.

The atmosphere started growing tense almost as soon as Game Six ended. I had made a really nice play in that game, diving to my right to stop a shot by the Marlins' Charles Johnson and throwing him out at first, so a lot of people were coming by the hotel room to congratulate me. But I really wasn't listening to what they were saying, because I was so focused on getting ready for the next game. It was a weird feeling.

I was thinking a lot about Bill Buckner, the first baseman who made the infamous error that helped cost the Red Sox the 1986 World Series. I can't imagine how he felt. The only thing going through my mind was being tough enough not to let something like that happen to me. I certainly didn't think it would. I live for pressure situations. In my first 55 playoff games, I made only one error.

For a shortstop, the ultimate pressure situation is one out, bases loaded, and the ball hit right at you. The spectacular plays are easier, in a way, because you're just reacting and nobody expects you to make them. The heat comes when you get a routine double-play ball.

It was funny: during the season, Jose Mesa's locker was right next to mine. He was having a great year. A couple of times during the summer, I told him, "I wanna see how tough you are in the seventh game of the World Series with the bases loaded and one out."

Sandy Alomar's locker was on the other side of me that year, and I said the same thing to him: "I want to see how tough you are when everything is on the line." Not everybody can handle it.

Mental toughness has been the story of my baseball career— and my life. I could go 0-for-40 and still believe I can bounce back and bring my average up. It doesn't matter how bad things are in the short run. It's a long season—and a long life.

A lot of guys have natural ability, but they freak out if they make a bad play or go into a slump, and their careers don't last. Others guys have solid careers but never reach their full potential. Take Manny Ramirez, for example. Manny is a great, great talent, one of the best hitters in the game. But he could be an even better ballplayer if he knew how to use his mind.

I heard an interview once with the American League's best pitcher, Pedro Martinez. He says he looks at the hitter's eyes during his first at-bat, and if he sees the hitter is frustrated, he *owns* that guy for the rest of the night.

It's a mind game.

And the biggest mind game of all is Game Seven. After 35 spring training games, 162 regular season games, and as many as 18 playoff games, everything comes down to a single game. One game out of 216 that will make or break the season.

When I finally got to bed the night before Game Seven, I had a lot of trouble falling asleep. I was playing the upcoming game in my imagination, going over every possible scenario. But when I finally drifted off, I slept like a bear in the winter. I think I logged 10 hours.

After I got up, I went with my family to a Cuban restaurant near the hotel for some Latin food. I got my usual—steak, rice and beans, and plantains. The food was good, but the meal wasn't very peaceful. Several fans recognized me and made a big commotion.

The biggest commotion was only a couple of hours away.

Pro Player Stadium doesn't have the ambiance of Jacobs Field. It's really a football stadium, and many of the seats are miles from home plate. But I was enjoying the place. This was a celebration. No matter who won, a big party was going to erupt.

You could gauge the importance of the event by the atmosphere in the locker room. For much of the previous eight months, our clubhouse was a fun, easygoing place, with guys constantly cracking jokes and playing music. But on October 26, 1997, as we pulled on our blue jerseys and gray pants, nobody said much of anything. The guys were in their own worlds. We didn't even crank up the music.

During batting practice, the field was a zoo. You see all kinds of people at the World Series who don't usually request media credentials—like Larry "Bud" Melman and Biff Henderson from the David Letterman show (Henderson interviewed our Bip Roberts—Biff, meet Bip. Bip, Biff.) Nearly 900 credentials were issued to organizations from all over the world, including Venezuela.

Salsa music was booming throughout the ballpark, the temperature was 80 degrees, and 67,204 people were in the stands.

What a contrast to the weather in Cleveland, where during Game Four the temperature was 38 degrees, the wind chill was 18, and everybody in the park was wearing heavy gloves and parkas. What are the odds of setting the record for the coldest game in World Series history, followed four days later by one of the warmest games in World Series history?

So we were prepared for anything.

We also had learned—the hard way—not to take anything for granted. In 1996, we won our division by 14 games and fully expected to wind up in our second straight World Series. But the underdog Orioles knocked us out in four games, the crowning blow coming off the bat of Robbie Alomar. I can still see that ball flying into the centerfield stands on a late, sunny afternoon at Jacobs Field.

By the time you get to the World Series, you have spent an entire month living on the edge. The fans love it. They tell me the playoff games are so exciting they get the chills. Well, me, too. It's every bit as exciting down on the field. Even though you have a job to do, even though you have to concentrate like crazy, you still feel the same emotions as the people in Row Z.

In fact, I even get the chills when somebody on the *other* team does something great. You feel good for the person who made the play, even though it hurt your own team. That's because you know how much pressure is on the guy. The average fan has no idea how hard it is to be in those situations, where everyone is looking at you and expecting you to excel. I admire every good play that anyone makes.

Mike Hargrove's decision to pick Jaret Wright as the Game Seven starting pitcher was controversial. Wright was just a kid, a 21-year-old who had begun the season on the mound in Canal Park in Akron, home of the Double-A Aeros. Hargrove could have chosen Charles Nagy, a 7-year veteran who had won 89 major league games and pitched in two All-Star games.

One school of thought says you go with people who have been there before. Another school says you go with the hot hand. Wright had been on fire. During the playoffs, he was 3-0. Hargrove went for the hot hand. I thought it was the right decision. When a guy has been going that well, you can't take the ball away from him.

Wright came through. Inning after inning, he mowed the Marlins down. Through six, he didn't surrender a run. Then he tired in the seventh, and the Marlins finally scored to pull within one. The drama continued to build.

I had pictured all of this so clearly in my mind's eye that when the game actually arrived, I felt like I was having a dream. I'd already been there. And when the scoreboard said 2-1 going into the bottom of the ninth, I thought I was going to find myself in the exact situation I had talked about all year. I thought I was going to be the guy to get the ball with the bases loaded and one out.

But Jose Mesa wasn't following the script.

Not long after I looked into his vacant eyes, he blew the save and the Marlins tied the game at two. And instead of that routine grounder coming to me, it went two innings later to second baseman Tony Fernandez—who booted it.

Tony is a great fielder. He owns four Gold Gloves, which are given annually to the best defender at each position. But in the bottom of the 11th inning, with a man on first, he got an easy ground ball that went right under his glove. I couldn't believe it.

The winning run scored a short time later when Edgar Renteria poked the ball up the middle past Nagy. The instant he hit it, I knew the game was over. It wasn't hit that hard, but nobody could get anywhere near it.

I felt horrible that we lost, but I felt even worse for Tony. The first thing I did after the game was go over and give him a hug. He is such a hard worker and such a good man. The only thing he cares about is winning.

Tony went through a really rough time when he was an Indian, trying to get some playing time from the manager. Hargrove just didn't trust him from the very beginning. Tony would start one game, then sit for three. But he hung in there and made some crucial plays for us. We wouldn't have gotten to Miami if he hadn't hit a homer in Game Six of the Baltimore series. Heck, he drove in both of our runs in that last World Series game, too.

After the loss, every person in our clubhouse felt as if his gut had been carved out. In 1995, when we lost to the Atlanta Braves in six games, most of the guys weren't too upset. We were thrilled just to have been in a World Series. But this time, we fully expected to get a championship ring. This time, we knew the drill. This time, we knew how to win—or thought we did.

If you felt lousy watching us lose Game Seven on television, imagine how we felt down on that field, nine months after the start of spring training, coming so close and not getting there.

For a long time after the game I sat alone in the dugout, watching the Marlins running around the field as Queen's *We Are the Champions* boomed from the P.A. system and the fans roared and showered the field with confetti. The Marlins' manager, Jim Leyland, ran a victory lap. It was painful to watch, but I wanted to know what the feeling was like for a team that had just won the whole thing in dramatic fashion.

On the bus back to the hotel, guys were crying. I was so upset I couldn't even talk.

I blew off the big rally held in downtown Cleveland two days after the game. I had a great time at the first rally, after the 1995 Series, but this was different. This time we should have won. Two outs away. I could taste it. Now I just couldn't bear the thought of going out in public and talking about that game.

I had to get away.

Way away.

I TOOK NICOLE AND NICO back to our off-season home in Seattle, then rounded up three pals and headed to the most remote spot I could think of: the Amazon jungle.

Venezuela is a beautiful country. My hometown, Caracas, is near the coast and 3,300 feet above sea level, so the climate is ideal—between 70 and 90 degrees all year. When you head southeast into the interior, though, you know you aren't far from the equator. You run into some of the heaviest jungle you can imagine. It's part of the largest unbroken expanse of tropical rain forest on the planet.

My destination was Angel Falls—the highest waterfall in the world.

Angel Falls is in such a remote location that it was unknown to Venezuelans until the 1930s. It's named after an American, Jimmy Angel, a bush pilot and adventurer who crash-landed near there while searching for gold. The falls are 3,212 feet high—about 20 times higher than Niagara Falls—with one uninterrupted drop of 2,648 feet—more than half a mile! I had wanted to see it for years. I'd seen so many beautiful pictures of it and heard so many great things from people who had been there.

The water rushes off the top of what we call a *tepuyi*, a huge rock formation that shoots almost straight up from the floor of the forest. These mesas are scattered about the Guiana High-lands, soaring above the greenery like giant anvils.

You don't stumble upon Angel Falls by accident. You need a plane, a canoe, and hiking boots. And a little bit of nerve, too.

I rounded up my best pal, Carlos Lopez, whom I've known since we played ball together at age nine; my brother, Carlos Vizquel, who is four years younger than us; and my cousin Cesar Ayala, seven years younger.

The four of us took off in a small plane and landed at a remote airstrip, where we were picked up in a 10-person Jeep and driven to some little cottages. When I walked into my room, the first thing I saw was a big lizard crawling up the wall. Clearly, I was no longer at the Bal Harbour Sheraton.

The room had nothing but a little bed and bathroom. No TV. No radio. The top quarter of the walls were made of concrete block with holes in the center and no screens. Lizards and all kinds of weird bugs had the run of the place.

Then things got really primitive.

To reach the falls, we headed up the river, against the current, in a narrow canoe. Two people were jammed side by side in this thing that was about 3 feet wide and 25 feet long. Its tiny, 45-horsepower engine was taxed to the limit. The guide steered around rocks and dodged other stuff and, after a while, we were certain the canoe was going to tip over and we'd be swept away by the current before anybody figured out what had happened.

At one point, we saw the other extreme: the water level dropped so far that we had to get out and push.

Finally, after moving upstream past a long series of waterfalls, we followed the curve of the river around this huge rock and—wham!—there it was.

Angel Falls is just humongous. I knew it was going to be big, but I was stunned at its size. I've never experienced anything like it. We couldn't even see the top when we first got there because it was surrounded by haze. So we stopped and ate breakfast. Several hours later, the clouds cleared out and we could make out the top.

To get a closer look, we walked for an hour through rocks and vines. We were having a great time, singing salsa music, swinging on vines and yelling like Tarzan, and just goofing around.

Halfway up the waterfall, there's a big, flat rock where people take pictures. Once we got there, the top of the falls cleared up completely and the scene was just magnificent.

This trip was just what I needed. As we hiked through the woods and saw the wild animals and tropical birds, I had a real sense of peace. It was a place where you could forget about everything else in the world and focus on what's right in front of you. The jungle offered a dose of quiet and isolation after the chaos of the playoffs. I was able to get away from baseball completely. With one notable exception.

There we were, slogging through the wilds of Venezuela, 2,700 miles from Cleveland, and I saw another group of adventurers, one of whom was wearing—I kid you not—a Cleveland Indians cap. I turned to my buddies and said, "Oh my God! Let's run away from these people." We were able to dodge them. We had to, because I still couldn't talk about that last game.

Our own guide was pretty funny. He was acting like a big science expert. We were constantly making fun of him because he was going way beyond what we needed to know. He'd explain the Latin name of the plant we were looking at and all this other stuff that nobody would remember 15 seconds later. We made so much fun of the guy that eventually he gave up. By the end of the trip, he would just say, "Okay, whatever you see, that's what it is."

But we actually learned a lot. We learned how the pre–Hispanic Indians lived during their time in South America. They used all sorts of wild plants for medicine. They had plants for pain and plants for burns. We tasted a few that numbed our tongues.

Most of what we put in our mouths was a pleasant surprise. Before the trip, I worried about the kind of food we might get. Food is very important to me. I love to cook, something I picked up from my mother. I was expecting the worst in the jungle, but this stuff was the best food I ever tasted. It was all natural. They grow the tomatoes and onions right there. They raise their own chickens. They have cabbage salads and all this unusual stuff. Oh, man, was it good! Even the breakfasts were great. We were served a little piece of bread that looked like a horn. It was like a croissant, but hard, with filling inside.

My friends kept wondering whether something in the jungle would make a meal out of *us*. All kinds of interesting creatures are roaming around in there, including jaguars. My country also ranks second or third in terms of poisonous snakes.

The jungle doesn't give you much room for error. When you're driving into it, all you can see is the road straight ahead of you. You feel as if you're at the point of no return. One time, we were driving along and ran over something. I asked the guide to go back, and we took a look. It was a coral snake—black, white, and red, one of the deadliest snakes in the world.

My only real letdown was not seeing an anaconda. The guide said the giant snakes usually come out at night and stay hidden during the day because of the heat. He showed me a couple of big snakes, but no anacondas.

My buddy Carlos kept asking me, "How come you're not afraid with all the danger that's out here?" I'd say, "Well, I'm just here to have fun. My mind is open. Whatever happens, happens. The World Series is over, so I can get hurt a little now and it won't be a big deal."

Besides, when I'm with a group of people, I'm pretty sure I won't be the slowest one in the group. If anybody is going to get eaten, it ain't gonna be me. You think I move fast when Frank Thomas is bearing down on me? Imagine how fast I could move with a coral snake ready to chomp on my butt.

CHAPTER 2
Making Mischief

MY EARLIEST MEMORY has nothing to do with baseball. It dates back to 1969, when I was two years old. That's when I decided it might be fun to put our cat in the washing machine.

Although I'm not a big fan of cats today, I don't think I was trying to be mean. Washing the cat just seemed like a logical thing to do at the time. For some reason, my mom didn't agree. Neither did the cat, who somehow managed to survive.

My life of crime soon escalated. About six months later, my mother and I went to visit a friend of hers who was wealthy. The woman had this really beautiful piece of glass she had bought in India. I pushed if off the table and broke it. I was not particularly popular at home after that. I remember lots of wringing of hands about where to find the money to reimburse the woman.

Fortunately, I never got into any serious trouble—never stole a car or robbed a gas station or anything like that. I just did dumb, obnoxious kid stuff. We'd get eggs and bury them in the dirt until they turned rotten. Then we'd dig them up, carry them to our third-floor apartment, and drop them on people walking by.

We had big mango trees outside our building. We'd climb up in the trees and shake the branches, and mangos would drop on people's heads. I thought that was hilarious. One time, though, the laugh was on me: I shook a branch and a swarm of bees flew out of a nest and stung me all over.

My childhood nickname was "Earthquake," because I never

stopped. I was always running around, jumping, or throwing something.

At school, I'd get in trouble for being a smart ass. A teacher would be writing something on the blackboard and I'd have a little piece of chalk and throw it against the board, then act like I didn't know who did it. I'd hide people's books. I'd sneak out of the building. I'd try to talk other kids into skipping class. I was the ringleader, the type of kid parents warn their own kids to stay away from.

Except none of the parents knew what a rotten kid I was. I was Eddie Haskell, the character in the old *Leave It To Beaver* TV show. Around the other kids' parents, I was very polite. But as soon as the adults were out of earshot, I'd turn to my friends and try to talk them into doing all kinds of bad stuff. Meanwhile, their parents were telling my parents what a saint I was and how they wanted me to come visit more often.

ALTHOUGH I NEVER OPENED A BOOK, I got passing grades. I have an excellent memory, and when I heard something in class, I'd retain it. So I suppose I was just bored.

The one teacher who held my attention was Raymond Grion, who taught Venezuelan history. I loved his classes, mainly because he acted like a normal person. He didn't intimidate you like other teachers. He talked like you'd talk to a friend, just telling great stories.

I rode a bus to school, but it didn't go all the way there. It stopped about three blocks from the building—and those last three blocks were straight uphill. I hated that walk. So pretty soon I figured out a way to hitch a ride. Every day a truck drove up the hill, very slowly, carrying big bottles of drinking water. I would grab onto the bottles and ride along.

The first time I did it, the driver yelled at me. He said it was too dangerous, and he was probably right. But I kept at it, and by the second week he gave up and let me hang on every day.

In Venezuela, we attend school through 11th grade. I graduated on time from Francisco Espejo High, at age 16, but the last three years were pretty rocky. I did some pretty rotten stuff. One day, on the playground, a history teacher that I hated was walking by. I threw a baseball at her and drilled her right in the back. She couldn't figure out where it came from, because there were about 200 kids all running in different directions.

Eventually, I pushed things too far.

Whenever you'd misbehave, the school would give you what was called a "negative note." After 10 notes, they'd call your parents. After 15, they'd throw you out of the school. Well, I got 10, and the principal called my parents. We had big discussions about how I had to behave and this and that. But I didn't listen very well, and pretty soon I had 15 notes. I was booted out for three days.

Dad is a pretty mellow guy. He didn't punish me much. Mom was the disciplinarian. She used to whack me with a belt. As I started getting older and stronger, the belt didn't have much effect. By the time I was 14 or 15, I was pretty strong. I had been lifting weights and doing a lot of ring exercises, and she couldn't hit me hard enough to get my attention. She'd bring out the belt and I would laugh. So she tried another technique: digging her nails into my arms. You can still see scars on the inside of both of my forearms, near the elbows, where her nails dug in. These days, somebody would probably phone the authorities and try to have her arrested. But Mom wasn't abusive. She was just trying to teach me right from wrong.

The worst punishment I ever suffered came when I was 13— and nobody laid a finger on me. I made the ultimate mistake of smarting off to my baseball coach. When he told me to pick up the balls after practice, I grabbed my crotch and said, "Pick up *these* balls." The coach didn't seem too upset, but my dad was at the field and heard me. He was livid. He was so mad he gave me the ultimate punishment, the one thing he knew would get my attention: he made me sit out the next baseball game.

That was a killer, far worse than any whipping. Baseball was my life. This was the only time my dad ever really disciplined me, but he certainly knew how to get through to me.

My parents' approach to raising me must have worked, because I have never gotten into any major trouble. I don't smoke. I don't do drugs. I don't drink. Well, sometimes when we go out to eat I'll have one beer or one glass of wine with my meal. But that's it. I value my brain and my body too much to mess them up.

MY FATHER WAS AN ELECTRICIAN and my mother was a homemaker. We were considered middle class. But middle class in Venezuela is certainly not the same as middle class in America. While I was growing up, we had one black-and-white TV. We didn't get a color set until I was 11 or 12. And I didn't have my own stereo until then, either.

Until I was 10, we lived in a big housing complex, called a block. We stayed on the third of four floors in Bloques C, Santa Eduugis. Our building housed 32 families. And there were six blocks just like that, one in front of the other.

With 35 or 40 kids in each block, I never had any trouble finding people to goof around with. We did classic little-kid stuff, like connecting cups with string between two blocks so we could talk to each other.

We didn't have the nicely manicured fields that you see in most American suburbs. We'd play ball in the street with a broom handle and a wad of tape. When a car would come, we'd all clear the street; the instant it passed, we'd all run back.

We got to be creative with our eating habits, too. We would go real late at night to a place where they sold rotisserie chicken—*hallaquitas*, we call them. They look kind of like a tamale. We'd show up at about one in the morning with the equivalent of two dollars and the guy would give us tons of food because he was closing.

When I was 10, we moved to the eastern part of Caracas to a building that was much nicer. This one was crowded, too, but not nearly as crowded as the first one. We were at Avenue Boulevard del Catetal Res Adriania, in Apt. 6-A. We were on the sixth of 10 floors, and again I shared a bedroom with my brother. We had lots of fun there, too. We'd go up to the room and mess around and, of course, drop things onto the people below. You probably wouldn't have wanted me for a neighbor in those days.

We'd get into a brawl every now and then, too. Sometimes a person would hit a friend of mine, and I'd punch the person and run away. I was one of the fastest guys around, so I didn't get caught much.

Sometimes in my neighborhood we'd have brawls in the street just for entertainment. A big group of people would stand in a circle running around and hitting each other. They called it "The Bomb." We'd get six or seven guys in the middle and hold hands and spin as hard as we could, then let each other go. We'd fly into people and knock them over. It was great fun.

MOST AMERICANS SEEM TO KNOW very little about my homeland. Some of them can't even tell you what continent Venezuela is on. For the record, it's right on top of South America, immediately east of Columbia, north of Brazil, and west of Guyana.

My hometown, Caracas, is the biggest city and the nation's capital. Caracas is like a small version of New York City: overcrowded, a lot of buildings, a lot of cars, a lot of pollution, and on-the-go 24 hours a day.

About two-thirds of the people in my country are *mestizo,* or mixed, the most common mix being American Indian combined with Spanish or Portuguese. Christopher Columbus "discovered" Venezuela on his third voyage. However, seeing as how the first cultures appeared there in 14,000 B.C., he was not exactly going where no man had gone before.

Columbus's men unilaterally awarded themselves the naming rights. On their second trip, a year later, they saw Indian houses on stilts around the edge of Lake Maracaibo and were reminded of the city of Venice, Italy. So they called the country Venezuela, or "Little Venice."

About half a million Indians lived there in those days. They were isolated from the better-known cultures of the rest of Central and South America, and were relatively primitive.

After Columbus, Venezuela remained a peaceful colony of Spain until the 1820s, when Simon Bolivar riled up the masses and tossed out the Spanish. Since then, much of the country's history has been marked by dictatorships and military rule. The first democracy wasn't installed until 1958. During the next quarter-century, five presidents were constitutionally elected.

In 1993, a military faction attempted a coup. It failed, and one of the ringleaders, Hugo Chavez, was jailed for two years. But he emerged as a folk hero because he was perceived as a champion of the poor. Thanks to a faltering economy, he was elected president soon after his release from jail. And in 1999, his leftist coalition pushed through a new constitution that eliminated the old congress and supreme court. He was overwhelmingly reelected to a six-year term in the summer of 2000.

A lot of Americans don't remember that Venezuela was a co-founder of OPEC, the group that helped create long lines at U.S. gas stations in the 1970s. Venezuela rode the oil boom until the 1980s, when the recession really hurt oil prices. Our economy didn't show many signs of life again until 1997—and it's still a long way from where it should be.

The coup attempt took place when Nicole and I were back in Caracas in the off season. I thought it was great entertainment. I was outside shooting the action with my video camera while the planes were flying over, blowing things up. Nicole wasn't nearly as amused; she hid under the bed. Well, not literally. But only because we were in a hotel, and you couldn't get under the bed. So she hid next to it. I don't think she has felt quite the same about Venezuela since then.

Still, I wouldn't trade my homeland for anything. Same goes for my childhood. I had several milestone experiences in Caracas—not the least of which were my first girlfriend and my first kiss. One of the biggest disappointments of my life took place there, too. When I was 13, my first girlfriend, Mary, broke up with me. I was devastated. People don't think that kind of thing means much to a kid of 13, but I remember it vividly. I may not have known much about real love, but I knew Mary broke my heart.

Other than that, I was a happy kid—and we were the happiest family around. We didn't worry about money. We didn't even talk about it much. We owned very few material things but took good care of everything we had. We learned to be creative, too. We'd build our own toys from stuff we found. I'd take pieces of wood and the wheels from an old skateboard and build my own car to slide down the hills.

In some ways, I was just like an American teenager. I had a poster of Davey Concepcion, the Cincinnati Reds shortstop, right above my bed. He was my hero, a fellow Venezuelan. I also had posters of Led Zeppelin, Van Halen, and Kiss. I was a real Kiss fanatic; I thought Gene Simmons and Ace Frehley were the coolest dudes around.

After I got my stereo, I would put my speakers right next to the window and crank up the volume, because I wanted the whole neighborhood to hear what I was listening to. Some of the neighbors weren't too thrilled; they'd throw stuff at my window and yell at me to turn it down. My dad would say, "Why do you listen to that music? You don't even understand what the hell they're saying!" He was right. I didn't know any English at the time, so I had no idea what these guys were singing about. I just knew I liked it. I sang away at the top of my lungs.

Years later, when I learned English, I was astounded by some of the lyrics. Even now I'll go on the Internet and download old rock songs with English lyrics to find out what I was listening to.

My buddies and I went to lots of concerts. At the time, a big rock movement was underway in Venezuela—not just American groups, but Spanish rock and roll. They'd stage all these mini-concerts with three or four bands at a time. Ten or 15 guys from the neighborhood would go together, all looking the same: long hair, cutoff sleeves, wristbands with spikes on them. We thought we were the baddest guys in Venezuela.

To get from the bus stop to the concert site, we'd have to walk through a street filled with transvestites and other weird people. After one concert, a guy I was with started taunting a transvestite, and the transvestite pulled out a gun and shot three times into the air. We were terrified. We probably set a world record for the 100-meter dash.

I was a real piece of work in those days. I had an old snakeskin that I'd use as a headband. One time, I was caught on camera wearing it in a rock video. My father said, "What the hell are you doing in there?" I said, "Dad, this is awesome! It's a rock 'n' roll thing!"

My bedroom had colored lights in each corner—one orange, one red, one green, and one blue. We'd steal the lightbulbs from the gardens of other buildings. My dad helped me wire up the sockets on the ceiling.

My hair was really long. I know that's hard to believe today, because I don't have much left under my baseball cap. But in those days, my hair was so long that it fell in my eyes. That's one of the reasons I used the snakeskin. Right up until the time I signed a professional baseball contract, my hair was down to my shoulders.

My hair started falling out at age 28. I think it had something to do with sweating inside a baseball cap nine months a year. Of course, other guys do that, too, and it doesn't seem to affect them. So I don't know. All I really know is that it bums me out. I'd still wear my hair long if I had any.

MY PARENTS SOMEHOW SURVIVED my musical head-banging stage. To tell you the truth, I think my family could work its way through just about anything. We've always been incredibly close.

My father, Omar Santos, is in his early sixties. My mother, Eucaris, is in her late fifties. They come to the States about once a year. Sometimes they'll go to spring training; other times they'll show up in the summer.

I am so fortunate to have those people for parents. They set a great example for me. Many of my friends didn't have that situation and, as a result, I had friends who got into drugs and alcohol. Although I never turned my back on those wayward friends, I never tried to do what they were doing because I had my parents to guide me.

Sometimes, being from a good family isn't enough. I have 23 cousins, and I'm close to all of them. But one cousin shot himself to death when I was eight; he was a drug addict. Another cousin is dying of AIDS in Brazil.

It certainly helps to have the right foundation, though. I grew up in a religious home. We were Catholic, like 96 percent of Venezuelans. We didn't go to church every Sunday, but we went often. I was baptized and received my first communion.

Everybody in my family calls me Kike (pronounced KEY-kay). That's a common nickname in our culture for Enrique, which is my middle name.

Because I was the oldest kid, I had to help Mom out around the house. I learned how to do all kinds of things—wash dishes, clean the floors, fold clothes. If you look at my closet today, it's impeccable. I fold all my shirts and pants, my socks, even my underwear. Everything has to be perfect.

Between the ages of 6 and 10, I spent a lot of time with my mom's mom. She used to be a teacher, so she'd come up with practice homework assignments. She was a tough woman. Her husband committed suicide before I was born, and she had to raise nine kids all by herself.

My father's mother wasn't tough at all. She was so laid-back that we'd tease her all the time. My father's father was fun, too. He was my godfather. When I was 15, he died suddenly. We were lying in bed watching a horse race when he had a heart attack.

Mom has always run the show. She's outgoing, likes to party, and makes all the plans for the weekend. My father just goes with the flow. I take after him, because I'm usually pretty easygoing, too.

I've already mentioned my brother, Carlos, who visited Angel Falls with me. I also have a sister, Gabriela, who was born 14 years after I was. She was spoiled rotten, because she was so much younger and the only girl. But Gabby turned out fine. She earned her teaching degree and is working with preschoolers in Venezuela.

I brought Carlos to Seattle when I was playing baseball there. He learned English and met a girl who was a graphic designer. He became so intrigued by graphic design that he earned a degree in the subject. But then he went back home and started dating a girl who was a seamstress. They started making bathing suits, and the suits started selling like crazy. Sales were so hot that he forgot about graphic design and plunged into the swimsuit business. It's going so well that they are expanding into Brazil and Italy.

Like most brothers, we had our share of fights. One time when he was running in the house I threw a pillow at him and tripped him, and he smashed into a table and had to get five stitches on his forehead. He still has the scar.

I have my share of scars, too. Once he threw a spoon at me and opened up a big cut on my nose. It was Christmastime. I was playing with a toy gun that gave off little sparks and I got too close to him and burned a hole in his new shirt. He was mad. As we were sitting at the table, I was laughing at him because of the hole and he threw the spoon and drilled me right between the eyes.

Another time we were racing around outside my grand-mother's house when I ran into an open window. The windows were low to the ground, and I was running around like a wild man with a bunch of other kids and just didn't see it. The glass fell on my hand and opened up a big cut. Fortunately, it didn't hit a tendon. One of the kids took me to his house, where his mom, a former nurse, sewed me up. She needed five stitches to close the gap.

Another time I got five stitches on the inside of the same hand—and additional stitches on my leg—because I was doing a baseball slide outside my house and hit a broken bottle.

And that's not counting the time I was little when I fell out of my stroller and needed stitches on the side of my eye.

For most of my youth, I was the undisputed ruler among the siblings. But when Carlos turned 18, I began to watch my step. By then he was taller than I was and about 20 pounds heavier. All of a sudden I became a lot more interested in the concept of brotherly love.

CHAPTER 3

Carrasquel to Aparicio to Concepcion

MY FIRST BASEBALL GLOVE was not exactly the best piece of gear in the history of sporting goods. It wasn't leather. It didn't even have a player's name in it. It was a blue vinyl job made by Tamanaco, the only glove maker in Venezuela. But that little glove was a gift from heaven. My dad gave it to me when I was eight years old, the first year I was allowed to play in an organized league.

You need to understand that baseball is king in Venezuela. In most Latin countries, baseball is popular, but soccer is even more popular. Not so in Venezuela, where soccer is a distant second. Baseball was introduced by American oilmen early in the 20th century, and it caught on faster than a refinery blaze.

The sport has never been more popular. Like basketball in America, baseball is seen by poor Venezuelan teens as a way to trade poverty for Porsches. My country is overrun with scouts from America looking for a scrawny kid with the potential to become the next superstar. Many major league teams have established baseball academies in Central and South America.

When I started, though, baseball was just a whole lot of fun.

My dad was a good amateur player. Although he was better at soccer than baseball, he was a solid shortstop with good hands and good speed. He took me to his games and was delighted that

I was interested. He loves the sport. Today, in his sixties, he's still playing softball.

But the main reason Dad encouraged me to play ball was to give me an outlet for my energy. I could never sit still. (Much like my own son, Nico, today.) I was always bouncing around, causing a ruckus and bothering people. Dad wanted me to burn off some of that energy on the diamond.

My dad is a really quiet guy. He always tried to show us the right way to play the game, but other than that he didn't talk much. He'd just sit and watch. And he never bragged about his kids. Other parents would go on and on and on about their kids, talking about how they were going to grow up to be stars. I'm so happy I didn't have one of those fathers. If I had, I probably would have been so turned off that I would have gone in another direction.

When I was little, I thought I wanted to be a catcher. I loved wearing the gear. I'd wear it all over the place. The night before a Saturday or Sunday game, I would actually sleep in my uniform. I just couldn't wait to get to the field. I wanted to play ball all day long. I'd even skip school to try to find a game. My brother was different. You had to beg Carlos to go to the games.

At first I wore No. 17, because Dad wanted me to. I didn't really know why at the time, but later I figured out that No. 17 was worn by Chico Carrasquel, the slick-fielding Venezuelan shortstop who played for the White Sox in the early '50s (and was later parodied on *Saturday Night Live* by Garrett Morris, who would answer every question with, "Beisbol been bery, bery good to me").

And in the early days, I was a second baseman. I wanted to play there. But my coach moved me to shortstop, because it was harder and he thought I was good enough to handle it.

Shortstop is the position of choice in Venezuela. The first great Venezuelan player in America was Luis Aparicio, who took over for Carrasquel in the mid-'50s, won nine Gold Gloves, and wound up in the Baseball Hall of Fame. Then came Dave Concepcion, the shortstop for Cincinnati's "Big Red Machine" in the 1970s.

Carrasquel and Aparicio were before my time. But I knew all about Concepcion. He wore No. 13, so pretty soon I wore No. 13. I still do, a quarter-century later. Americans sometimes ask me whether I worry about wearing an "unlucky" number. No wonder. In America, people are so superstitious that they skip No. 13 when numbering the floors of a hotel. But in Venezuela, we don't think that way. It's just another number. Actually, it's better. It's the number of Concepcion—and Vizquel.

My ultimate goal as a kid was to become Davey Concepcion or Tony Armas or Manny Trillo, fellow countrymen who were playing in the big leagues. Today Venezuelan kids want to grow up to be Andres Galarraga or Omar Vizquel. That's a big responsibility, and I take it seriously.

The first glove I owned with a player's name on it was, oddly enough, that of a pitcher. I had a Jim Palmer autograph model made by Rawlings, the people who custom-make my gloves today. I didn't care that he was a pitcher. I just knew he was a star for the Baltimore Orioles. I bought an Orioles hat, and I wore it constantly for five years. My friends kept telling me that if I didn't take off that hat once in a while, my hair would fall out. I guess I should have listened.

I always took good care of my glove. Although I never used oil on it, like American kids did, I'd put a softball inside it, wrap a sock around it, and put it under my bed. I'm not sure what I thought that was going to do, but all my friends were doing it, so I figured I'd better do it, too.

Still, I was different from most of my friends. You'd ask them what they wanted to be when they grew up, and they'd say "fireman" or "doctor" or something else traditional. I'd always say "baseball player." They'd laugh at me.

The first time I genuinely thought I might have a chance to achieve my dream came when I was 12. In the middle of a game, I made a tough stop between short and third and threw out the runner. A man stood up in the stands and said, "Who are the parents of this kid?" My dad didn't say anything, but my mom raised her hand. "That kid is awesome," the man said. "I've watched a lot of baseball, but I've never seen that kind of play at this level. That boy is going to make it to the big leagues some day."

I wasn't sure about that. But the idea of playing in *Las Grandes Ligas* certainly sounded good.

Every athlete should have a fallback position. You never know what might happen, so you have to be prepared if your dream falls short.

During my last year of high school, I applied for admission to a school that trained people to work in customs. That kind of work always intrigued me. I don't know why. Nobody in my family did anything like that. Maybe it's just because I love boats and harbors. I always loved the area near Caracas—La Guaira—where all the ships come in. I always wanted to be there doing something. If not there, maybe working customs at the airport, with all the comings and goings and the fast pace.

My baseball fervor was fed by some early successes. They held big tournaments for even the youngest kids. At age nine, I was chosen from 150 hopefuls to be the starting shortstop for the state of Caracas in the nationals. I played in that tournament three times, and once, when I was 10, we won the championship. What an incredible experience. Six thousand people were in the stands watching, plus the TV, radio, and newspaper people. I never expected to see my picture in the newspaper, much less get interviewed by all these grownups. As a reward for winning the title, the president of the country flew us to Miami with one member of our family. We were summoned to the Venezuelan White House to pick up the tickets.

Running around Miami at the age of 10 was a blast. I got lost for a while with my friend Carlos Hernandez (who would play 10 years in the National League) and one of our coaches. The three of us headed out to some stores and couldn't find our way back. None of us spoke English. My mom was waiting at the hotel, growing increasingly frantic. She was looking for me all over the place. Then she called the police. They couldn't find us, either. Finally, about 6 P.M., we were able to make our way back.

In spite of that experience, I've never been afraid to get out and explore new cities. Even when my English wasn't so hot, I'd hit the streets to see what each new city had to offer.

That championship youth team had some real talent. In addition to Hernandez and myself, we had another player who would eventually make it to the bigs for a time—Luis Vasquez of the Red Sox.

When I got a little older, one of the guys I played with in Caracas was Andres Galarraga, who became a star with the Atlanta Braves and, later, with Texas. An amazing hitter, he is known as "The Big Cat." Well, he wasn't very catlike when I first knew him. In fact, he was a nerd—an honest-to-goodness, hopeless, bigtime nerd. The guy belonged in *Dexter's Laboratory*. He played outfield in those days, rather than first base, and he was worthless. He was chunky and had really thick glasses, and every time somebody hit a fly ball it would go right over his head. But I liked him a lot and got to know him really well. We would hang out later on, go to nightclubs and restaurants.

As a young teen, the most dramatic thing I could imagine was the Venezuelan nationals. The nationals are held every two years. Two years after our championship, we made it to the finals again. This time we didn't win, but I was named the "champion infielder" and the "champion base stealer," the equivalent of a Most Valuable Player award in specific categories.

I was pretty good at other sports, too. The guy who taught physical education at school called me "the Iron Horse" because I won a marathon and played almost every sport there was. I played a lot of soccer, usually as a striker, and scored plenty of goals. I was the third-highest scorer on my school's basketball team and, despite my lack of height, a good rebounder. I couldn't dunk, but I could touch the rim. I played some volleyball, too.

My true love, though, remained baseball. I couldn't get enough.

Because we didn't have any decent fields, we had to improvise. I knew a guy who sold bottles of soda at ballgames. He would open the bottles for his customers, and the caps would drop into a big box below him. He saved those caps for me, and every weekend I'd go collect them. I'd take them home and play games with my dad and my brother. One of us would throw the caps and another would try to hit them with a broomstick. The caps would slide and move like a curveball, so you really had to pay attention. We played all the time in the parking lot next to our building. The neighbors would scream at us because we'd play early in the morning and you could hear the pinging of the caps all over the place.

In those days, I swung strictly right-handed. If I'd try to swing left-handed, my dad would yell at me.

Even when we got to use an actual baseball field, the conditions were terrible. Dad used to take Carlos and me to a place about five minutes away from our home that was nothing but rocks and bushes. He'd hit ground balls to us, and the ball would take terrible hops. But I was never afraid of it. I got in the habit of getting in front of the ball and blocking it like a catcher.

It's hard to convey just how bad these fields were. One day, shortly before a game started, I was playing around with some teammates and I stepped on a piece of glass. It flipped inside my baseball shoe and gave me a big cut on the ankle. I didn't want to miss the game, so I just put some paper inside my sock to try to hold down the bleeding. When the game started, I hit a double and scored. My second time up, I hit another double. But my sock was soaking wet. I told my coach, "Hey, man, I'm sorry, but I'm bleeding." I had to go to my mom and dad to get permission to leave the game. When I took my shoe off, my mom almost fainted. I needed four stitches to close the cut.

But the fields of my youth helped turn me into the fielder I am today. People make a big deal about me using my bare hand to field grounders, but I've been doing that since I was a kid. The ball would take a bad hop, and I'd reach up and grab it. Today, stopping a ball that's traveling 70 MPH is routine. I don't do it to show off; I do it only when I have to save a fraction of a second to catch a speedy runner.

I also played a childhood game that, in retrospect, I really think helped my fielding. Two of us would play. I'd stand about 15 feet away from a wall and throw a ball against it and try to make the other guy miss. If he caught it, he'd wing it back against the wall and try to make me miss. We played it all the time. I played it by myself, too. I'd fire the ball again and again, throwing and catching, as fast as I could, until it became a cardiovascular workout, too.

By the time I was 16 and the coaches were talking about moving your feet and getting in front of the ball, I was already doing it.

Footwork is underrated. People always talk about good hands, but footwork is what gets you to the ball. If you don't get into a position to catch it, it doesn't matter how good your hands are. I tell kids that the most important thing in playing defense is your feet.

As far back as I can remember, I was the best player on my teams. At age 13, the coach made me a captain. I took it seriously. But other guys on the team would tease me about it. They started calling me "Captain" all the time, and it made me mad.

When I was 16, I had my first encounter with the legendary Carrasquel. At that point he was the manager for the Caracas team. They were holding a workout, teaching young players how to field, and I caught his eye. He told me, "Hey, kid, you've got good hands." That was the highest praise in the world. I will never forget him saying that. That was like Eddie Van Halen saying you play a mean guitar, or Picasso saying you really know your way around the canvas.

It was not unusual for the Venezuelan professional teams to show up and stage a big workout, trying to uncover hot prospects. At the first camp I went to, the man running it said I was too small. He told me I'd be better off becoming a jockey.

To narrow down the prospects, they had all the third basemen and shortstops stand on the third-base line and throw to first as hard as they could. I threw the ball fine, but the man told me I was too short. He wanted to cut me. I think there were so many kids that he was just trying to weed some out as fast as he could. The only thing that saved me was that I had been recommended by one of the owner's friends. So they kept me for another three days and I got a chance to show what I could do.

A Red Sox scout saw me at a workout and liked my ability but said I was too young. He was afraid that if I went to the States at that age and was cut, I would have a hard time getting another chance when I was older. He wanted me to be patient.

But I wasn't particularly interested in being patient. And when a scout for Seattle came around about three months later and wanted to sign me right away, I jumped at the chance. We met with my parents that very day.

His name was Marty Martinez. He was Cuban, so he spoke Spanish. And when he went to my house, he raved to my parents about the opportunities I would have in America. I was thrilled. My mom and dad turned to me and said, "Is this really what you want to do?" I said yes, and they said, "Okay, go for it." I signed immediately.

It wasn't exactly a blockbuster contract. Here were the terms:
– $2,500 signing bonus
– $500 bonus if I made it to Double-A ball for 90 days
– $500 if I made it to Triple-A for 90 days
– $1,000 if I made it to the big leagues

I never did get the $500 for being in Triple-A, because I didn't stay there long enough. But I guess I've been reasonably well compensated since then.

Marty Martinez was an important person in my life. He really believed in me. Though not as much as he believed in another guy he signed at the same time. Marty was infatuated with this other kid, but the other kid got into trouble with the law and never went anywhere. The hotter prospect was caught stealing at the mall. He took perfume and socks and other weird stuff that you'd never even dream of taking if you thought it might end your baseball career. He was with two other guys, and both of them got caught stealing, too. I almost went with those guys that day. They asked me to go, but I was tired and said I was just going to stay at the hotel and get some rest. Best move I ever made.

The key to the whole thing was my parents. They have always been extremely supportive. They knew that letting me head off to America at the age of 17 was a big risk. They knew I had never even lived away from home in Venezuela, much less in a foreign country. But they knew that baseball meant the world to me, and they thought I should give it a shot.

They were in the minority in our family. My mother's big brothers were urging her not to let me go. They said I was too young. They said I should get a college education. They said I had no chance of getting to the major leagues.

Now they're calling me for tickets.

CHAPTER 4

Coming to America

TODAY IT SOUNDS LIKE A COMEDY SHOW. But it didn't seem very funny at the time.

I'm 17 years old.

I don't speak a word of English.

I arrive in America and they send me to Butte, Montana.

Now, if you've never been to Butte, Montana, you should know that in Butte, Montana, a person from Great Falls, Montana, is considered a foreigner. The population is about 25,000—and 24,000 of them wear cowboy hats and chew tobacco.

I was scared to death. Imagine being a 17-year-old Venezuelan who speaks nothing but Spanish.

Actually, I did know some English. I knew one word: eggs.

Every time I went to a restaurant, I'd say, "Eggs." They'd ask me how I'd like my eggs cooked, and I'd reply, "Eggs." They'd ask me if I wanted anything with them, and I'd say, "Eggs." My cholesterol level must have been 400.

Soon I started going to Denny's because their menus had pictures. I could just point at the food I wanted. Denny's quickly became part of my daily routine.

Fortunately, my misery had company. I came to America with two other Venezuelans. The manager of the Butte team, Manny Estrada, picked us up at the airport and drove us to a house where seven other Latin players were living. When I walked in, everybody was speaking Spanish, which made me feel right at home. A big party was under way. I thought it was a special welcoming party for us, but I soon discovered it was just a typical day. The place was one big, nonstop party.

The three of us from Venezuela took it easy in the partying department. We knew what we were there for, and it wasn't parties. It was baseball. The two other Venezuelan kids were from good families, too, and they kept their priorities straight.

Even with the other Latin players around, life was tough. I got really homesick. Sometimes I would just sit and cry. But I never thought about leaving. Not once. I knew that making the adjustment to America was part of my job. And I was willing to pay almost any price to reach my goal.

Most of the other guys in that house were gone within three years. In fact, I was the only one in the whole house to make it as far as Double-A ball.

Living there was a great experience, though. It was like a little United Nations. We had Venezuelans, a Mexican, a Puerto Rican, a Dominican . . . guys from all over.

In retrospect, the most important person I met in Butte was a girl from Mexico. I was coming out of a movie theater one day and heard her speaking Spanish. Believe me, you don't hear many people speaking Spanish in Butte. So we struck up a conversation, and soon we were hanging out constantly. She knew how to speak English and would teach me a little every day. I can't even remember her name. But she helped me so much. She even did my laundry. She was a saint.

Another way I picked up the language was watching television. But when I first turned it on, I was stunned to see the cartoons I grew up with. I always assumed that Batman and Robin, Superman, Tom and Jerry, Bugs Bunny, Popeye and all those guys were Venezuelan. I turned on the TV and they were all speaking English! I couldn't believe it.

Even *Sesame Street* was American. I almost died when I found out *Sesame Street* wasn't made in Venezuela. All the names were different, and a lot of them didn't translate from one language to the other. For example, in Venezuela, Kermit the Frog was Rana Reneé. Bert and Ernie were Beto and Enrique.

The show that got me most was *Zorro*. I swore Zorro was Venezuelan. When I turned on the TV and he was speaking English, I wanted to fall on his sword.

STILL, LEARNING ENGLISH seemed like a worthwhile thing to do, and I kept my ears open. Some people just have an affinity for languages, and I guess I'm one of them. Although I speak only English and Spanish, I can understand bits and pieces of Italian, French, even Japanese.

When I was on a two-week goodwill tour of Japan with a group of major leaguers in November of 2000, I was able to pick up many Japanese phrases. After one week, I was ordering my food in Japanese. And not just eggs.

Learning a new language isn't that hard if you really pay attention to what people are saying. I'm surprised at how many of my Latin teammates have no interest in learning English. I have tried to help a number of them, but they're kind of shy. They feel embarrassed when one grown man is trying to teach another grown man how to write. I don't have a problem with that. I wish they wouldn't, either. It would be an honor for me to help Bartolo Colon, Ricardo Rincon, or Einar Diaz learn to write English or just to talk a little better. But they're simply not interested.

I think part of the reason for the lack of enthusiasm is that a lot of Latin players who come to the States are so proud of who they are and so proud of their countries that they don't want to absorb too much of the American culture. After each season they go back and live a happy life in their native country, and they figure that's good enough.

To a degree, I can understand that. I was a little bit like that at the beginning. In the minor leagues, I'd be on a plane back to Venezuela one millisecond after the season ended. But then I started getting more involved with the community and felt the need to develop my language skills.

Of course, a lot of Americans don't make much effort to accli-
mate themselves to foreign countries, either. Everywhere you
guys go you expect everyone to speak English. When they don't,
you have a hard time coping.

The U.S. players in Japan couldn't even leave the hotel without
a guide. For me, Japan was easy. I'd just hop into a taxi and get out
wherever the cab driver wanted to drop me. I was used to wandering around in a strange environment.

LANGUAGE WAS ONLY ONE of the big adjustments I had to make in
Butte. The biggest difference between our countries is actually
the food. We eat a lot of spicy stuff and a lot of rice, and Butte
didn't have much of either. My body took a while to adjust.

After living in the U.S. for nearly 20 years now, the biggest difference I notice between my people and Americans is that Latin
people tend to be warmer. They hug more, they hold hands more,
they kiss more. They show their feelings. We're not as locked into
rules, either. We tend to be more freewheeling—which can be
good and bad.

Americans have a lot more freedom at an early age, though. In
Venezuela, most kids continue to live with their parents until they
reach age 20. Even when you're 21 or 22, you still have to ask your
parents for permission to go to a party. But there I was in America, at age 17, essentially on my own. It's no wonder some Latin
players just pack up and go home. But most of them are willing to
gut it out because baseball is so important to them.

Latin players have become increasingly important to baseball
as well. From 1978 to 1998, the percentage of foreign-born Latin
players in the major leagues grew from 7 to 17 percent. Part of the
reason is that baseball executives have found that whenever they
import a Latin player, the guy can really play. We know the game.
We work hard at it. So a lot of teams started going to Latin America to find more talent.

Another reason Latinos are more prominent in baseball is because kids in the United States have a million other things they

can do. It's easy to lose focus on baseball when you have all the crazy sports you have here, things like skateboarding and motocross.

In Venezuela, it's only baseball, basketball, and soccer—or the informal stuff played on the street. In my country, you can't just go out and buy a new toy every week.

Latin players tend to band together in the States and help each other. Some people call it *La Cadena*—Spanish for The Chain. It's nothing formal; just a feeling of obligation the older players have toward the younger ones.

Unfortunately, most Venezuelan kids who come to the States don't make it to the majors. I was lucky. For every player like me, there are 100 other talented kids who, for one reason or another, don't make the grade. Maybe they get hurt. Maybe they're lacking a key ingredient, either mental or physical. Maybe they just have bad luck; sometimes you have to be with the right organization at the right time and be seen by the right people. And sometimes they just can't handle the culture shock.

When you can't read a menu or the lease for an apartment, and you can't understand your teammates, you're starting with two strikes against you. The language barrier hurts in more subtle ways, too. I can remember walking out of a hotel in my baseball uniform and having the other players laugh at me. They were all in their street clothes. I had misunderstood the instructions and thought we were supposed to dress in our rooms, not at the ballpark.

Scouts sign hundreds of Latin players every year, most of whom immediately quit school. They come to America believing they will be superstars. When they're cut, their lives are over. They have no baseball career and no education.

Current major league rules prohibit a scout from signing anyone under the age of 16, but each year dozens of top kids are signed under the table. In 1999, commissioner Bud Selig fined the Atlanta Braves $100,000 for signing a 15-year-old Dominican shortstop and banned the Braves from recruiting in the Dominican Republic for six months. The Los Angeles Dodgers got a similar penalty for signing an underage third baseman.

It's an old story. In fact, a generation ago, so many kids were being taken advantage of that, in 1981, a concerned American formed a group called the Latin Athletes Education Fund. Based in San Jose, California, the group brings poor but promising ballplayers to the States for college and athletic training.

The head honcho is a man named Don Odermann, a California stockbroker who used to be a Peace Corps worker. When he was stationed with the Corps in Puerto Rico, he watched, disgusted, as one slimy scout after another swooped down on 15-year-old athletes and signed them to dirt-cheap contracts. Odermann wanted to send a message to Latin players: if you want to keep playing baseball, you don't have to quit school and go straight to the minors. Instead, you can go to college, get a solid education, play ball against decent athletes, and get acclimated to life in the States. And if you sign a pro contract after that, all the better.

One of the trustees of the group is Juan Escalante, a childhood friend of mine. Juan is a product of the program. He was a good ballplayer, but not quite good enough. Because he got a college education through the Latin Athletes Education Fund, though, he was well prepared for life after baseball. Today he is a successful international businessman in New Castle, Indiana.

The group is relatively small, with about a dozen players enrolled in college each year, many from the Dominican Republic. But it's an effective program and one of my favorite charities. These people do good work, and I like to support them.

IN BUTTE, in 1984, I was barely supporting myself.

Playing in the Class A Pioneer League with a bunch of other rookies, I hit .311 in 45 at-bats. My fielding was only so-so, but not because the fields were bad. The minor league diamonds were as smooth as bowling alleys compared to the ones I was used to.

The travel certainly took some getting used to, though. In the minors, a 10- or 12-hour bus ride is not uncommon. You're packed in tighter than a fat lady in Spandex, and sleep is tough to come by. Because I'm so short, I would sometimes climb up in the luggage racks above the seats and take a nap up there.

I learned one other important lesson while living in Montana: don't chew tobacco.

About 90 percent of the people in Butte seem to chew, some of them for breakfast. So I figured I'd give it a try. I put in a wad and lost my mind. I got dizzy and wanted to throw up. It was awful. The next day, I got to thinking that maybe snuff would work better. So I tried a dip of Copenhagen. That was even worse. I didn't know how some of those guys I saw with big wads did it, but I was certain from that day forward that I'd never have a bulge in *my* cheek.

The year after Butte, 1985, I was off to Bellingham, Washington, home of another Class A team, this time for a full season.

During spring training that year, they took us to see a big league practice. I remember it well, because that day was the first time I knew in my heart that I was good enough to play in the majors. When I saw them taking ground balls and swinging the bat, I realized they were normal human beings and that I could hold my own if I just played my game.

That year also marked the first time I lived with Americans. I stayed in a house with a host family and a teammate. The other player was a catcher from Boston, Bob Gibree, a guy taken in the third round of the draft, and he got to live upstairs in the nice part of the house. I lived in the basement with the rats. But I didn't care. I had all my pictures of my girlfriend from back home and did just fine in my little basement. The best part was that my American hosts gave me lots of leftovers, so I didn't have to worry about cooking.

The next year, 1986, it was off to Wausau, Wisconsin and my first stay east of the Mississippi. Fortunately, I went there with an outfielder named Jorge Uribe, who was from a poor town in Venezuela. We had a blast. We did everything together and became really close. We lived in a little apartment three blocks from the ballpark. I loved that guy. Still do. He was so down to earth. Having come from a little town, he was humble and naïve and innocent. It was just fun being around him.

Two floors up were two other Venezuelans. We'd all go shopping together and cook together. That was the first year I was essentially living on my own. And that was the first time I really felt like a man.

But in one game that year, I felt anything but manly.

A runner was on first when the batter hit me a grounder. I got ready to scoop it up and start the double play, but the ball took a funny hop and hit me under the chin. When I looked down for the ball, I couldn't find it. The second baseman was yelling at me, but at first I couldn't understand him. Finally I figured out that he was telling me to look inside my shirt. The top button of my jersey was unbuttoned, and the ball had hit my chin and rolled down my front. I didn't know what to do. The runner on first was already at second, and he figured that, with the ball inside my jersey, he might as well head for third. So I ran over and hugged him. I figured that would count as a tag.

The umpire didn't know what to do. Nobody had ever seen anything like that before. Eventually, the ump decided to call the runner safe. The other guy ended up on second.

In spite of adventures like that, I continued to work my way up through the organization.

In 1987, it was Salinas, of the California League. Again I lived with Americans. That was a good experience, because the Collins family helped me understand a lot more about American living. My English really started coming around.

The Collinses were a strong Christian family who prayed before they ate. I used to take care of their yard, a big lot on a corner.

One of my good buddies in Salinas was Jeff Nelson, who went on to pitch for the Mariners in the early '90s, played for those great Yankee teams of the late '90s, and came back to the Mariners as a free agent in 2001. His wedding reception was held at the Collinses' house.

Jeff is 6-foot-8, 235 pounds. When we hung out together, we were a sight.

Jeff is a great guy, but in those days he couldn't throw a strike. He'd drive me crazy. Every time he would pitch, I'd get mad. His wife, Colette, would sit there and yell, "Come on, Big Daddy, throw strikes!" Apparently, he never heard her, or any of the other people who were urging him to get the ball over the plate. He was a starter in those days, but he usually didn't last more than a few innings because he'd throw 50 pitches every inning.

The man was a riot, though. His wedding was at the ballpark in Salinas. He and Colette took their vows right on the mound in front of one of the biggest crowds of the year. Instead of walking down the aisle, they walked under a row of raised baseball bats. After the ceremony, a limo drove in from behind the fence to chauffeur them away.

I didn't ride in any limos that year, but I did get my first car. When I returned to Caracas after the season, I bought a used Renault Fuego. Paid 250,000 B's for it. That's bolivars, Venezuela's basic monetary unit. In American dollars, the price wasn't quite as impressive, maybe $2,200.

The following year, 1988, Jeff and I were on the move again. His next stop: San Bernardino, California. My next stop: Vermont.

Burlington, Vermont, to be precise, home of the Double-A Vermont Mariners. The M's had just signed an agreement with the team, which had previously been a farm club for the Cincinnati Reds.

I was reunited with my good buddy, Jorge Uribe. We lived in a little place above a restaurant called the Rusty Scupper. It had one bathroom, a tiny kitchen, and two beds in the same room. Every night when we came back from the game we could smell clam chowder and steaks cooking downstairs.

When it was too hot to sleep, we'd open a window that was right next to a fire escape. Anybody could have climbed right in during the night. But we never worried. In fact, I never worried at all about my safety in the minors. I never realized how dangerous life can be away from the field. Minor leaguers are just like any other high-school-age kids: you think you're invulnerable. It's amazing any teenager survives.

Our ballpark, Centennial Field, was on the campus of the University of Vermont, and early in the season we had to fight for field time with the college team. The city used the field, too.

The distance between the locker room and the diamond seemed like 20 miles. The stadium was old, and not exactly plush. The place operated like a drive-in movie. Fans arriving for a game would buy their tickets while they were still in their car, then drive around looking for a place to park. Parking was a nightmare, because there just wasn't enough room. The road behind the field was dirt, so it was either a dust bowl or a water-soaked quagmire. The bathrooms were port-a-pots. And, in a stadium that seated 5,000 people, there was exactly one concession stand.

The neighbors hated the place. They hated the traffic and the glare from the lights during night games. The houses were incredibly close to the field—so close that foul balls sometimes nailed them.

Still, I loved playing in Vermont. We had some talent on that team—Ken Griffey, Jr. was with us for a little while—and we played well, winding up with a record of 79-60, good for second place.

I had so much fun there. I met a woman there named Sonya who let me borrow her stereo. To this day, I talk to her. My wife knows her, too. She lives near Boston, and when we play the Red Sox, I always leave tickets for her. Jorge used to date Sonya's best friend, and the four of us would go out together.

Those were the days. Life was so simple. I didn't have much and didn't want much. I was only making $800 a month, plus a whopping $12-per-day meal money on the road, but in some ways I was never happier. Jorge and I went half-and-half on all the expenses and never felt we were missing a thing. As a matter of fact, late that season, when the Mariners told me they were moving me up to Triple-A, I started crying.

Only one month remained in the 1988 season, and I fully expected to stay right where I was, just as I had during all my other minor league seasons. The Vermont team was doing great, and I was perfectly happy.

A lot of people pray for a call-up, but I was devastated. We were in New Britain, Connecticut, playing against the Red Sox affiliate, when the manager took me to his office and told me to pack for Calgary, Canada.

I called my mother and said, "I don't want to go. I want to stay right here and finish the year." She said, "No, you can't do that! You have to go to Triple-A!" So I headed off to Calgary, leaving Jorge and my other friends behind.

Calgary was awful. I hated the place from day one. Froze to death. The food was terrible. I had to live in a little hotel all by myself. I realize this means I will never be offered a job by the Calgary Chamber of Commerce, but everything about Calgary bummed me out. Maybe things seemed worse than they were because I had been so happy in Vermont. That last month seemed to take a year. As soon as the final pitch was thrown, I was on a plane back to Venezuela.

EVERY WINTER THROUGH 1995, I would come home and play in Venezuela's professional league. My first couple of years with the Leonese of Caracas were rough, because I was one of the youngest players on the team. People called me Menudo, after the teenage pop singing group (the one Ricky Martin was in). I did look young. There I was, 18, 19 years old, playing with guys who were in Triple-A and the big leagues, guys like Tony Armas and Bo Diaz.

The Venezuelan winter league has eight teams that play from mid-October through the end of January. The biggest rivalry, by far, is between my old Caracas team and the Navegantes de Magallanes, from the city of Valencia. Those games make Yankees–Red Sox games seem tame.

Eventually, after a decade, I had to give up playing winter ball at home, because it just wore me down too much. We played 60 games in the winter. By the time I got through spring training in the States and then into the regular season grind, I was wearing out by July, and I'd be terrible in August and September. At first I was afraid that the fans in Venezuela would be mad at me, maybe think I suddenly considered myself too good to play there. But I think they understand that my body just couldn't handle it.

In some ways, playing in Venezuela is tougher on your head than playing in the American minor leagues. The fans in Venezuela are outrageous. When they get on a guy, they don't stop. One fan always stood behind home plate and screamed the entire game. He hated our second baseman and rode him constantly.

The abuse wasn't just verbal. The ballpark sold lots of oranges. They were sold in halves, and the fans would peel them, eat the inside, and save the peels for when somebody made an error. They threw beer at you, too. The outfielders had to wear batting helmets to protect themselves from the junk that would fly out of the stands.

We quickly learned to expect that kind of behavior. That's why there was so much pressure every time you took the field to avoid making an error. Maybe that's why I enjoy playing in Yankee Stadium and Fenway Park. Those fans get on you pretty good, too. When I was in Fenway one time, I took off my batting helmet in the on-deck circle and rubbed my bald patch, and some guy yelled, "Hey, Vizquel, you building a runway up there?"

Made me feel right at home.

CHAPTER 5

Seattle

I F NOTHING ELSE, the Seattle Kingdome was unique.

From the air, it looked like a giant mushroom that had sprung up from the banks of Puget Sound. From the inside, it looked like a big green carpet laid out in somebody's unfinished basement.

When the Kingdome opened in 1977, the whole region was excited. Not only was Seattle getting a new stadium, the city was back in the major leagues after an absence of eight years.

Seattle's professional baseball history dates all the way back to 1890, when the Seattle Reds played in the Class-C Pacific Northwest League. But in all those years, fans got only one big-league season—1969, when the expansion Seattle Pilots stumbled to a 64-98 record in old Sicks' Stadium. The team was broke and moved to Milwaukee, where they became the Brewers.

In 1977, Seattle returned to the majors with a new team—the Mariners, named through an essay contest that drew 15,000 entries—and a brand new dome that would guarantee they could play 81 home games without regard to the weather.

But by the time I arrived, people were complaining about the weather *inside*—dark and dank every day. By then, the dome was widely regarded as a gray concrete hulk with no charm. One of the kinder nicknames was "the Concrete Cupcake."

I disagreed. I loved the place. Even with its bland interior. Even with its rock-hard Astroturf. I was sad when it was blown up in 2000, to be replaced by Safeco Field a few hundred yards away. As far as I was concerned, the Kingdome was nirvana.

Of course, I felt that way about every ballpark I played in during my first few years in the majors. Each time we would arrive in a new city, I'd go right to the stadium and walk all over the place, inside and out, up and down the aisles, sitting in different seats and taking pictures of everything. I couldn't believe I was actually going to play in the same places I had seen on television back in Venezuela. Every ballpark was awesome. I even liked the Metrodome in Minneapolis, which all my teammates hated.

The Kingdome may not have been the prettiest ballpark, but no place was louder. When there was a full house—something that admittedly didn't happen much when I was a Mariner—the fans could leave your ears ringing for hours. During the 1995 American League Championship Series, someone took a decibel meter to Game Six and tracked the noise level. During the early innings, when things were going the Mariners' way, the meter consistently hit 106 decibels, about what you'd experience standing next to a small chain saw.

Compared to the fields I grew up with, and the ones I played on in the minors, every major league park was a work of art. Every game was a thrill. Just putting on the uniform increased my heart rate. I was in the big leagues. I had achieved my childhood dream.

MY BREAKTHROUGH YEAR was 1989—and it was completely unexpected.

When I headed to spring training that season, I thought I had virtually no chance to play for the big club. The Mariners had Rey Quinones as the starting shortstop and Mario Diaz as the backup. At best, I was the third-stringer. But Quinones decided to hold out for a better contract, and Diaz hurt his elbow. Talk about being in the right place at the right time.

Twenty-four hours before spring training ended, manager Jim LeFebvre called me into his office and said, "Omar, I think you're gonna be my Opening Day shortstop, because we're going to trade Rey Quinones. So we want you to be mentally prepared."

That was a shock. I was 21 years old, and in one day I would be starting in the bigs.

We opened the season on April 3 in Oakland in front of 46,163 fans. The A's were a glamour team, big and bad, featuring muscular bashers Mark McGwire and Jose Canseco. They made it to the World Series the previous year, losing to the Dodgers, and were in the midst of a three-year run as American League champions. Playing against them helped make my first game the thrill of a lifetime.

The pregame show was wild. There to throw out the ceremonial first pitch was . . . an elephant. Honest! The beast ambled out to the mound and tossed the ball with its trunk. (I'm guessing he threw a spitter.) The other highlight was a high-wire act. The wire was strung between home plate and the top of the big scoreboard in centerfield. The acrobat started at the scoreboard and walked all the way down. It was awesome. Then fireworks were blasted off along the first-base and third-base sides of the field. The whole thing gave me the chills. I was deliriously happy. It was beautiful.

The game itself was not so beautiful. Our starting pitcher was Mark Langston, and he's probably still mad at me.

Although I handled the first big league ball ever hit to me, I choked in the clutch. The game was tied at one in the seventh inning when Canseco hit me a grounder. It was a simple play: I went two steps to my right . . . backhanded the ball . . . picked it out of my glove . . . and threw it into the stands. Then McGwire came up and hit a homer. We lost, 3-2.

But the manager kept me in the lineup. What else could he do? He was already down to the third-string guy.

That game was also the first opening day for another notable rookie: Ken Griffey, Jr., who went on to become without a doubt the best player in baseball. During our five years together in Seattle, I saw him do things in centerfield that nobody else could do—even Kenny Lofton, who has been a marvelous outfielder.

Griffey started in center that day and batted second. I hit in the ninth spot, right behind another future star, Edgar Martinez. Unfortunately, I didn't do much hitting that day. Or the day after. My first major league hit didn't come until the third game of the series. It was a double down the left field line against Oakland's Storm Davis. Someone retrieved the ball and gave it to me. I still have it at home in Seattle.

I have a lot of autographed baseballs, but I don't save many balls from personal achievements. The only other ones I kept are from my first home run (off Jimmy Key of Toronto on July 23, 1989) and my 1,000th hit.

I also have a ball autographed for me by McGwire and Sammy Sosa at the 1998 All-Star game. That was my first All-Star Game, and the year McGwire hit 70 homers and Sosa hit 66. I also have some balls from the two World Series I was in, but they're not connected to anything I did personally. I'm not sure what my next personal milestone ball might be. Maybe my 500th home run.

Okay, maybe not.

Anyway, one week after my major league debut, I got some rotten news: I was being sent back to the minors. Quinones had decided to end his holdout. Suddenly I was back in Calgary, my city of nightmares, looking for a place to live. Fortunately, I decided to stay in a hotel, rather than lease an apartment, because a week later the Mariners traded Quinones to Pittsburgh and called me back up.

This time I was in the majors to stay.

Unfortunately, I was still learning how to hit. Only four months before my major league debut, I started switch-hitting. I had always batted right-handed. In fact, when I was a kid, my dad would yell at me if I turned around and tried to hit lefty. I was a good hitter, and he didn't want to mess with my swing.

But the hitting instructor in Seattle's farm system, Bobby Tolan, told me he wanted me to start switching. He pointed out that, by hitting from the left side against right-handed pitchers, I could take full advantage of my speed. When you hit lefty, you're a couple of steps closer to first base.

The main reason to switch, though, is so you can stand on the opposite side of the pitcher's arm. Inside pitches are less intimidating, and you can usually get a better look at the ball.

Most switch-hitters learn as youngsters, and it becomes second nature. But at the ripe old athletic age of 21, I was suddenly watching the ball from a whole new angle. Although the transition was difficult, I honestly don't think I would have made it to the majors if I hadn't started switch-hitting. I'm proud that I stuck with it. A lot of guys who were urged to switch tried it for a while and gave up.

Casual fans may not notice, but this righty-lefty business is a big deal among managers. It makes so much difference that many managers will "platoon," or play certain players only against righties and certain players only against lefties.

In 1999, Richie Sexson drove in more than 100 runs for the Indians during the regular season. But in the playoffs, against the Red Sox, he couldn't crack the starting lineup until the third game because the first two Boston pitchers were righties. When you switch hit, you don't have to worry about that.

I get more comfortable with switch-hitting every season. Oddly enough, during the past several seasons I've hit much better left-handed than right-handed. The biggest reason, I suppose, is that most pitchers are right-handed, which means I don't swing from the right side nearly as often.

When I first started my experiment, in winter ball, my manager was Bill Plummer (who would be hired to replace LeFebvre as manager of the Mariners in 1992). He knew I was a work in progress, and he kept playing me every day even though I was hitting about .180. I worked hard at batting left-handed. Away from the ballpark I'd walk around using a left-handed swing with broomsticks and anything else I could get a hold of.

That first year with Seattle I was okay at the plate, all things considered, hitting .220 in 143 games. I also recorded a .971 fielding percentage, sixth best among American League shortstops. But I knew I could do better, both in the field and at the plate.

As we headed into the 1990 season, I was eager to prove that. But in a meaningless spring training game, as I was trying to turn a double play, Carlos Baerga—then in his first season with the Indians—barreled into my knee. It was a real cheap shot. The score was 5-0, and he had no reason to go at me that hard. I had an instant hatred for him. Every day during my six weeks of rehab, I got boiling mad just thinking about the guy.

Ironically, after I was traded to Cleveland four years later, Carlos and I turned into best friends. I still keep in touch with him, even though he hasn't played in Cleveland in years. Looking back on it, I figure he was just playing hard because he wanted to make the team. But I held that incident against him for a long time. I just didn't trust him.

Because of Carlos, I began the year on the disabled list with a sprained medial collateral ligament. In May I went back to the minors to play myself back into shape. When I was finally called up on July 5, we were playing Cleveland—and I hit a homer and a double off their knuckleball pitcher, Tom Candiotti.

During my second season in Seattle, my game continued to improve. Although I hit only .230 in 1991, I began to get a reputation for clutch hitting, batting .311 with runners in scoring position. In a game against Milwaukee, I went 5-for-5, tying a team record for hits in a game. My fielding kept improving, too; during the last 50 games of the season, I made only two errors.

The following year, I added 64 points to my batting average, hitting a solid .294, and led all shortstops in fielding percentage. One of my biggest clutch defensive plays came in the bottom of the ninth in a game against the Red Sox. We were leading 7-0, but our starter, Chris Bosio, had a no-hitter going.

Only one pitcher in the history of the franchise had thrown a no-hitter (Randy Johnson, in 1990). Bosio needed one more out to get the second. As Boston's Ernest Riles dug into the batter's box, I was hoping he would hit the ball to me. I want *every* ball hit to me. So when he hit a little chopper, I was ready. I dashed in, barehanded it, threw to first in one motion and nailed him. It was a great feeling to contribute to such a rare moment.

People asked me after the game how I had the nerve to bare-hand a ball in that situation. Well, that's the only way I could have made the play. I'd rather risk dropping the ball than conceding an infield hit.

THE 1993 SEASON WAS MEMORABLE for another big reason: that's the year I met Nicole Tonkin.

When people ask how I met my wife, I usually just say we met at a health club. That's not exactly true, but the real story is too complicated. You almost need a scorecard to follow along. Hearing the full story, you might be amazed that Nicole and I ever got together.

Our backup shortstop at the time, Jeff Schaffer, had a girlfriend in Seattle named Christine. Christine worked out at a health club owned by Nicole's uncle. Christine and Nicole got to know each other at the club. In the spring of 1993, Christine went to the Mariners' spring-training site near Phoenix to visit Jeff. At the same time, by pure coincidence, Nicole went with a girlfriend to visit friends at Arizona State University. Christine and Nicole ran into each other one day, and Nicole invited Christine to go swimming at her hotel. When Christine left to pick up Jeff at the ballpark, Nicole rode along in the back seat. She was half-asleep after a long day in the sun. When they drove up, I was walking out of the ballpark, and Jeff called me over and introduced me to Nicole.

With one look, I was in love.

Nicole was wearing a really cute outfit—an orange shirt with multicolored shorts. She had the most beautiful eyes I'd ever seen. I immediately asked whether she wanted to go to a movie with me the next day. She agreed.

Things didn't exactly get off to a marvelous start. On our first date, I stood her up.

I didn't mean to. Earlier that day some friends invited me to go to the ostrich races—seriously, *ostrich* races—and the affair ran later than I expected. I didn't have Nicole's phone number, so I couldn't get in touch with her. And by the time I got back, she wasn't around.

The next day she flew back to Seattle as planned, before I had a chance to talk to her. So I tracked down Christine and got a number for Nicole in Seattle. I called and asked her to meet me at the airport when the team returned from training camp.

From the airport, I took her to a Mexican bar called Tlaquepaq (pronounced ta-LOCK-ee-POCK-ee), where a friend of mine was the bartender. I hadn't been in the joint since the end of the previous season, and when we walked in, lots of my old pals were there, drinking and carrying on. They swarmed around me. Although I don't drink, some of my friends do, and these guys were getting pretty loose. They had a ritual where they'd pound a shot glass on a big wooden board to make the mixture fizz, then fire it down. The whole place was loud and rowdy.

I really wanted to impress Nicole with my dancing, so I got out there and showed off a little. It's not really a dance place; it's just a bar. But when you gotta dance, you gotta dance, right?

On the surface, this was a strange relationship. That first night, we were in a place that featured blaring salsa music, which she knew nothing about, and everybody was jabbering in Spanish, which she didn't speak. The poor woman didn't have a clue what was going on.

She had even less of a clue when it came to baseball. In fact, she told me later that when we first met, she thought I was lying to her because I told her I played shortstop for Seattle. She knew Jeff Schaffer played shortstop, because Christine had told her so. How could I play shortstop, too? To check her instincts, she asked her brother how many shortstops play on a baseball team. Naturally, he said one. So she figured I was a fibber.

That was probably part of why she appealed to me. I knew she didn't like me just because I was a baseball player.

We did have plenty of things in common. I love to dance, and she had taken formal dance instruction from the age of 3 to 17. She studied everything under the sun—ballet, jazz, tap, gymnastics. When I taught her the salsa and the meringue, she was a quick study.

Nicole somehow survived the bash at Tlaquepaq, so I asked her to come watch me play on Opening Day.

That game—April 6, 1993, against Toronto—was the first baseball game she had ever seen. Randy Johnson was pitching, and 55,928 people were packed into the Kingdome. We won, 8-1. When she saw me introduced as the leadoff hitter and the starting shortstop, she realized I hadn't been lying.

But that's about the only thing she understood that day. Baseball is a complicated game. For a person who didn't grow up with the sport, the first game must look like nuclear physics. Nicole says she spent a lot of the game staring back at the other players' wives, who apparently were spending a lot of time trying to figure out who she was.

Since then, Nicole has gotten a pretty good handle on baseball. She watches all our games and knows what she's talking about. But in the early days of our relationship, I'm sure she felt the same way I did when I was looking at a menu in Butte, Montana.

Four-and-a-half months after our first date, I proposed. I guess I didn't really "propose" in the traditional American sense of the word. What I did was ask her to lunch and then walk her to the courthouse to apply for a marriage license. She agreed, and we were married within days.

The wedding was in a little church near her house in front of five people. My brother was the best man. Nicole brought her mom and dad and her best friend, Laurie Ulrich. The honeymoon had to wait until after the season. Eventually, we went to Puerto la Cruz, a resort town just east of Caracas, right on the Caribbean Sea.

Puerto la Cruz caters to tourists. The main drag, Pasco Colon, runs right along the beach. One side of the street is packed with shops, hotels, and nightclubs, while the other is filled with seafood restaurants, outdoor cafes, and people peddling their art-work. Palm trees line both sides of the street. The atmosphere is festive. The whole place is hopping day and night. I couldn't think of a better place to take Nicole.

Since that time, unfortunately, the water near the beach has become too polluted for safe swimming. My country has an on-going problem with pollution of all kinds, partly because it isn't up to speed on modern treatment technology and partly because of its economic problems.

Even in 1993, Nicole had to deal with culture shock. You've heard of casual dining? One day I took her to a restaurant that was accessible only by a small boat. All she was wearing was her bathing suit. We went into the place and her eyes got wide. Chick-ens were walking around inside the restaurant. When we sat down at the table, they started pecking at her feet. She was also a bit surprised by the food presentation—they just flop a whole fish on your plate, eyes and gills and everything.

Nicole wasn't prepared for some of Venezuela's mainstream entertainment offerings, either. I took her to a bullfight, and—well, let's just say she exhibited great sympathy for the bulls.

Every major city in Venezuela has a bull ring. The one in Va-lencia is the second largest in all of the Americas. In Caracas, where we went, the fights are held on Sunday afternoons in the Plaza de Toros Nuevo Circo, and the crowds are huge.

When the action began to unfold, Nicole cried. And cried and cried and cried. She bawled so much that I was embarrassed. A woman in front of us kept turning around, trying to console her. She'd say things like, "It's okay, honey. You eat steak, don't you?"

Not for a while.

Nicole will admit that Venezuela offers the best lobster she's ever eaten. And she's fond of plantains, a small fruit that resem-bles a banana. But, understandably, I'm much more comfortable in Venezuela than she is.

Nicole Tonkin was raised in an upper-middle-class family that made its money by owning a variety of businesses. Her father operated a hair salon, a dry-cleaner, and bars. Her dad's uncle jumped in on the ground floor of TacoTime, a fast food chain that is the Northwest's equivalent of Taco Bell, only with better food. Frank Tonkin, Sr. began franchising the restaurants in 1962. Today the family controls about 75 of them.

When Nicole was 10, her father moved out of the house. But he and Nicole's mother didn't officially divorce until 17 years later, when, Nicole claims, her mom got tired of doing her dad's tax returns. For most of those years, Nicole lived with her mom, who ran a pizza restaurant. I see both of her parents regularly, and I get along great with them. Nicole jokes that her parents like me more than they like her.

Nicole went to Kentridge High School in Kent, about 25 miles south of Seattle, where she was on the swimming team. She was a diver, both springboard and platform. From there she enrolled at Highline Community College in Seattle, then moved on to the University of Washington, where she majored in English literature. She quit school in her senior year after we met and never did get her degree. She talks about going back and getting it some day. I hope she does.

Both sides of Nicole's family have roots that reach a long way into the Seattle soil. How rooted is she? Well, her mother's great, great, great, great grandfather was Chief Seattle. Yes, *the* Chief Seattle, the guy they named the city after.

On Nicole's father's side, the family heritage is Danish. But they're not exactly newcomers, either. Nicole's paternal great, great grandfather was born in Seattle. That branch of the family was heavily involved in newspapers and coal mines, and they were so influential that local books have been written about them.

Little wonder Nicole is so infatuated with the Emerald City.

Our first place in Seattle was an apartment on Alki Beach, a beautiful area on the shore opposite downtown. As you look across Elliott Bay from Alki you see all the skyscrapers. Alki's waterfront is beautiful, too. It has everything from hamburger joints to upscale gourmet restaurants. The public beach there is often packed with people biking, running, rollerblading, and playing volleyball. Even though we don't live there anymore, it's still one of our favorite spots in Seattle. (Another of our favorites is Pike Place Market, the big public market right in the heart of the city. We eat there often when we're in town.)

From Alki Beach we moved to Bellevue, where we bought our first house. That was the first time in my life I lived in a single-family house, and it took me a while to adjust. It's funny—having always lived in places where other people were right beside me, above me, and below me, I just didn't feel comfortable living in a self-contained building.

We lived in Bellevue for five years and really enjoyed it. It's a nice, upscale suburb just east of Seattle. While we were living there, we were able to save enough money to start thinking about building our dream house (which I'll tell about in a later chapter).

In Seattle I fell in love not only with Nicole but with the city itself. The first time I saw the place was 1985, when I drove down from Bellingham, Washington, with a minor league teammate to watch some Mariner games. I liked the place immediately. When I actually started living there, I liked it even more. I love the big buildings and the views from the highways and all the water and the lights at night and the fact that you can see Mount Rainier hovering out there in the background, with the snow on top.

The three of us—Nicole and Seattle and I—were a perfect match. I hoped it would last forever. But soon I would get a phone call that would turn our lives upside down.

CHAPTER 6

Off to Cleveland

THE CALL CAME AT MIDNIGHT. When a phone rings at that hour, the caller usually is not delivering good news. And that held true on December 20, 1993. Or at least it seemed that way at the time.

I was in Venezuela, playing winter ball and enjoying my first year of marriage. We had our own apartment, but it was a long way from the ballpark, so we often stayed in the team hotel in the heart of the city. That's where we were when we heard the news.

My agent, Adam Katz, was on the line. He informed me I had just been traded to the Cleveland Indians for shortstop Felix Fermin and designated hitter Reggie Jefferson.

I was crushed. I loved Seattle. I didn't want to leave. My wife wanted to leave even less than I did.

When I hung up the phone and told Nicole, she started to cry. And she didn't stop for a long time. She had just assumed we would always live in Seattle. Cleveland was 2,400 miles away. To her, Cleveland sounded like Antarctica.

I tried to console her. I told her we were going to get a new start with a new team, that they had a new ballpark, and that we'd find new friends and create new adventures. But nothing seemed to make her feel better.

She didn't hate Cleveland. She hadn't heard the jokes and the stories about the burning river. She simply hadn't been there and didn't know anything about the place.

My own memories of Cleveland were sketchy. I remembered

walking from the team hotel to the old ballpark and seeing virtually nothing of interest. No intriguing buildings, hardly any people, nothing cool at all. Being from a big, crowded, peppy city like Caracas, I was afraid Cleveland would be a snore.

But maybe the new stadium would perk the place up. I knew the city was building a fancy ballpark that would be open in time for the coming season, and I hoped it would bring a whole new flavor to the downtown.

The trade wasn't a blockbuster in either city. These days, the team would call a press conference and people would take pictures of you putting on a new cap and jersey. But I wasn't a big enough star in those days to cause any fuss. Although I had won a Gold Glove in Seattle, my hitting was still a work in progress, and most Cleveland fans probably figured they were essentially exchanging one light-hitting shortstop for another.

In *The Plain Dealer*, Paul Hoynes wrote that the Indians "didn't receive the starting pitcher they so desperately need from Seattle in exchange for Fermin and Jefferson. What they did receive was Omar Vizquel. Yes, he's a Gold Glove shortstop. But he's still another shortstop."

In the *Akron Beacon Journal*, Sheldon Ocker wrote, "Vizquel is the closest thing in the American League to Ozzie Smith in his prime," but in the same story asked, "With all of Vizquel's flashy defensive credentials, why did [General Manager John] Hart expend his energy in a deal for another shortstop rather than concentrating on grabbing a starting pitcher or bullpen stopper?"

After the trade, Hart flew down to Caracas to meet with me. He took me out to lunch and told me about his plans for the team and what I could expect to find in Cleveland. We even talked a little about a new contract. During his three-day visit, he also showed me pictures of the new stadium, which was nearly finished. (Maybe he shouldn't have. In the photos, the field was covered with a foot of snow.)

I was impressed that Hart made an effort to get to know me.

IF YOU LOOKED AT THE FINAL STANDINGS from the 1993 season, there was no particular reason for me to feel good about coming to Cleveland. In '93, the Indians finished sixth, 19 games out of first place—business as usual. During the previous 25 years, the Tribe had never finished higher than fourth.

Still, the team had picked up some promising young players, like Sandy Alomar and Carlos Baerga, both of whom arrived from San Diego in a trade for Joe Carter. Baerga was coming off his second straight 200-hit season. The Indians had two other young stars: Albert Belle, who led the league with 129 RBIs, and Kenny Lofton, whose 70 stolen bases also topped the American League.

Lofton is an amazing athlete, one of my favorite players ever. I watched him do so many great things over the years—in the field, at the plate, and on the bases. I'd rank him as the fourth best player of the 1990s, behind only Ken Griffey, Jr., Ivan Rodriguez, and Alex Rodriguez. The man did everything well and really put on a show. I would have paid money to watch him play, and I can't say that about too many people.

The winter of my trade, the news coming out of Cleveland was exciting. First, Hart signed Dennis Martinez, a smart, veteran pitcher who knew how to win. Then he signed Eddie Murray, a future Hall of Famer who would step right in as a designated hitter and sometime first baseman. Owner Dick Jacobs was one of the richest men in the country and, now that the Indians were moving into a new ballpark and had enough good players to really compete, he was clearly willing to spend some of that cash.

In fact, the Indians traded for me partly because of their relative wealth. Seattle's ownership had ordered the M's general manager, Woody Woodward, to keep the 1994 payroll at $28.5 million. My contract was ending, and I was eligible for arbitration. Given the fact that I had just won a Gold Glove, it was likely that my $1.3 million salary would nearly double if I went to arbitration. Meanwhile, Seattle had just spent close to a million dollars to sign a hot young shortstop prospect by the name of Alex Rodriguez. They figured he was so good that he would be ready for the big leagues as early as 1995. So Woodward wanted to unload my salary, and Cleveland was willing to pick it up.

Those kinds of things didn't usually happen in Cleveland. For a quarter-century, the Indians had been the ones dumping big salaries, rather than taking them on. But everything about Cleveland baseball was starting to change.

Even if it weren't, I had no choice. I was going to Cleveland anyway. Trades are part of the business, one of the few downsides of a career where the average salary is two million dollars.

If I hadn't gone to Cleveland, I probably would have been shipped to New York. I learned later that the Mets were trying to trade for me, but the Indians got there first. Apparently, the Mets had been talking to Cleveland about trading Fermin for a pitcher, and then shipping Fermin to Seattle for me.

Nicole wouldn't have been one bit happier going to New York. The problem was less where she was going than what she was leaving. In my view, Cleveland or New York wouldn't have made much difference, either. All I wanted was to be in the big leagues. You can adjust to any place.

One great thing about coming to Cleveland was the way the team treated Latin players. Since the early '90s, Cleveland's roster has been packed with Spanish-speaking players, and they have been treated extremely well. Believe me, word gets around.

I've never seen another team do the kind of things the Indians do. They make us feel right at home, even providing our kind of food. They employ Spanish-speaking psychologists, they offer English classes . . . all kinds of stuff I never had in Seattle.

When we talk to the young Latin kids in the Indians' farm system, we tell them they should never complain about the way they are treated. Compared to the way things work on most other teams, those guys are spoiled rotten.

Still, I was a little worried about coming to a place where I hardly knew anyone. Fortunately, a friend of mine, Alvaro Espinoza, had joined the Indians the previous season. Espy was born in Valencia, Venezuela, and played for the Twins and Yankees before coming to Cleveland. Even if everybody else hated me, at least I'd have Espy.

The first day of spring training was awkward. But Espy introduced me around, and I pretty quickly began to feel at ease. About a month into the season, I was completely comfortable.

WHEN I ARRIVED IN CLEVELAND after spring training, everybody in Northeast Ohio seemed excited about the upcoming debut of the new ballpark. I was, too. But, frankly, I really didn't mind the old park. I have good memories of Cleveland Stadium. In 73 at-bats there, I hit .301. The old stadium was far enough away from the rest of downtown that you didn't have distractions. You could concentrate completely on baseball. Sure, I hated the food they served us in the clubhouse after the games. It was consistently lousy. But I loved the smell of barbecue that wafted from behind the left-field wall during the games. And I didn't mind the tiny clubhouse or that long, dark tunnel you had to walk through to get from the clubhouse to the field.

The only real negative was that, toward the end of the season, the field would get mangled by the Cleveland Browns. The football and baseball seasons overlapped by about a month, and you'd see leftover yard lines in the middle of the outfield and big holes all over the place from football spikes.

I'll never forget one game there at the end of the 1992 season. The Mariners were approaching 100 losses and the Indians were closing in on 90. About 4,000 fans showed up —this in a stadium that could seat more than 80,000. During this Battle of Losers, the players could hear every word the fans were saying. It was like putting on a game in a library.

When I first saw Jacobs Field a few days before the 1994 season opener, it knocked my socks off. Everything was first class. There wasn't one single feature that stood out; rather, it was the overall feel. It didn't remind me of any other ballpark; it was unique. It was just a beautiful place to play ball.

The new clubhouse at Jacobs Field was literally four times larger than the one at Cleveland Stadium. The place was—and is—stunning, featuring plush burgundy carpeting (since changed to navy), leather couches, big wooden dressing cubicles, subdued lighting, and eight Sony TV monitors suspended from the ceiling. That's just the clubhouse. There's also a huge weight room . . . a huge aerobics room . . . a players' kitchen . . . a manager's suite . . . a coaches' suite . . . a room dedicated solely to analyzing videotape . . . and a training room the size of Parma, filled with the latest high-tech rehab equipment. Heck, even the batboys have their own quarters.

When one of our pitchers is sent to the showers, he has 14 showerheads to choose from, compared to five at the old place. Even the hallway between the clubhouse and the dugout is carpeted, wide, and well-lit. Rather than the monstrous bugs that hung out on the walls of the old tunnels at Cleveland Stadium, these tunnels are covered with photos of the top players from Cleveland's 100 years in the American League.

Jacobs Field has the best clubhouse in the American League. (The worst is Boston's, in 89-year-old Fenway Park. It's about the size of a phone booth.)

The new digs brought the team more than aesthetic improvements. Just behind our dugout are four batting cages, where we can crank up the pitching machine before games and even between at-bats.

I felt as if I had died and gone to Cooperstown. And if the players were in heaven, the fans were just as happy. Cleveland fans were certainly ready for this place. They started packing it from the very beginning. Within a year, they were filling Jacobs Field to capacity, night after night after night.

In 2001, owner Larry Dolan made a great move by retiring the number 455—the consecutive sellout streak at Jacobs Field that began June 12, 1995, and ended April 4, 2001. That's nearly six years of sellouts, an all-time baseball record that may never be broken.

Winning cures a lot of ills, but the ballpark was also a key factor in the streak. It's just about perfect for a fan. With a capacity of about 44,000, it's big enough to be exciting, yet small enough to be intimate. The design is dominated by big steel beams that remind you of the city's bridges. The design is a tribute to Cleveland's industrial past, but the park has all the modern amenities.

Ironically, one of the first things you notice inside the ballpark is the outside. It reaches out and pulls in the surrounding city.

Jacobs Field has some special seating. In the "dugout suites" at ground level, some fans are actually closer to home plate than the pitcher is. Each of the 10 suites has 12 seats, a private bathroom, a wet bar, refrigerator, telephones, and a private dining area. To rent the suites, companies had to sign a 10-year lease, for $100,000 per season. And all 10 suites were leased right away.

Sometimes, these dugout suites helped *me* enjoy the games more, too. When you're walking up the tunnel behind our dugout to the locker room, there's a doorway on the left that leads to another tunnel that runs behind the dugout suites. Well, don't tell anybody, but on occasion, when I wasn't in a game, I would walk through that door, sneak down the hallway, and check out the big dessert carts that are brought around to the patrons of the dugout suites. The waiters or waitresses would be so shocked to see me standing there in my uniform that they'd give me a free dessert. Those chocolate cakes with strawberries—man!

Since those days, the team has mounted video cameras in those hallways. I hope they weren't installed because the team was losing too much money on free desserts.

Obviously, my main interest at the new stadium was not the condition of the dessert trays but the condition of the infield. In the early years, the field itself was outstanding, the best in the league. It's still good. But during the last couple of seasons, the infield has gotten a bit too hard for my liking. I'm not sure what happened, but I'd say our infield now ranks behind the ones in Baltimore and Chicago.

The worst infield in the league, without question, is Tampa

Bay's. For 2001, they installed a new type of fake grass called Field-Turf that cost $1 million. It's not smooth like Astroturf, which they had the previous two seasons and cost about $200,000 less; it looks and feels a lot like natural grass. But it's strange. The fake grass gives you weird hops from time to time. Plus, the infield dirt is all chewed up. Every time the ball hits the dirt it does something odd.

The infield in Kansas City is bad, too. It is so soft that your foot sinks in every time you take a step. I'm surprised the Royals' former shortstop, Rey Sanchez, was so good with all those holes out there. When he was traded to the Braves in the middle of 2001, he must have been the happiest player in the league.

Jacobs Field has another big advantage over most parks: I've never seen a place that handles water better. The day of our first playoff game in 1995 against Boston, it rained hard for eight hours. You would have thought we were playing in Amazonas, the site of a lush rainforest in southern Venezuela. The start of the game was delayed for 40 minutes. Every so often, the grounds crew would have to dump the water off the tarp so it wouldn't get too heavy to move. They would empty it in shallow left field—and the field would suck it right up. Under the grass are perforated drain lines that run across the field horizontally every 20 feet. There's six inches of gravel under that, then a layer of peat moss mixed with sand. The head of the grounds crew, Brandon Koehnke, says this setup allows the field to absorb 12 inches of water per hour.

COMING FROM SEATTLE, Nicole and I didn't have any trouble with Cleveland's rain. Our problem was the odor.

People keep talking about how Cleveland's economy has moved away from manufacturing, but there's still plenty of heavy industry around. And when the conditions are right, it can give off a funky odor.

The first week we were in town, we were staying at a downtown hotel and the stink was so bad that we had to put towels under the door. We thought, "Oh, man, what have we gotten ourselves into?" But that only happens on certain days. And once you get away from the downtown, you never have that problem.

Cleveland's suburbs were a pleasant surprise. We had no idea how many nice ones the city has. That first season, we rented an apartment in Westlake, at a place called Hunter Chase, off Detroit Road. We were there for about three years, then bought a small house in the same area. A couple of years after that, we moved to the larger house we have now. It's about 3,500 square feet, a brick two-story on a corner lot in a nice neighborhood. There are plenty of kids in the area for our son, Nico, to play with.

Nicole really likes living in Westlake during the summer. She says it reminds her of the community where she grew up in Seattle. But I don't think she'd have much interest in living there during the winter. Neither would I. I hate cold weather. Seattle can get pretty dreary in the winter, too, but at least you don't freeze to death there.

Almost all of the Indians live on the West Side. Suburbs like Westlake and Bay Village offer plenty of nice neighborhoods and are close to the airport. When you travel as much as we do, and you're getting home at literally all hours of the day or night, you don't want to be too far from the airport. A few players have lived on the East Side. One of them, Jack McDowell, lived all the way in Chagrin Falls, as far from Hopkins International as you can get and still be in Cuyahoga County. Getting to the airport from there is no treat. Maybe that's why Jack had arm troubles—too much time spent shifting gears.

But I'm not one of those "West Side Only" people. I know the people of Cleveland think of themselves as either West Siders or East Siders and don't cross over much. But I frequently venture into foreign territory. When I'm in the mood for a great lunch, we head to Little Italy, an East Side neighborhood with great restaurants. One of my favorites is La Dolce Vita, owned by a good pal of mine, Terry Tarantino. Every time we have some kind of special celebration, we ring him up. When it comes to Italian food, he's a purist.

Little Italy is also near the Cleveland Institute of Art, and I'll frequently make a side trip to enjoy the exhibits. There's a glass gallery, too. It's a really neat area, one of the things that makes Cleveland special.

Cleveland's best-kept secret, in my opinion, is it's historic churches. The town has so many wonderful old churches. People don't seem to pay any attention to them, but these are beautiful, unique places with great architecture. You couldn't possibly duplicate them today.

In the summertime, I spend a lot of time on Lake Erie. I bought a pair of jet-skis, and if we have a day off I'll go hit the water. We live only about five minutes from the lake, so I'll drop them in at Edgewater Park or Whiskey Island or in Rocky River.

One of my jet-ski adventures didn't go too well. I was hanging out with Kenny Lofton, and we were in the little harbor near the Rock and Roll Hall of Fame. I was on one of the jet skis and Kenny was on a boat. As I threw him a line, my keys got caught on the rope and fell into the water. I didn't have one of those floating key chains, so they sank right to the bottom. I kept diving down to try to get them, but it was nasty down there, real muddy, with all kinds of garbage. Kenny was laughing like crazy. I didn't think it was particularly funny. I ended up having to call someone to go to my house and get another set of keys. It took me about three hours to get back in action.

I never did find those stinkin' keys. Somewhere on the bottom of Lake Erie, about five feet into the muck, is a set of my keys. And that bum Lofton is still laughing about it.

He shouldn't be laughing at anybody. Heck, *I'm* not the one they used as the model for Willie Mays Hayes in the movie *Major League*. Check it out. That's Kenny. The way he talks, the way he acts. Willie Mays Hayes.

THAT FIRST YEAR WITH THE TRIBE, I also became close to Dennis Martinez, the fiery pitcher from Nicaragua. Dennis broke into the big leagues with Baltimore in 1979 and had seen just about everything baseball has to offer. He had played in both leagues, starting his career in Baltimore before being traded to Montreal. He had pitched in a World Series and three All-Star Games.

I also admired him for his ability to overcome his personal demons. From his early 20s until the age of 30, he had a terrible problem with alcohol and, to a lesser degree, with drugs. It not only hurt his baseball career, it nearly cost him his life. The guy was a mess. But he got help and overcame it. He was able to keep his marriage intact, too.

When he joined the Indians in 1994, Dennis was turning 40. By the end of that year, he was a grandfather. He had seen and done so much, inside and outside of baseball, and I loved hearing about his experiences.

Dennis lived in Miami during the off-season but frequently went back to his native Nicaragua on goodwill missions. Between the 1991 and 1992 seasons, he flew to Managua to play in a couple of exhibition games to raise money to build a cathedral. He also worked with Nicaraguan refugee aid groups in Miami.

When we were on the team plane, Dennis was always reading books about politicians, and I'd always kid him about it. I knew he wanted to become involved with politics in Nicaragua. He was a smart man, and he got stronger as time went by.

He didn't talk about his former alcohol and drug problems very much. Occasionally if he was in the back of the plane and somebody was drinking too much, he might mention something about what alcohol does to the body. But he didn't badger anybody, and the guys really respected the fact that he had pulled his life together.

On the field, Dennis was a warrior. By the time he signed with the Indians, his arm had a lot of miles on it. He had been in the big leagues 18 seasons and had thrown 220 innings or more during nine of them. But what his arm had lost, he made up for with his head and his heart. Dennis kept badgering manager Mike Hargrove to put catcher Tony Pena in the lineup whenever he pitched. Dennis didn't think Sandy Alomar was intense enough. Martinez and Pena really had a thing going. I loved to watch them work as pitcher and catcher. They communicated so well that Tony didn't even need to flash a signal half the time. They'd just look at each other and know what the other guy was thinking.

The player I was the least comfortable with initially was the guy who played right next to me—Carlos Baerga. I'll readily admit it took me a while to warm up to him. When a guy crashes into your knee like he did mine, threatening your career, it's hard to trust him. I hated him so much at the time of the injury that I couldn't imagine ever becoming his friend. When I came to the Indians, I wasn't sure I even wanted to talk to him because I still hated him so much. But after a couple of months, I realized he's a great soul. He has a smile that's contagious. He'll talk to anyone. As I've mentioned, we turned into great friends and we still keep in touch.

My biggest surprise in Cleveland was the fans. In Seattle, unless you were Ken Griffey, Jr., nobody cared. But in Cleveland, even the backup players are recognized whenever they leave their houses. Northeast Ohioans love the Indians, and they'll come right up to a player and say hi.

Even after a guy's hair falls out.

CHAPTER 7

Strike Three

M Y FIRST GAME with the Cleveland Indians was also the first Opening Day at Jacobs Field—and it was an event to remember. The weather was sunny and unseasonably warm, and management had pulled out all the stops to christen the new ballpark in suitable style.

For me, the day was even better because we were playing my old team. The bad news was that my old team still had Randy Johnson, the snarling, 6-foot-10, wild-haired lefty who could throw a baseball through a phone book.

It took Randy a while to get out on the mound, because the pregame ceremonies went on and on. The game was scheduled for 1:05 P.M., but didn't start until 1:20. Our starting pitcher, Dennis Martinez, later complained that he had completed his warm-ups at the scheduled time and then had to sit around cooling off for 15 minutes. Of course, Dennis was always complaining about something.

The aesthetics that day were marvelous. As we ran onto the thick, emerald grass wearing our spotless white uniforms, with red script lettering on the chest and bright red shoes, hundreds of red, white, and blue balloons were released into the blue sky.

The 41,459 fans applauded frequently, but for most of the day there was no sign of a fan frenzy. They seemed to be rendered speechless by the new ballpark. After all those years of sitting inside crumbling Cleveland Stadium, they sat looking around, not quite believing what they were seeing, pinching themselves to make sure they were actually sitting in downtown Cleveland.

President Bill Clinton received a mixed reception when he came out to throw the first pitch. He was the first sitting president to attend an Indians game. As the Beatles' tune *Twist and Shout* blared from the sound system, he jogged from our third-base dugout to the mound. The big lefty stretched his arms above his head and lobbed his pitch to catcher Sandy Alomar, who caught it without having to move.

Ohio Governor George Voinovich tossed a second ceremonial pitch. He was on target, too.

Ironically, the third tosser, Hall of Fame pitcher Bob Feller, was the only one to mess up his throw. He bounced it in the dirt. Of course, he was working with a major age disadvantage.

Clinton hung around near our dugout for a while. I was among the players who shook his hand. We didn't talk much, because I wasn't a big fan of his. At least not in those days. After I heard about the Monica Lewinsky thing, I started to like him a lot better.

Anyway, my brief meeting with the president went better than Buddy Bell's.

Not long before the game began, Bell, a former Indians third baseman who was our infield coach that year, went down the steps from our dugout to the restroom just behind it. While taking care of business, he heard someone try to open the locked door. He mumbled something about being out soon. When he opened the door 30 seconds later, still buckling up his uniform pants, he came face to face with the most powerful man on the planet. Bell was startled, but managed to exchange a brief pleasantry with Clinton and go on his way.

In the interest of good public relations, Clinton wanted to wear the cap of the hometown team. But that created a political problem. The Indians have worn the Chief Wahoo emblem since arriving at Jacobs Field. Clinton didn't approve of that. He thought it reinforced a negative racial stereotype. So he wore an older Cleveland Indians cap, one that carried only the letter C.

Chief Wahoo has been the subject of controversy for years. Almost every Opening Day, protesters stage a demonstration outside the ballpark, and the 1994 opener was no exception. About 200 people from the United Church of Christ were protesting, as well as a group led by Michael Haney of the Northeast Ohio Coalition on Racism in Sports and the Media.

Personally, I don't see anything wrong with Chief Wahoo. It's an image with a long history and it has come to represent a first-class franchise. All of the players respect it, because it symbolizes our team. We care about it. Every time we put on our uniform, we wear Chief Wahoo with pride.

The chief is known internationally. In a travel guidebook about Venezuela that is sold in the big American bookstore chains, there's a picture of a boy leading a mule train through the remote Sierra Nevada de Mérida. He is posing in front of a panoramic view of valleys and mountain peaks, with no sign of any other humans. The boy is holding a wooden staff and wearing a blanket—and on the front of his beat-up, red-and-blue baseball cap is Chief Wahoo.

On Opening Day, though, I wasn't giving much thought to the chief. Too many other things were going on. Even after the game began, another ceremony broke out.

After one inning, play was halted so that our new teammate, Eddie Murray, could be given a trophy for playing more games at first base—2,369—than any other person in major league history, including Lou Gehrig. First base was removed from its peg and given to him as a souvenir.

I suppose I could have come away with my own souvenir two days earlier, because I got the first hit ever at Jacobs Field. Unfortunately, it was only an exhibition game. We were playing one last preseason tune-up against the Pittsburgh Pirates (and giving the stadium operators a chance to make sure everything would be in order for the real opener). In the first inning, I lined a single over the shortstop's head. I didn't bother to get the ball because, to me, it was a meaningless game.

For the record, I was also the first Indian to have his name misspelled on the scoreboard. At the start of the Pirates game, I was listed in the Indians' lineup as V-I-*S*-Q-U-E-L. Soon they figured out that the *S* should have been a *Z*.

Two days later, my teammates and I were having considerably more trouble figuring out Randy Johnson. Through the first seven innings, we didn't have a single hit. The same thought was going through all of our minds: Oh, man, we can't get no-hit in our first game at the new ballpark!

Finally, five outs away from a no-no, Sandy Alomar singled through the right side of the infield to break the spell. He then scored on a clutch double by an unknown rookie named Manny Ramirez.

The '94 opener offered a preview of the Manny Ramirez of the next six years. At times, Manny was clearly the best player on the field. And, at other times, he was just as clearly the worst. In the opener, we saw seemingly unlimited hitting potential side-by-side with seemingly unlimited boneheadedness. Moments after his picture-perfect swing produced that eighth-inning double, he was picked off second base, killing a promising rally. And earlier in the game he nearly crashed into center fielder Kenny Lofton when Lofton was settling under a routine fly ball that was clearly his to take.

But Manny's double tied the game at two and gave a tiring Randy Johnson a chance to test out the new showers.

Things didn't get any easier after Johnson left. In the top of the 10th, Ken Griffey, Jr. beat a throw to home plate to give the Mariners a 3-2 lead. The crowd seemed to sense defeat, runs having been so hard to come by. But in the bottom of the inning, we came right back and tied it.

The key hit was a double by Jim Thome—a hit that proved that the move to Jacobs Field was more than purely cosmetic. That's because immediately before his turn at bat, Thome spent 20 minutes in the indoor batting cages, fine-tuning his timing. He said that warm-up was a tremendous help when he came to the plate.

One inning later, Eddie Murray doubled, moved to third after a fly ball, and scored on a single by Wayne Kirby, who had come on earlier as a pinch-runner for Ramirez.

Tribe wins, 4-3.

For once, Indians fans went home thrilled about their ballpark and thrilled about their team's immediate future. But nobody loved the new park more than the players who had been in the organization for a long time. Charles Nagy said: "If I could get a bed here, I would."

Mike Hargrove, a tough Texan who at that point had been in the major leagues 15 years as a player or manager, was moved to tears the first time he saw it. Six days before the opener, as he and his wife, Sharon, looked into the park from behind left field, he choked up thinking about how far the franchise had come since his arrival in 1979.

Indians owner Dick Jacobs also acted out of character that week. I heard that during the exhibition game against the Pirates, on a sun-drenched Saturday not long after he agreed to spend $14 million of his $275 million fortune to name the place after his family, he spent several innings hanging out in the low-rent section, the bleachers. He didn't want to sit up in his loge behind home plate, or in his dugout suite down at field level. He wanted to mingle. He was approached by a steady stream of fans who asked him to autograph their ticket stubs and programs.

Jacobs is a pretty quiet guy. He's from the old school—he keeps to himself, and his handshake is his word. Although I didn't have much contact with the man, I respected him.

OUR SECOND GAME AT JACOBS FIELD didn't take place until three days after the opener, on April 7. That's when I got my name in the record book.

I became the first player to steal a base at Jacobs Field.

To be honest, I don't even remember it now. Until somebody showed me the listing, I had just assumed Kenny Lofton did it, because he was stealing so many bases in those days. But I'll take it—especially in view of the fact that, nine days later, I played the worst game of my entire life.

Seriously. I'm talking about the worst baseball game in the history of Omar Enrique Vizquel, dating all the way back to the age of eight.

On April 16, we were at home, playing the Kansas City Royals on a sunny Saturday afternoon. In the third inning, Greg Gagne hit me a grounder—and I dropped it.

Now, I don't make too many errors, but every time I do, I hope hard for the next ball to be hit to me so I can redeem myself. And that's exactly what happened. On the very next pitch, another grounder headed my way. I prepared to scoop it up, turn the double play, and erase the mess I had made. But I dropped this one, too.

Two pitches, two errors.

That led to four unearned runs. I was bummed.

Still, we held leads of 8-5 and then 9-8, so nobody was ready to shoot me. That would come later.

In the eighth inning, with two outs, somebody hit a routine fly ball in my direction. I caught it—and dropped it. Everybody safe. Two runs scored. The next batter singled home yet another run.

After my third error, the 36,439 Indians fans were booing me like I was a child molester. Who could blame them? My errors cost the team seven runs—and the ballgame.

In the next day's papers, writers compared us to the fictional Indians in the recently released comedy movie *Major League II*.

But the papers also contained something that made me feel better: I was praised for standing up and taking my medicine during the postgame interviews. I didn't try to sneak out the back door, like some players do after being identified as the goat. When the people with notebooks and microphones approached me cautiously in the locker room, I answered every one of their questions. In various ways, I offered the same story line over and over: "My errors cost us the game." I didn't offer any excuses.

I suppose I could have. I had the flu that day and didn't take pregame infield practice for the first time all season. I had a fever and felt weak, but I figured I would have enough strength to play in the game if I didn't use up all my energy during warm-ups. That may have had something to do with my problems. But I certainly wasn't going to say that. People don't want to hear excuses. I'm paid to catch the ball, and I didn't catch the ball. Simple as that.

I think athletes have a responsibility to take the heat when they deserve it. Some guys love the TV cameras after they get three hits, but if they strike out three times, they act like cockroaches racing to hide from the light.

I had to take out my frustrations on something, though. So I threw away my glove.

That's not something I did lightly. With that one exception, I use just one glove every season, which I then retire to a safe place at home. Oddly enough, I had been in love with this particular glove. It was a black Rawlings I had used in winter ball, where I made only two errors all season. I kept using it during spring training, and it felt great. But after making three errors in a single game, I didn't even want to look at the thing.

I tried not to show how upset I was about that game, but it really bothered me. Dropping a pop-up? I felt like I was in the *Twilight Zone*.

That evening, I called my dad at his apartment in Caracas. As we talked, he was looking at my Gold Glove, which was sitting on a table across the room. He reminded me of the trophy and told me not to worry. He said I knew all the proper fundamentals and that I would bounce right back. Dad reminded me to do what I'd always done: look the ball into my glove, take my time, plant my feet, and make a good throw.

I already knew all that, of course, but hearing it from him—my original coach—helped immensely.

As Dad predicted, I did bounce right back. I had promised publicly that I would never have another game like that one, and I never even came close. I didn't make another error for 51 games, and I made only three more the rest of the 1994 season.

Unfortunately, the 1994 season only lasted until mid-August. And I missed a good chunk of it because of a cheap shot by one of the game's best players.

On April 24, I went on the disabled list with a third-degree sprain in the medial collateral ligament in my right knee and didn't return until mid-June. It was similar to the Baerga incident—but this time I knew it was no accident.

We were playing in Texas, which had opened its own new stadium that year, the Ballpark in Arlington. In the seventh inning, our pitcher, Jack Morris, nailed Ivan Rodriguez in the left triceps. Rodriguez was hot. He figured Morris drilled him on purpose—even though it was late in the game, the score was tied, and Morris was clearly tiring, as witnessed by his previous pitch, which had bounced 20 feet in front of home plate.

The next batter bunted. Catcher Sandy Alomar pounced on the ball and threw to second to force Rodriguez. Rodriguez was determined to take somebody out, and that somebody happened to be me. I took the throw, stepped on the bag and quickly stepped backward. He slid way past the bag and rolled into me. It was a really dirty play.

To this day, I have not heard one word of apology.

Rodriguez said after the game that he was just trying to break up a potential double play. But our manager, Mike Hargrove, disagreed. He snapped to reporters: "You saw what happened. I think that's enough said on that subject."

But the next day, Hargrove was still steaming. "I thought it was a cheap shot," he told reporters. "I have no problem with hard-nosed, clean baseball. But that slide was beyond good, hard, clean baseball. From the looks of it, Rodriguez went in with the intent of hurting somebody, and he succeeded."

It was hard to think otherwise. I was five feet behind the bag when he got there, and he still plowed right into me.

Tongues were wagging when Rodriguez took himself out of the lineup the next two games of the Cleveland-Texas series, claiming to have a bruised elbow. Many people in the clubhouse and the media speculated his move was more an issue of self-preservation.

But he could only hide for so long. A week later, Texas came to Jacobs Field for a three-game series. At that point, I was wearing a cast from my right ankle to my thigh. And in the seventh inning, Charles Nagy nailed Rodriguez with a pitch. Rodriguez didn't charge the mound; instead he merely picked up the ball and flipped it underhand to Nagy, as if to acknowledged that he knew he had it coming.

I returned on June 13 and soon got back into the swing of things. My defense held up and my hitting continued to improve, especially in the clutch. I wound up batting .369 with runners in scoring position, sixth best in the league.

The team was on a roll, too. On June 22, we were five games behind the White Sox. But within a week, we had cut that in half. We stayed close the rest of the way. When we beat Toronto 5-3 on August 10, we were only one game out of first. We had won six of our last nine games. But that would be the last game we'd play in 1994.

On August 12, the strike went into effect and wiped out the rest of the season, the playoffs, and the World Series. Baseball had experienced plenty of labor-management problems before, but nothing like this. In the previous 89 years of major league baseball, nothing had wiped out a World Series—not depressions or natural disasters or even world wars.

When we cleaned out our lockers at Jacobs Field, I was horribly disappointed. For once I was in a real pennant race, with a great team and a great stadium. This couldn't have happened when I was with the Mariners and we were 4,000 games out of first place? No. It happened with my team only one game out with six weeks to go. Had the season ended on August 12, we would have qualified as the Wild Card team, putting me into the playoffs for the first time.

I didn't think the strike would last more than a week. But I was still steamed. The only thing I wanted was to play baseball. Most of the other guys felt the same way. At that point, I was only 27 and didn't fully realize the importance of sticking together as a team. But the older guys prevailed and made it clear we needed to stay united.

Nicole and I packed up and went to a house we owned in Sarasota, Florida. A few years earlier we had visited friends in Sarasota, liked the area, and bought the house. It was on Cleveland Street, appropriately enough. During the strike, we lounged around, entertained friends, and played in the water. But, without any income, we eventually started running out of money and had to sell the house.

Well before that, I started getting antsy. Things had been going so well in Cleveland, for both me and for the team, that I couldn't wait to start playing again.

It would be a long wait. The strike carried over into the following season, wiping out the first 18 games.

The owners' attempt to use replacement players caused major rifts down the road. A buddy of mine, Edgar Caceres, who was in the Kansas City organization, called me for advice. He was 32 years old and had been playing Triple-A ball forever. He didn't seem to have a shot at the major leagues. I told him he may as well put on a big league uniform during the strike, because he probably never would otherwise. He became a replacement player, made some money, and showed enough talent that after the strike he stuck with the big club for about three months. Predictably, he was an outcast, totally shunned by the other players.

Despite the disappointment of the summer of 1994, I got a glimpse of the possibilities of my own team—and the pent-up enthusiasm of Indians fans. The new ballpark wasn't the only thing that was lighting their fire. With our .595 winning percentage—highest for an Indians team since 1955—we had gotten their attention because of our accomplishments. When the strike came, we were leading the league in runs, hits, doubles, homers, and slugging percentage. We had the best home winning record in all of baseball, at 35-16. Our .290 team batting average was the highest for a Tribe team since 1936.

Although I wasn't fully up to speed at that point on the history of the franchise, I could sense how ripe the town was for a winner. Within just a few months, the fans had embraced us. Unlike my former team, which has been in existence only since 1977, Cleveland has been in the American League since 1901, and for most of the second half-century had played dismally. The town was lugging around heavy baseball baggage. When we started winning, the fans started to erupt like a can of Coke that had been shaken for decades.

If they were reacting this way just to a pennant race, how would they react if we actually won something?

We were about to find out.

CHAPTER 8

1995

THE FIRST TIME I knew the 1995 Cleveland Indians were more than just a very good baseball team was the day I saw the tattoo.

We were in Baltimore to play a regular-season series against the Orioles. At the team hotel, the Stouffer Harborplace, I stepped into an elevator with several other players. A Tribe fan got in, too. She was excited to see me. How could I tell? Because she eagerly pushed down the side of her pants and showed me a tattoo of my autograph on her butt.

That wasn't the only skin that would be flashed at the players in 1995. Before one home game, while I was signing baseballs and caps along the left-field line, a woman asked me to autograph her boobs. I politely declined. I also declined a request during an off-the-field autograph session to sign another woman's panties.

I pass along this information only to illustrate the frenzy that developed around the 1995 Cleveland Indians. The season turned into a wild road show with all kinds of unexpected twists and turns. We were like rock stars being trailed by groupies. Ted Nugent would have been proud.

But we're getting ahead of the story.

The amazing saga of the 1995 season actually began on April 8, before we had played a single game. That's when the Indians signed veteran pitcher Orel Hershiser.

In a normal year, the season would be under way by April 8.

But the labor dispute was still raging, and the games wouldn't start for several more weeks.

And in a normal year, hot free agents like Hershiser simply wouldn't settle for less money to play in Cleveland. The fact that he did was another indication that people were finally taking Cleveland baseball seriously.

Orel Hershiser had been to the mountaintop. In 1988, he won 23 games for the Dodgers, the most since the immortal Sandy Koufax, and took home the Cy Young Award in a rare unanimous vote. He pitched a complete-game victory in the deciding match-up of the National League Championship Series, a complete-game victory in the deciding match-up of the World Series, and was named MVP in both. He was absolutely dominant that year, at one point putting together a record 59 consecutive scoreless innings.

So we knew he had the heart. The only question was whether he still had the arm. Orel had had major shoulder surgery in 1990 and battled back gamely, but he hadn't had a winning season since the injury. Plus, he was 36 years old.

In his first 12 starts with the Tribe, he was pummeled. The tall, thin righty had a 6.64 ERA, and opposing batters were hitting .341 off him—good enough to win a batting title. But he kept fighting, and eventually things began to click. In July, after missing several starts with a back injury, he started humming and just didn't stop. He finished the regular season with 16 victories. Even when he didn't win, he kept us close: during his last 31 starts, the team went 22-9.

Orel made things happen. He was also a great tutor for some of the younger guys on the team, including me. He taught me a lot of baseball. He's also a devout Christian. He worked hard to keep everybody together. If we had a problem, he'd call a team meeting to try to iron it out. Not that we had many problems—only once did we lose as many as four games in a row, and only twice did we lose three straight.

But in April our problem was just getting the season started.

The owners recruited "replacement players" and made a show of starting the season on time. But everybody knew that was going nowhere. Eventually, a judge ordered the season to begin, and the real players reported for an abbreviated training camp before resuming the original schedule on April 27.

By then, 18 playing dates had simply been washed away.

Our Opening Day lineup looked like this:

Kenny Lofton, CF
Omar Vizquel, SS
Carlos Baerga, 2B
Albert Belle, LF
Eddie Murray, DH
Jim Thome, 3B
Manny Ramirez, RF
Paul Sorrento, 1B
Tony Pena, C
Dennis Martinez, P

That lineup was largely unknown outside of Northeast Ohio. But it wasn't long before it started getting more national attention than any Indians lineup in decades.

By Memorial Day, we were leading our division by five games. By the Fourth of July, we were up by 11 games. By Labor Day, we were 21 games ahead. And by the last day of the season, we were an incredible, unimaginable, record-breaking 30 games ahead.

The mark we broke went all the way back to the 27-game lead of the Pittsburgh Pirates of 1902.

I knew we were going to field a strong team, but I didn't have a clue we could be that good. It was a dream season. Whenever we needed a base hit, we got a base hit. Whenever we needed a strikeout, we got a strikeout. If we needed a wild pitch, we got a wild pitch. We could make a bad mistake and then come right back the next inning and get three or four runs. Everything was falling our way. Every little break, every call from the umpires, absolutely everything. We began to think nothing could go wrong.

It rarely did. We won 27 games in our last at-bat, and we came from behind 48 times. We had eight players hit over .300. We led the league in runs, batting averages, steals, homers, ERA, and just about every other offensive or defensive category you can think of.

The 1995 season was the most amazing one I've ever been through. I also had more fun that year than any other year I've spent in the big leagues.

Almost from the start, the team was worshipped in Cleveland, and soon people around the country started hopping on the bandwagon. It was the classic worst-to-first story. For nearly half a century the Indians had been the American League's version of the Chicago Cubs, who couldn't win a pennant even if the Baseball Fairy gave them a five-game lead with six games to play. Only they weren't loveable like the Cubs, and they never even got within five games of a lead. Now, as we marched toward a record-setting season, beating the other teams to death and setting up big expectations for the playoffs, we developed quite a following.

But we also turned some people off. The longer the season went on, the worse our press clippings got. By the end, I almost felt as if I were playing for the Oakland Raiders. In many parts of the country, the 1995 Cleveland Indians were the Team America Loves to Hate.

Granted, some of our players could have used a lesson or two from Miss Manners. Albert Belle, for example, was consistently surly to the public and the press. Eddie Murray didn't want to be quoted, and his attitude seemed to reinforce a standoffishness in some of the younger players, like Kenny Lofton.

But for every Albert Belle, smashing other people's belongings with his bat, we had a Wayne Kirby, an Alvaro Espinoza, and a Dennis Martinez. For every Eddie Murray, lips sealed near reporters, we had an Orel Hershiser, seemingly born with a lapel mike clipped to his chest.

But among ourselves—in the dugout, in the locker room, on the team bus, on the charter flights—we were having a blast.

The '95 edition of the Indians scored as many practical jokes as runs. Kirby and Espy were the masters of goofy stuff. They'd be sitting next to someone in the dugout, and when the other player wasn't looking they'd put a big, blown-up wad of bubble gum on the top of his cap. Sometimes it would stay there for a long time. TV cameras would pan the dugout and catch the victim, oblivious to the wad.

Espy and Kirby also used bubble gum to attach matches to the back of guys' shoes and light them. You'd see people with their shoelaces on fire. They'd put holes in the drinking cups, and when you poured in the water, you'd end up soaked. They hid shaving cream on towels and telephones.

Occasionally, this caused problems. Everybody has a different idea of what's funny and what's not. You have to know which people you can pull these jokes on, because some guys just don't go for that kind of humor. Sandy Alomar didn't like to screw around much. Obviously, Albert was not a constant target, either—although there were actually times that he would smile and laugh like everybody else.

I never initiated much of the practical joking, and I do even less of it today, having become, in baseball years, about 127. But I will admit to doing a lot of laughing in 1995.

The best part of that team was the way things went on the baseball diamond. When we stepped onto the field, everyone knew exactly what he was going to do. It was an unreal collection of talent, and all the pieces fit.

One of the keys to our success was the emergence of Jose Mesa as a top-flight relief pitcher. Many fans don't remember that Mesa was a starter before coming to Cleveland from Baltimore. Even after he got to the Tribe in 1992, he was used as a starter. As late as 1993, Mesa started 33 games. But in '94 he was converted to a reliever, and in '95 he really got the hang of it. As it turned out, Jose was a born stopper—if for no other reason than he had a hard time concentrating for more than one inning.

Jose would lose his focus a lot. You always had to go out there and remind him of things. Phil Regan was the pitching coach that year, and Phil worked wonders with Jose.

Our starting pitching was spectacular as well. Our two senior citizens, Hershiser and Martinez—a combined 77 years old—rang up a combined record of 28-11.

And, of course, 1995 marked the breakout year for Albert Belle. I didn't know much about Albert personally, because he just couldn't communicate with anyone. But whenever he came to the plate, it was an event. After a while, you began to think only one of two things was going to happen: he'd either hit a double or a home run. He did each of those 50 times during the season, the only time anyone did that in a century of baseball.

Albert is so intense. He would go 3 for 4 and be livid that he wasn't 4 for 4. He was thrilling to watch. Fans said they would time their restroom visits to make sure they wouldn't miss Albert at the plate, because you never knew what the guy might do— good or bad. Well, his teammates felt the same way.

In some ways, Albert was very businesslike, showing up every day, ready to play, going through the same routines. He was the key to an offense that just wouldn't quit.

You could put together a full-length highlight film just from a handful of our games:

May 9: We come out in the first inning and score eight runs before Kansas City can record a single out.

June 4: Trailing 8-0 in the third inning against Toronto, we come back to win 9-8. We do it in the most thrilling manner possible: with a ninth-inning, two-out, two-run homer by Paul Sorrento.

June 30: Eddie Murray becomes only the 20th player in baseball history to collect 3,000 hits when he slaps a grounder through the right side of the infield on the Minneapolis turf. The first person to hug him is teammate Dave Winfield—the previous player to reach that milestone.

August 5: We strike terror into the hearts of our divisional rival, the White Sox, by hitting six homers in one game, two by Albert and one each by Murray, Sorrento, Lofton, and Baerga.

Everybody in the world knew we were going to win the pennant. The only drama became how soon we would clinch.

The magic moment came September 8, after only 123 games.

We were at home against Baltimore, and the Orioles were playing us tough. The game came down to the final out in the ninth inning, with us clinging to a 3-2 lead and Mesa on the mound. Jose got Jeff Huson to hit a foul pop-up, which third baseman Jim Thome snared easily. The crowd went ballistic. And no wonder: it was Cleveland's first baseball championship of any kind since 1954.

Strangers in the stands hugged each other. Drivers honked their horns throughout the city. Television stations ran bulletins, and newspapers began to assemble special editions.

Clinching the title meant just as much to the guys on the field. After Thome's catch, the whole team ran to the center of the diamond to celebrate. Then we went into the locker room and put on white hats and white T-shirts reading "Central Division Champions." It was like we had just won the World Series. Everybody was hugging and throwing around champagne. With the exception of guys like Murray and Hershiser, we had never been in the playoffs, and the feeling was almost indescribable.

After about five minutes inside, we went back out on the field to share the celebration with the fans. Mark Clark, Alvaro Espinoza, Julian Tavarez, and Manny Ramirez paraded the pennant out toward the flagpole on top of the scoreboard in left-center, followed by the whole team. When the flag was hooked to the clips, Murray pulled it to the top. What a sight. You spend your whole career playing for moments like this.

Clinching with several weeks left in the season gave us time to rest and get mentally prepared for the postseason. Some observers wondered if clinching that early was good, because we would be coasting along while other playoff teams would be growing accustomed to playing under pressure. But we didn't care when we clinched. We just wanted to get there. And we certainly didn't ease up after locking up the division. In fact, we picked up seven more games on second-place Kansas City. Our final record: 100-44. That's almost 7 wins in every 10 games.

Northeast Ohio was on fire as the playoffs approached. You could almost feel the emotion in the air. Unfortunately, the rest of the baseball world didn't care so much. Nationally, attendance and TV ratings were way down because of fan resentment over the strike. But in Greater Cleveland, as we prepared to open the first-round series against Boston, every newscast and every conversation seemed to center on the Tribe.

The day of the Indians' first playoff game in 41 years, the skies over Cleveland decided to imitate the Venezuelan rain forests. Driving rain and thunder pummeled the city for eight hours. The only thing stirring on the field was the grounds crew, messing with the tarp.

Finally, the weather broke, the tarp was removed, and the game began, 39 minutes late.

Ace Roger Clemens started for Boston against Dennis Martinez. The Red Sox jumped to a 2-0 lead . . . we came back with three in the sixth . . . and the Sox scored again to tie it. Then the skies opened up again, forcing another, 23-minute delay.

The tie lasted until the top of the 11th, when Boston scored what appeared to be a crushing blow on Tim Naehring's homer. But we weren't finished. Albert came up in the bottom of the 11th and jacked a homer to tie the game yet again.

The game went on and on. Finally, in the 13th inning—five hours after the start—backup catcher Tony Pena was at the plate with two outs. With the count at 3-0, he got the "take" sign from the third-base coach. But he either missed the sign or ignored it, because he swung—and lifted a game-winning homer into the bleachers.

The clock read 2:08 A.M. And the magic was still with us.

What a fabulous contest. The longest playoff game in major league history. Incredible drama. Every pitch meant something. I love those kinds of games. And when you win the first game in a five-game series, it takes a huge amount of pressure off, especially when you're playing at home.

The next night was a more traditional game. It lasted nine innings and was over in an hour and a half. We won 4-0 behind Hershiser. But the game didn't lack excitement—particularly for me.

The score was 0-0 in the fifth when I came to the plate with Paul Sorrento on third and Lofton on first. Both of them had been walked by Boston starter Erik Hanson. The count went to 1-and-1, then Hanson threw me a fastball down the middle. I cranked it into the gap in left-center, clearing the bases with a double. To that point, it was the biggest hit of my career.

We added two more runs in the eighth, then headed to the airport to fly to Boston.

We were in perfect shape, needing only one victory in the next three games. But why wait? We got right down to business at Fenway Park against knuckleballer Tim Wakefield, who usually gave us a lot of trouble. On this night, though, we erupted in the second inning. I can still see Jim Thome's blast into the right field stands, arcing high into the October night, so high you thought it was going to hit the moon. When it came down, we were ahead 2-0.

We put the game away in the sixth when we scored five more runs, two off my bat. At that point, many of the 34,211 customers started heading for the exits. Final score: 8-2. For the Red Sox, it was three-games-and-out. For the Tribe, it was the first playoff sweep in 95 years.

Our pitching and defense were superb. Boston's big sluggers, Mo Vaughn and Jose Canseco, went a combined 0-for-27.

Now we could sit back and wait for our next opponent.

MEANWHILE, ONE OF THE BEST playoff series in baseball history was unfolding in a coast-to-coast marathon between Seattle and the Yankees. Looking dead-and-buried after losing the first two games of the five-game series, the M's won three straight times to stun the Yanks. No true baseball fan will ever forget Ken Griffey, Jr. scoring the winning run from first base on Edgar Martinez's double and the happy pile-up of players that followed.

The instant Griffey touched the plate, our next mission became clear: beat Seattle.

During the playoffs, almost everything changes. Even the atmosphere in the locker room is different. During the regular season, the guys straggle into the clubhouse talking about cars and golf and stuff like that. But in October, everybody is talking about the game and how to approach the opposing pitcher. It's wall-to-wall intensity.

As we arrived in Seattle for the first two games of the seven-game American League Championship Series, I was happy for my ex-teammates in the other dugout. I knew how frustrating some of their previous seasons had been. The Mariners lost 98 games in 1992, 80 games in 1993, and 63 games in strike-shortened 1994—and now they were on as big a roll as we were.

I talked to a lot of my old teammates in the outfield before the first game and compared notes about how exciting the whole thing was. One topic was the noise level in the dome. With 57,000 people screaming at the top of their lungs in what was basically an enclosed room, the crowd could sound like a fleet of 747s taking off from the nearby Boeing plant. So the Indians had to be ready.

Obviously, you can overcome a hostile crowd. Players do it all the time. But it requires sustained mental toughness.

Everybody deals with it in his own way. Baerga started wearing earplugs. Hershiser said he programmed his mind to convert the soul-jarring roars at the Kingdome into the sound of soothing ocean waves—long, smooth waves of water washing over him and keeping him calm. For me, the key is concentrating so hard that everything outside of the white lines just disappears. Most of the time, when the game is on the line, I'm not even aware the fans are there.

The Kingdome crowd didn't have much to hoot about at the beginning of Game One. We were throwing our ace, Martinez, and poor Seattle—burned out by the Yankee series—was trotting out an unknown rookie named Bob Wolcott. The first thing Wolcott did was walk the bases loaded. But then he got Belle, Murray, and Thome without giving up a single run. Against all odds, Wolcott went seven innings and gave up only two runs. The M's won, 3-2, wasting six solid innings by Martinez.

We returned to form in the second game. Manny hit two homers and got two other hits to lead us to a 5-2 win. Hershiser earned his second straight playoff win as an Indian—and his seventh straight dating back to his Dodger days. We hopped on the plane back to Cleveland in good shape.

Game Three illustrates why it's so important to be mentally tough. Seattle right fielder Jay Buhner looked like a hero when he hit an early homer. Then he looked like a bum when he dropped an easy fly ball in the eighth, allowing us to tie the game. But he kept his head on straight and, in the top of the 11th, hit a three-run homer to give the bad guys a 5-2 win. It was our first loss in 15 extra-inning games in 1995. And it hurt. The almost-unhittable Randy Johnson was their starter, and we let him off the hook.

Game Four, obviously, was crucial. And we had to play it without Albert and Sandy, who were both hurt. Albert showed up on crutches. He had turned his ankle the night before while trying to get out of the way of an inside pitch. He finished the game, but the ankle swelled overnight.

The game-time temperature was in the 40s—not exactly ideal for a team with a lot of Latin players. But we jumped on starter Andy Benes right away. Murray ripped a three-run homer in the first inning, and we went on to wipe out the M's, 7-0. One of the RBIs was mine. The series was tied again, with one more huge game in Cleveland.

The next night, we looked like Little Leaguers, committing four errors. But we hung in there, made some big plays when we had to, and Thome came through with a sixth-inning homer to lead us to a 3-2 win. We were heading back to Seattle needing one more win in two games.

But winning even one out of two in the Kingdome wouldn't be easy. In Game Six, Johnson would again be on the mound—against a sore-armed Dennis Martinez. And if the series went to seven games, Charles Nagy—who was horrible in domes—would be our pitcher. (Charlie's dome problems weren't just psychological; a sinkerball pitcher causes batters to hit a lot of ground balls, and those grounders are more likely to find holes on the lightning-fast artificial turf.)

Besides, in Game Six, the pressure would be on the M's. If it went to Game Seven, the pressure would be on us.

As Johnson—AKA the Big Unit, a 6-foot-10 bat-eating machine—prepared to throw his first pitch, the noise was deafening. How deafening? Glad you asked. One reporter brought a decibel meter to the game, a sophisticated piece of equipment that is used most often to monitor noise levels in the workplace. And in the first inning, when Johnson struck out Lofton, the meter hit 109 decibels—the equivalent of standing right next to a chain saw.

Soon, however, Lofton would be personally responsible for cutting the decibel level nearly to zero.

In the fifth, Kenny singled home our first run. Three innings later, the score was still 1-0, and Kenny was about to pull off one of the most spectacular plays in Indians history. I had a front-row seat.

The eighth inning started with a double by Pena. Ruben Amaro pinch-ran for him. Lofton tried to sacrifice Amaro to third, but Johnson was so slow in fielding the bunt that Kenny beat it out. With runners on first and third, it was my turn to hit. On the first pitch, a ball, Lofton stole second so easily that he didn't even draw a throw. Johnson threw me another ball. On his third delivery, he unleashed a high fastball that ticked off catcher Dan Wilson's glove and rolled to the wall near the Indians' dugout.

Amaro scored easily from third. And Lofton, seeing Wilson casually jogging after the ball, hit third and just kept going. When Wilson picked up the ball and turned around, he was shocked to see Lofton streaking home. So was I. So was everybody else in the ballpark—including Johnson, who was covering home. Wilson hurriedly fired to the plate but his throw was late. Tribe 3, M's 0. At that point, the game was essentially over.

Kenny said later that he was just going to bluff coming home. But when he saw Wilson taking so long to get to the ball, he took off.

I'll never forget Kenny's play, and neither will most Tribe fans.

And a lot of Tribe fans were watching that night. Not in Seattle but 2,400 miles away in Cleveland, at home in front of their televisions. The TV ratings in Northeast Ohio averaged 58.2 percent. That means 58 of every 100 households in the region were glued to Game Six.

Johnson seemed shaken by Lofton's dash. Although he got me to fly out to left, the next batter, Baerga, drove a homer over the center-field fence to really lock up the win.

I had an excellent game in the field. I made two barehanded stops, one of which started a double play. And I started the bottom of the eighth by diving into the hole, popping up, and throwing out Alex Diaz.

We were heading to the World Series!

Although I certainly didn't want to trade places with them, I felt sorry for my old teammates. Half the team was crying in the dugout, including my old tough-guy manager, Lou Pinella. The M's had gone through an incredible season. They had been 13 games behind in August, and nobody thought they had a prayer of making the playoffs. But they won 20 of their last 24 regular season games, then won a playoff game against California to qualify. Next, they had to pull off that miraculous upset of the Yankees. Now, suddenly, their season was over.

Later I read that, a few minutes after the final out, when the P.A. announcer said: "Let's hear how you feel about the 1995 Seattle Mariners," the fans burst into a standing ovation that lasted 16 minutes. The guy with the decibel meter clocked the initial roar at 110.

Some of Seattle's players appeared to be nearly overwhelmed by the outburst. Vince Coleman picked up a bunch of baseballs and tossed them into the stands for souvenirs. Then he tossed a bunch of batting gloves. Then he took off his jersey, wadded it up, and threw that into the stands, too. The rookie pitcher, Wolcott, fired baseballs all the way into the upper deck.

A huge banner was unfurled in center field that read, "Thanks for the memories." The banner was in the same spot where the first "Refuse to Lose" sign had shown up during the summer, a phrase that quickly become the city's battle cry. "Refuse to Lose" was on T-shirts, posters, and bumper stickers. During the ALCS, it was in huge letters on the cover of the weekly *Hispanic News* ("Rehusadose A Perder") and it even flew from a banner atop the Space Needle.

Refuse to Lose. As if the whole city could simply *will* the Mariners to win.

Well, they finally lost. But during an amazing six-week period, they created an incredible trove of baseball memories for a city that sorely needed some. I was happy for them.

SHORTLY BEFORE they blew up the Kingdome to make way for
Safeco Field, the city held a sort of memorial service at the building and invited in the public to watch a special highlight film. The
movie included action shots of the M's and the city's pro football
team, the Seahawks, who played there a couple of years longer
than the Mariners did. I was told that I appeared on that tape
three times—one of them being the barehanded scoop that saved
Bosio's no-hitter.

But the big highlight reel in my memory banks will always
contain a play that didn't make the Mariners' movie: Kenny
Lofton's mad dash home from second base on October 17, 1995.

I also will not soon forget the crowd that greeted us at Cleveland Hopkins International Airport when we finally got home.
Because of our big locker-room celebration, we bussed to our
charter flight later than usual and had to fly throughout the night.
We were astonished when we arrived and saw thousands of people pressing against the fences, cheering and waving. The time
was 6:55 A.M. They had stood there all night long for a three-
minute glimpse of the team buses passing by.

And our biggest adventure was yet to come.

CHAPTER 9

The Whole World's Watching

URING THE POSTSEASON, even the players turn into fans. We stay up late watching other games in different time zones, partly to scout the competition but mostly just to see how things turn out.

With each round of the playoffs, everything grows bigger. The media coverage. The pageantry. The fame. The money. The pressure.

By the time you get all the way to the World Series, the game becomes bigger than just sports. Suddenly, even people who can't tell a curveball from a cue ball are riveted to their television sets.

In America, the World Series is one of only a handful of events like that, along with the Super Bowl, the Olympics, the Kentucky Derby, and the NCAA Basketball Finals. (Maybe someday the World Cup will be added to that list. But no time soon.)

Baseball has become such an international attraction that media from all over the world cram into the clubhouses and interview rooms. In Atlanta in 1995, two television networks and more than 400 reporters from as far away as Japan analyzed our every move.

For the third straight playoff series, we had the home-field disadvantage, simply because of the bad luck of the draw. In those days, all the match-ups were prearranged, regardless of who had the better record. And 1995 was the National League's turn to start hosting the World Series, meaning that the first two games would be in Atlanta—enough to set the tone for the Series.

The Braves' ballpark, Atlanta-Fulton County Stadium, which has since been torn down in favor of a new park next door, was nothing special. It wasn't a bad stadium; it just wasn't particularly distinctive. The only thing I remember about the facility itself was the really cool World Series logos that were painted on the fences and on the grass behind home plate. It was a classy logo for the classiest event in my profession.

My family came to Atlanta, along with a bunch of friends from Venezuela. I was thrilled with the whole situation.

Braves fans didn't seem nearly as thrilled. Atlanta had been in the two previous World Series (losing both), and their fans seemed a bit jaded. When they weren't doing that moronic "Tomahawk Chop," they were mostly sitting on their hands. The crowd was so quiet for most of the first two games that you'd have thought they were watching an exhibition game.

I just hated the "Tomahawk Chop." Fans would raise their right hand, spread their fingers slightly, and move their hand forward in a chopping motion while droning along in a fake Indian chant. It was incredibly annoying. I'd say the same thing if I were playing for the Braves. Heck, even organ music would be better than that stupid chant.

The first game was a nail-biter—as would be the case throughout the Series. Atlanta's ace, Greg Maddox, was virtually unhittable. We collected a grand total of two singles off him. Still, we were able to score two runs because of Atlanta errors and great baserunning by Kenny Lofton. Orel Hershiser pitched six strong innings, giving up only one run. But Atlanta manufactured two runs in the seventh off three walks and a squeeze bunt, and nipped us 3-2.

In Game Two, I was reminded why it is possible to both love and hate Manny Ramirez at the same time.

Atlanta was ahead, 4-3, in the eighth inning, thanks mainly to a two-run homer by catcher Javy Lopez off Dennis Martinez, who had struggled. Manny singled to center, putting the tying run on first. But then he wandered too far from the bag and was picked off on a snap throw from Lopez.

The guys in our dugout were ready to kill him. How could he be so careless in a one-run ballgame with the whole season on the line? Well, we got our answer soon enough. Manny came back and sat down between Sandy Alomar and me. We were steaming, but we didn't say anything. Manny broke the silence.

"I was thinking about Ricky Henderson."

As mad as we were, we couldn't help but crack up.

The rest of the game wasn't as funny. The Braves hung on to win behind Tom Glavine, and we headed home trailing two games to none.

Even though we were coming back to Cleveland deep in the hole, the city was exploding with enthusiasm. Game Three marked the first World Series game in Cleveland in 41 years, and everybody wanted to be a part of it.

Five hours before the game, hundreds of fans were walking up to the park, without tickets, just to look inside the gates at an empty field. Just to be there. Some took pictures; most simply stared. As game-time neared, fans honked their horns on the way into the parking decks.

During pregame introductions, the 43,584 patrons stood screaming the entire time—even cheering lustily for trainer Jimmy Warfield. When a 73-year-old fan named Sam Danze attempted to throw a strike into a net and win $1 million in a promotional gimmick, they chanted, "Sammy, Sammy, Sammy . . ." And when Chrissie Hynde, the lead singer of the Pretenders, walked onto the field to sing the national anthem, they roared.

(For the record, she was considerably better than Joe Walsh, the Cleveland native and former Eagle, who butchered the anthem before Game Five. The best anthem performer during our playoff run was Bruce Hornsby, who accompanied himself on the piano before Game Six in Seattle. But then again, I may be prejudiced. Hornsby is a good friend of former Mariner and Indian

Mark Langston, who introduced me to him and took me to some of his concerts.)

The pregame noise was subtle compared to the sound that erupted when Albert Belle ripped a single to give the Tribe a 4-1 lead in the third inning.

When somebody does something great and the crowd goes wild, I literally get the chills. It doesn't just happen when one of *our* guys makes a spectacular play; it can happen even when a player on the other team does. That might sound odd, because a big play by an opponent can hurt us. But having been out there, I realize what it takes to make a huge play in a clutch situation, and I feel good for that person on a basic human level.

A couple of hours after Albert's single, the noise inside Jacobs Field grew even louder. Atlanta had staged a rally and tied the game. Lose this one and we'd be facing a sweep. But in the bottom of the 11th Eddie Murray came through with a single, scoring Carlos Baerga. Indians win, 7-6.

It was the first World Series victory for a Cleveland team since 1948.

I felt good about making some key defensive plays in that game. Out-of-town writers were starting to refer to me as "the next Ozzie Smith."

I was happy that people were noticing my ability on a national scale. When you play in a place like Seattle, as I did for the first part of my career, you can get lost simply because you're in the Pacific time zone. Your home games don't end until maybe 1 A.M. eastern time, meaning you don't get on the mainstream sports highlight shows and you don't get into a lot of newspapers in the eastern half of the country. When I was in Seattle, the only Mariners known to most U.S. fans were Randy Johnson and Ken Griffey, Jr.

The postseason spotlight makes me play better. Playing in big games is almost easier than playing in a regular season game. Every pitch, every out, every chance means so much that you know you have to stay focused the whole time. I can get in a zone where I block everything else out and concentrate so hard that I'm not even aware of my surroundings.

I LOVE THE PLAYOFFS. Love the attention, love the commotion, love the pressure.

The only thing I don't love is that, because of television, you find yourself playing in some really ridiculous conditions.

By late October, after the sun goes down, cities like Cleveland get cold enough to freeze Gatorade. When you're playing a baseball game and can literally see snow in the air, as was the case in 1997, something is wrong.

I've played in a number of playoff games in conditions that are barely fit for football. For the first pitch of Game Three of the 1995 Series, the windchill factor was 29 degrees. Obviously, both teams are saddled with the same conditions, and all you can do is your best. But it's frustrating to play crucial games in horrible conditions.

The best weapons against the cold are Spandex outfits like the ones Fernando Montes, our conditioning coach, ordered from California. They have long sleeves and long legs and are worn under our uniforms. They stretch so well you can barely tell you have them on. We have heaters in the dugout and hot-water bottles, and a lot of guys carry little hand-warmers in their back pockets. Some guys—not me—even put Vaseline on their bodies and plastic bags around their feet to seal in the heat.

During pregame warm-ups in '95, a lot of us wore ski masks. But Mike Hargrove wouldn't let anybody wear them during the game, even if you were just sitting on the bench. He thought that would make us look too intimidated by the weather.

Between innings, we could go into the tunnel behind the dugout and stretch our muscles using "flex bands," which are like little bungee cords that we wrap around various body parts to provide resistance, somewhat like isometrics.

But even when the weather is warm, your play can suffer in October because of the starting times dictated by television. In the early playoff rounds, when the networks are showing several match-ups per day, some games start at 4 P.M. That creates horrible problems with the sun.

I hate 4 o'clock starts. The shadow from the stadium is covering home plate but the pitcher is standing in bright sunshine. It's hard enough to hit a ball that's coming at you at 95 MPH. Imagine how tough it is when the ball is coming out of the sunlight and into a shadow.

You've played 162 games that started either at night or at 1 P.M., and suddenly—facing the most important games of the season—you have to play when nobody can see anything.

The problem is not just seeing the ball when you're hitting. The half-shadow affects your defense, too. You don't hear much talk about that, but it's a big factor. If you don't follow the ball really closely, you can lose track of it just enough to miss a play you'd usually make. Most fans don't notice when it happens, because it's not a question of not seeing the ball at all; it's that you can't get the kind of jump you normally get.

We lucked out in '95 and played all our games at night, mainly because the networks saw us as an exciting team with the best record in baseball.

Unfortunately, much of the media also saw the 1995 Indians as a pain in the butt.

Before Game Three, Albert erupted in his infamous tirade against NBC reporter Hannah Storm (more on that in the next chapter). Although Storm didn't file a formal complaint and the incident wasn't much more than a minor distraction to the players, it pushed more people onto the anti-Cleveland bandwagon.

The media already weren't fond of us, because some of our top stars were standoffish or downright hostile. *Sports Illustrated* ripped us. "Not the kind of team you'd want to take home to mom," the article said. "Hanging in their clubhouse is a framed and matted essay called *The Art of Getting Along* by Wilfred Peterson. Now, if they would only read it." As another writer noted,

If you can't have fun during spring training, when can you? I was feeling especially good when this was taken, at the beginning of 2001, having just signed a contract extension that boosted my salary and meant I could probably finish my career as a Cleveland Indian. (Akron Beacon Journal, Phil Masturzo)

Here I am checking out the South American bathing beauties. I've always loved the sun, sand, and water. Although Caracas is not right on the Caribbean, it isn't far away, and I used to hit the beach often when I lived there. I still like to swim, water ski, and jet ski. (Vizquel family)

I was raised by leopards in the wilds of Venezuela, then captured at age 2 and sent to a zoo. Okay, maybe not. This might have been Halloween. Judging by my expression, I don't think I cared much for the outfit. (Vizquel family)

I acquired a taste for sports cars at an early age. Here I am firing up a Ferrari on the balcony of our apartment in Caracas. I haven't lost my love for fancy wheels. These days, I usually drive around in a yellow Porsche. (Vizquel family)

Now here's a double-play combination. My younger brother, Carlos, looks like he isn't quite sure of the game plan. Within a few years he was joining me on the ball fields. I picked on him a lot, but by age 18 he was taller than me and about 20 pounds heavier. (Vizquel family)

The big guys had nothing on us when it came to blowing bubbles. Here I am with second baseman Richard Blanco, one of my earliest double-play partners. We were on a team that won the Venezuelan World Series. He later became quite a basketball player. (Vizquel family)

Check out the Montreal Expos batting helmet. Before this, I used to wear a Baltimore Orioles hat. Like almost every other kid growing up in Venezuela, my dream was to make it to the Major Leagues. This is at Disney World in Orlando, which we visited after winning a youth championship. (Vizquel family)

I'm the one without the ears. The rodent is Gabriela, my sister. Check out my T-shirt. That's Pat Benatar, the American rock singer who was big in the 1980s. I grew up with American rock 'n' roll and loved it—even though I had no idea what the lyrics meant, because I didn't speak English at the time. (Vizquel family)

I loved playing for the Vermont Mariners in Double A ball. Even though I was making only $800 a month and sharing a tiny apartment, I had a great time. When I was called up to Triple A late in the 1988 season, I didn't want to go! (Seattle Mariners)

Looks downright prehistoric, doesn't it? Note the high stirrups. Number 42? Well, you can't be picky when you're a raw rookie. This is from my first week in the bigs, in April 1989. I actually had hair at the time. (Seattle Mariners)

I'm probably in the minority, but I have good memories of Cleveland Municipal Stadium. In 73 at-bats in the old ballpark, playing with the Mariners, I hit .301. This photo is from 1993. That December, I was traded to Cleveland, just in time to help christen Jacobs Field.

(Gregory Drezdzon, courtesy of Seattle Mariners)

Until Nico was born, I used to return every winter to play for Caracas in the Venezuelan winter league. Baseball is by far the most popular sport in my homeland. The fans are so rowdy they make Yankee Stadium seem tame. (Vizquel family)

Jim Thome congratulates me after I scored in the third inning of Game Three of the 1995 World Series against the Atlanta Braves. We went on to win a thriller in 11 innings.
(Akron Beacon Journal, Phil Masturzo)

A couple of days after the 1995 World Series, Indians fans jammed Public Square for a welcome-home rally. It made the players feel great to see all those people turn out even after we had lost. I had fun in front of the microphone that day. (Akron Beacon Journal, Lew Stamp)

I had to backhand this ball hit into the hole by Toronto's Homer Bush. The best shortstops make all the routine plays and make the hard plays look easy. (Akron Beacon Journal, Phil Masturzo)

What a great moment! Oct. 6, 1997. We had just beaten the New York Yankees in Game 5 of the division series in a thrilling 4-3 comeback win. I went 9-for-18 in the series, including the winning hit in Game Four. Nico, barely two years old, helped us celebrate in the clubhouse. (Akron Beacon Journal, Phil Masturzo)

When people ask me to name the best play I ever made, I tell them about this one. It wasn't the most spectacular play physically, but it was tough enough, and it came at an absolutely crucial time against the Marlins in Game Six of the '97 World Series. If I had missed the ball or thrown it away, we may not have gotten to Game Seven. (Akron Beacon Journal, Phil Masturzo)

It was painful to watch the Florida Marlins and their fans go crazy after Game Seven of the 1997 World Series, but I sat in the dugout for a long, long time—I wanted to get a feeling for what it would be like to win the championship in dramatic fashion. I was so bummed out on the ride back to the hotel that I could hardly talk. (AP Photo / Roadell Hickman, The Plain Dealer)

If you're going to get mugged onfield, it may as well be by the best player in the game. Ken Griffey, Jr., my former teammate, was still playing for Seattle when he got me in this bear hug before a 1999 game at Jacobs Field.
(Akron Beacon Journal, Phil Masturzo)

Nomar Garciaparra of the Red Sox is not only one of the best players in the game but one of the nicest. I really enjoyed hanging out with him during practice before the 1999 All-Star Game at Fenway Park in Boston.
(Akron Beacon Journal, Phil Masturzo)

Troy O'Leary of the Red Sox came in hard during the eighth inning of a game at Jacobs Field in September of 1998, and we couldn't turn two. We would get the last laugh that year, though. In the first round of the playoffs, we beat Boston in four games. (Akron Beacon Journal, Phil Masturzo)

Hitting a game-winner homer was the easy part. Living through the celebration was the hard part. I got a traditional rowdy reception after my ninth-inning grand slam beat the Detroit Tigers on a beautiful Sunday afternoon at Jacobs Field in May of 1999. (AP Photo / Tony Dejak)

One of the reasons I have spent a lot of my career hitting second in the lineup is that I'm a good bunter. You have to be able to move the leadoff guy along to set things up for the big guns who hit three, four, and five. I've also collected my share of bunt hits.
(Akron Beacon Journal, Phil Masturzo)

In spring training, representatives from the big glove manufacturers come around and give you a choice of gear. Every spring I pick out a new Rawlings. I use it throughout that whole season and then retire it. I use one of the smallest gloves in the majors because I don't want the ball to get lost in the pocket when I'm trying to pick it out. (Akron Beacon Journal, Phil Masturzo)

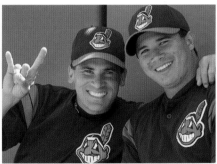

Einar Diaz has become one of my good buddies on the team. He took over as the starting catcher during the 2001 season and quickly showed he has a cannon for an arm and a strong bat.
(Akron Beacon Journal, Phil Masturzo)

Playing a little baseball Hacky Sack during a spring-training water break in March of 2000.
(Akron Beacon Journal, Phil Masturzo)

When my son, Nico, was 4, we got a miniature greyhound. They seem to strike identical poses during a summer day in 2000. Nico is the one on the left. (Phil Masturzo)

During the season, I don't get too much time to work on my painting. But when we're not on a road trip, I'll sometimes get in a couple of hours of work before driving to the park.
(Akron Beacon Journal, Phil Masturzo)

When we play in Seattle, I stay at our home in Issaquah, about 20 minutes from Safeco Field. This photo was taken on an off-day. I'm sitting near the front door of the 10,000-square-foot house I designed. (Phil Masturzo)

Backstage at the 2001 Tribe Jam with my wife, Nicole. (Phil Masturzo)

At one end of our Seattle house is a room that's all mine. That's where I keep autographed baseballs, my Gold Glove trophies, all kinds of photos and posters, plus one of my prized possessions, an autographed Michael Jordan jersey. (Phil Masturzo)

Here's a painting I was working on in August of 2000. I've tried a number of styles over the years. During the season, my studio isn't very fancy—I use the garage. But it works fine. I like the natural light that comes pouring in the open garage door. (Phil Masturzo)

Guess who? I really like the lighting in this shot. It was taken before a 2000 home game in the tunnel leading from the clubhouse to the Tribe dugout. (Akron Beacon Journal, Phil Masturzo)

Three-quarters of our 2000 infield won Gold Gloves, awarded annually to the best defensive player at each position in the league. The trophies were handed out before a game in May of 2001. Second baseman Robbie Alomar (left) won his ninth, third baseman Travis Fryman (right) won his first, and I collected my eighth. Robbie and I won again for the 2001 season. (AP / Tony Dejak)

Carlos Lee tries to take me out as I start a double play against the White Sox at Jacobs Field in 2001.
(Akron Beacon Journal, Phil Masturzo)

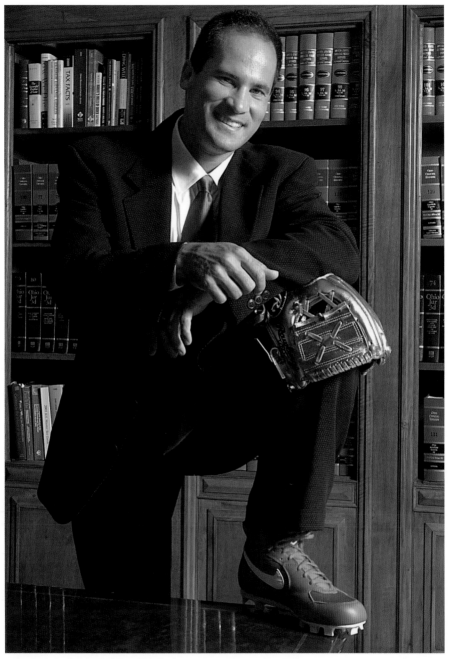

I earned my ninth straight Gold Glove during the 2001 season, tying me with Hall of Fame shortstop and fellow Venezuelan Luis Aparicio. The only shortstop in the history of the game with more is Ozzie Smith, who was named to the Hall of Fame in 2002. Ozzie retired with 13 Gold Gloves.

(Akron Beacon Journal, Phil Masturzo)

I was worried about the reception I would get in March, 2001, when we played two sold-out exhibition games in Valencia, Venezuela, but the fans were great. Vizquel jerseys were everywhere, even hours before game-time—in spite of the fact that my old team, Caracas, is Valencia's archrival. (AP / Juan Carlos Solorzano)

Crank it up, baby! Here I am at the 2001 Tribe Jam at Nautica in the Flats. The annual July event raises money for Cleveland Indians Charities. (Don't tell anybody, but the red pants I'm wearing belong to Nicole.) (Akron Beacon Journal, Phil Masturzo)

During spring training at Winter Haven, I sometimes give fielding clinics for kids. Here, I'm showing how to get in position to backhand a ground ball. (Akron Beacon Journal, Phil Masturzo)

Sometimes before a home game I'll wander over to the stands on the third-base side of the field and sign autographs. Unfortunately, you never have enough time to sign them all. I collect autographed balls myself, so I know how much it means to people. (Akron Beacon Journal, Phil Masturzo)

In 2001 my son, Nico, made his debut as a bat boy. He worked several games at Jacobs Field and even got into action on a road trip. Here he is at Safeco Field in Seattle, joking with Robbie Alomar. I'm on the left, waiting to hit while Seattle changes pitchers. (AP / Cheryl Hatch)

more words may have been spoken and written about our team's off-the-field surliness than were used to describe our efforts against the Braves.

That was hard to take for the average guy on our team, because the average guy on the 1995 Indians was just as nice as the average guy on any other team. The media tarred everybody with the same brush. Part of it, I think, was that the team was so powerful that we generated a lot of resentment. In other words, some of it was simple jealously. But some of it was clearly deserved.

So when we lost Game Four, 5-2, press row wasn't exactly suicidal. It was the only game in the entire Series decided by more than one run. More importantly, it left us only one game away from a long winter vacation.

The situation certainly wasn't hopeless. Six teams had been down 3-1 in a World Series and ended up wearing championship rings. In 1985, Kansas City rallied to beat St. Louis. In 1979, the Pirates did the same against the Orioles.

Still, to survive the next game we would have to get past the amazing Maddux, who mowed down Indians like a grounds crew mows down grass. But in the bottom of the first, Albert lit up Maddux for an opposite-field, two-run homer. We got two more runs off him before Thome knocked him out in the eighth with a homer.

Hershiser was superb again, going eight tough innings, and we hung on to win, 5-4, sending everybody back to Atlanta.

Meanwhile, the Braves were dealing with a small media problem of their own. Midway through the Series, one of their players, David Justice, ripped his own fans for being so laid-back. He said the Cleveland fans were louder and that the Braves fans were spoiled from seeing three World Series in five years. He backpedaled a bit before Game Six, telling reporters that, although he didn't deny making the comments, he didn't mean them to be as strong as they were.

The first two times he came up to hit, he was booed. But it's amazing how quickly people forget. In the sixth inning, when he led off with a homer against reliever Jim Poole—it would be the lone run in the deciding game—the cheers were thunderous.

Our offense went with barely a whimper: one hit, a bloop single. Even though I made what some called the defensive play of the Series—a flip from my glove to Baerga, which he barehanded and threw to Murray for the double play—you just can't win without scoring.

Our season was over. We went into the clubhouse to pack while the Braves partied. After the initial clubhouse celebration and interviews, they went back out on the field for at least 90 minutes. Players and their wives were walking around the diamond with beer and champagne. Everyone from owner Ted Turner to the batboy was hugging everyone else. Several Braves walked slowly around the field, as if trying to lock the moment into their memory banks.

Although the loss stung, given our high expectations, the pain passed relatively quickly. Unlike the 1997 Series, when I would be emotionally crushed, in 1995 I was happy simply to have gotten to a World Series. A lot of great players never do.

WHEN I THINK BACK TO 1995, I think about magic. I think about all the big rallies and the comeback wins and what a joy it was to play on a team that good.

That joy came through two days after we returned from Atlanta and headed to a big rally at Public Square in downtown Cleveland. Although the weather was cold and drizzly, an estimated 40,000 people turned out to cheer us. Probably 30,000 of them were skipping school or work. One police official said it was the biggest crowd for a downtown event he had seen since joining the force in 1969.

Confetti and streamers fell to the ground as balloons soared into the sky. High school marching bands paraded ahead of our bus as it crept west from Euclid Avenue and East 22nd Street to the square. Bells on the landmark Old Stone Church played *Take*

Me Out to the Ballgame. Governor George Voinovich, Mayor Mike White, team owner Dick Jacobs, and a bunch of other dignitaries were on hand.

White took delight in reciting the Justice quote about Cleveland fans being more enthusiastic than Atlanta fans. "He was right," said the Mayor. "But, David . . . we've got the best team, too."

Manager Mike Hargrove thanked the crowd and praised the fans who showed up at the airport early Sunday morning to welcome us back the night of the loss. "I have never been so excited in my entire life, to see you people at the airport for us," he said.

That airport scene really was amazing. At 2:40 A.M., in a cold rain, people were standing five deep along a 550-foot fence at the I-X Jet Center. Authorities estimated the crowd at 6,000. Over and over they chanted, "Thank you, Tribe. Thank you, Tribe." Instead of getting right off the plane and onto the buses, as usual, we went over to chat and touch hands through the fence. I wasn't expecting that at all. I was blown away by their loyalty.

Caught up in the community spirit, I hitched a ride back in a police car. I had always wanted to do that.

Now, at the noontime rally two days later, about 20 players were on hand, including all of the regulars except for Albert and Manny. We sat on a grandstand in the heart of the city. Several of us were asked to take turns in front of the microphone. When I started to speak, I just couldn't stop.

Two parachutists had dropped into the square to deliver an American flag and an Indians flag, so I said: "We're still waiting for Julian Tavarez and Manny Ramirez. They were supposed to jump from the airplane. They're probably in Lake Erie somewhere."

I told some anecdotes about the "glory" of playing in a World Series, including this one:

"I was in a store in Atlanta buying a shirt. A sales lady asked me if I was a ballplayer. I said that I was. She said, 'Oh, I love how you play!' I thanked her and bought the shirt. On the way out, I heard another sales lady say, 'Who was that man you were talking to?'

The first lady said, 'Oh, that's Mark Lemke, the second baseman for the Braves.'"

The crowd was eating it up. But I rambled on so long that Hargrove started to make slashing motions, urging me to cut off my monologue. I figured the season was over, so I didn't have to catch every sign from the manager, and I kept on going. Finally, Wayne Kirby, who was carrying an umbrella with a curved handle, grabbed me by the neck and started to pull me away from the microphone, just like they did in the old vaudeville days.

I didn't want to leave without sharing all the stuff that happened. You don't get to play in a World Series every day. And, as I told the crowd that day: "We lost the World Series, but I don't think anyone can beat you guys."

I meant it.

CHAPTER 10

Albert and Other Clubhouse Characters

I DIDN'T HATE ALBERT BELLE. But he was certainly a difficult guy to like.

During the three years I played with him, Albert would talk easily to me about anything involving baseball—the pitchers, the hitters, whatever. But the instant somebody came around who wasn't wearing a uniform, he completely changed. He'd stop talking, sit down, and turn his back. He just didn't want to meet anybody new. He didn't want anybody to know his life. I don't know why, but for some reason he just wanted to talk to his teammates. As long as he was doing that, he was a regular guy—at least most of the time.

When Albert got mad, though, even his teammates were the enemy.

If he was struggling at the plate, you didn't want to be anywhere near him. He would come back to the clubhouse and just start trashing stuff. He'd take a bat to a nice spread of food . . . to the thermostat on the wall . . . to anything he laid his eyes on. One time he even smashed a trophy of mine that was sitting inside my locker.

I cherished that trophy because nobody on earth expected me to win it—including me. Clearly, I'm not the world's biggest home-run threat. But in 1996, we were playing an exhibition game against our Triple-A affiliate in Buffalo, and our media relations director, Bart Swain, was having trouble rustling up enough guys to participate in a pregame home run contest. They needed one more guy. So I half-jokingly told Bart, "Put me in there." He did—and I ended up winning. I hit eight balls over the fence, compared to seven for Albert. The other guys hit five or six. So they gave me a trophy and I put it in my locker.

About a month and a half later, Albert came into the clubhouse after going 0-for-4. He was in a rage. He started trashing everything in sight. At one point, he clobbered my trophy. Knocked the little batter guy right off the top.

Albert didn't say a word to me about it. Not that day, not ever.

As a matter of fact, Albert never apologized for anything. Heck, he wouldn't even admit to doing anything wrong, much less apologize for it.

Remember the corked bat episode? If you're an Indians fan, I'm sure you do. Well, to hear Albert tell it, the whole thing was a setup. The White Sox stole his bats, corked them, then framed the poor soul. Right.

Believe me, I was as surprised as anyone. Today I'd say the same thing whether I was chatting in a restaurant, writing my autobiography, or testifying under oath: I had no idea his bat was corked.

It's July 15, 1994. We're in the middle of a pennant race with our increasingly bitter rival, the Chicago White Sox. Albert is tearing up the league. The night before, in the first game of a four-game series at Comiskey Park, he blasts a 425-foot homer, his 26th of the season.

Now, in the top of the first inning, we already have a run home and Carlos Baerga is standing on first. As Albert strolls to the plate, White Sox manager Gene Lamont approaches home-plate umpire Dave Phillips and asks him to confiscate Belle's bat. (The rules allow a manager to do that once per game.)

Phillips looks at Belle's bat and doesn't see anything wrong with it. The top of the barrel, where a hole would have been drilled to insert the cork, looks okay. It's smooth and not missing any paint. But Phillips has had previous experience with doctored bats, and he knows the lengths players will go to get a little more pop. In 1974, he was umpiring a game involving the Yankees when Greg Nettles swung, broke his bat, and six Super Balls flew out.

So Phillips hands Albert's bat through the screen of the backstop to an assistant, who takes it to the umpires' dressing room and locks it up. The suspicious bat will be sent to the league office in New York, where it will be x-rayed or sawed in half.

In the dugout, guys were saying, "Oh my God! The bat is corked!" My response was, "What?" I felt a little bit like the way I felt when I first heard the true identity of the Tooth Fairy.

I can be naïve at times, but I'm not stupid. Certainly not stupid enough to steal Albert's corked bat and replace it with one that looked completely different—one that was autographed by Paul Sorrento. That wasn't even a nice try.

The problem, of course, was that *all* of Albert's bats were corked.

Obviously, we didn't want to see our best hitter suspended. So one player took matters into his own hands. I didn't discover the identity of the culprit for about a week. It took five more years for him to come forward and tell his tale to the public. Pitcher Jason Grimsley finally confessed to the *New York Times* that he was the one who crawled through the ceiling from our clubhouse to the umpires' room and switched the bats.

"That was one of the biggest adrenaline rushes I've ever experienced," Grimsley told the *Times*. He was a spot starter for us in those days, and he wasn't pitching that particular game. He remembered that the visitors' clubhouse had a drop ceiling with removable panels, and he knew the umpires' quarters were on the same level of the stadium. What could prevent him from crawling along the top of the cement-block walls and swooping down into the umps' room? Well, wires and pipes and darkness and danger. But he was in the mood for adventure.

Grimsley grabbed a bat and, with a flashlight in his mouth, crawled 100 feet along an 18-inch-wide wall to where he thought the umps' room was. When he removed a ceiling panel, he realized he had miscalculated slightly, because he saw a member of the grounds crew sitting on a couch. He knew the umps' room was right next door, so he crawled a few more feet and lifted another tile. Bingo. He dropped onto a refrigerator, then onto a countertop, then onto the floor. He hastily switched bats and began his retreat.

As soon as he climbed back up into the ceiling, somebody came into the room. Grimsley had to sit up there in the ceiling, completely still, for several minutes before the person left and he could start the long crawl back.

Given the fact that Grimsley was 6-foot-3 and 180 pounds, this may have been one of our more remarkable athletic feats of the season.

The scam took about four innings to complete. When Grimsley returned to our dugout, he told the people who were involved that everything was taken care of.

Not quite. The bats were so different that the umps and the White Sox instantly knew something was rotten. They didn't know how we had managed to pull the switch, but they knew it had taken place. Indians officials were eventually informed that the person who switched the bats would be suspended if the proper bat were not returned. They knew fingerprints would have told the real story, if things came to that, so they caved in and turned over the real bat. Albert got a 10-game suspension, which was reduced to seven after an appeal.

Following the game, in which Albert went 1-for-4, striking out twice, he finally talked to reporters, because he wanted to set the record straight: "It's all [bleeping] bull[bleep]," he said.

Right.

"Batgate," as it was dubbed, has since entered into baseball lore. Looking back on it, Albert's episode was much funnier than the one involving Cincinnati's Chris Sabo, who was caught doing

the same thing two years later. Sabo insisted he was using someone else's bat and had no idea it was corked. Not much imagination there.

But even Belle's affair wasn't quite as amusing as a 1997 corking incident involving Dodger rookie Wilton Guerrero. Guerrero
broke his bat while hitting a grounder and, instead of running to
first, he ran around near home plate, frantically scooping up little pieces of cork, apparently believing he could hide the evidence.

The idea behind corking a bat is that, by replacing wood with
cork, the same size bat will be lighter, which means the hitter can
generate more bat speed, which means he can send the ball farther. They open a hole deep in the top of the bat, then stuff cork
in. Then they glue a piece of wood in the top of the hole, sand it
smooth, and repaint it.

As you can probably tell from my home run stats, I haven't
personally done it. But, believe it or not, I was accused of it. Yes,
me, Omar Vizquel, a guy with fewer than 50 career taters.

In mid-July of 1999, on a Saturday afternoon, we were playing
Cincinnati in front our usual sellout crowd at Jacobs Field. It was
a long, wild game. We were behind for most of the way and
needed a three-run rally in the seventh just to pull within one
run. In the eighth, Manny Ramirez tied the game with a homer.
But the Reds scored in the top of the ninth to take a dishearten-
ing 10-9 lead.

In the bottom of the ninth, I came to the plate with two outs.
John McDonald was on first, pinch-running. The first pitch from
Cincinnati's Scott Williamson was a ball. On the next pitch, I
smacked a homer into the right-field stands, giving us an 11-10
win. The place went nuts. After I crossed the plate, Jim Thome
picked me up and carried me around.

But in the next day's papers, their pitcher, Williamson, accused me of cheating. "Let's check their bats," he yelled to reporters in the clubhouse afterward. "I thought it was a routine
pop-up. I didn't think a little guy could hit a low-and-away pitch
like that."

Believe it, pal.

Besides, this was no pop-up. It was a line drive. I was running hard to first because I wasn't sure it was high enough to clear the eight-foot wall in right.

The accusation was actually kind of flattering. At that point in the season I was batting .352 with runners in scoring position, so opponents were worrying more and more about how to get me out. But seeing as how that was my third homer of the season, after nearly four months of action, I'm not sure how anyone could accuse me of juicing my equipment.

ALBERT DID ALL KINDS OF THINGS I would never dream of doing. Case in point: the infamous Hannah Storm episode, which nearly upstaged our play in the World Series.

As usual, I had a front-row seat—like it or not.

An hour or so before the third game of the 1995 Series, Storm, a reporter for NBC, was sitting in the corner of our dugout with a camera crew, waiting to interview Kenny Lofton. Belle was walking off the field to the clubhouse when he just started unloading on her, calling her the vilest names in the book.

The scene was pretty bad. She hadn't done anything to provoke him. She wasn't even trying to talk to him. She was just trying to do her job by talking to another of our players before a big game on national television—a game NBC had paid a ton of money to televise. Belle simply lost it. He started swearing a blue streak, and just kept going.

About 20 reporters were in the dugout at the time. So even though Storm didn't file any official complaint, word got around quickly. Eventually, the commissioner fined Albert $50,000.

Who knows what triggered that explosion? It was odd behavior even by Albert's standards. And those were high standards.

Before I arrived, Albert was suspended three times. The first time, 1991, he drilled a heckling fan in the chest with a baseball. In 1992, he was suspended for charging the mound after he thought a pitcher threw at him. In 1993, ditto. I understand he was even suspended in the minor leagues for eating a hot dog in the dugout, then getting into a scuffle when his manager confronted him.

After I joined the team, things got even more interesting. In 1995, Albert climbed into his SUV and chased down some teenagers who had egged his house as a Halloween prank. In 1996, he threw a ball at a photographer who dared to aim a lens at him. A month later, he was suspended for throwing a vicious forearm at Milwaukee's Fernando Vina, a friend of mine, while running to second base. And one month after that, he threw a cup of Gatorade on a TV cameraman in Chicago.

Albert's resume also includes: slapping a drunk with a ping-pong paddle during an evening in the Flats, destroying two thermostats (because he thought the clubhouse was too warm), and insulting more autograph seekers than perhaps any player in baseball history.

Most of the time, though, when he was around us, he seemed reasonably happy. And, man, could that guy hit the ball.

For a great example of his impact, look at the second-to-last game he ever played for us. It was Game Three of the 1996 Division Series against the Orioles.

After being upset in the first two games in Baltimore, we needed a win to keep from being swept. We held the lead briefly, then Baltimore went ahead, then we fought back to tie it. In the bottom of the seventh, with the bases loaded, Albert ripped a pitch from Armando Benitez into the bleachers that put the game away. Jacobs Field went absolutely crazy. The noise was so loud you could feel it vibrating your chest.

By that point in his career, Albert had turned around so many games with one swing that he could write his own ticket. Which, of course, he did.

I wasn't at all surprised when he left for Chicago with a five-year deal worth $55 million. He said it wasn't about the money. Obviously not. It must have been his love affair with the White Sox, the team that got him suspended two years earlier.

The first time Albert returned to Jacobs Field after signing with the White Sox, he was a marked man. I was beginning to think I was back home in Venezuela—people were throwing golf balls, batteries, and half-filled cups of beer. Someone even threw his own foul ball back at him from the upper deck behind home plate.

In the second game of the series, Albert was hit by a Jose Mesa pitch. The next batter, Harold Baines, hit a grounder to Tony Fernandez at second, who flipped it to me. Albert came at me with his spikes high. Fortunately I was able to jump over him. I figured he would do something like that, and I was ready for him.

What a difference a year made to the fans. The people on the terrace in left field who once worshipped Albert were dropping dollar bills onto the field, taunting him about caring only about the money.

A lot of people seemed surprised when he took the big paycheck and ran. But I saw it coming. Just like I saw Manny Ramirez's departure coming five years later.

During Manny's last season with the Indians, as he came closer and closer to free agency, he kept walking around saying, "I'm going to break the bank. I'm going to break the bank." Manny didn't talk like that. It just wasn't a phrase he would use. To me, it was obvious somebody had planted that seed, and the seed had taken root. The only mystery to me was what team he'd end up with and how much he'd get. (He wound up with the Red Sox at $160 million over eight years.)

Manny is wacky, but he isn't a bad guy. I enjoyed him as a teammate. We hung out together sometimes, and he was a whole lot smarter than most people thought. I still consider him a pal. But there was a screw loose somewhere.

Most guys are very particular about which bat they use. Each player gets his own custom-made bats, and we agonize over the length, weight, and shape. But half the time, Manny didn't even use his own bats. In batting practice, he would grab six bats from six different players and see which one felt best. Even when a bat felt good, he wouldn't necessarily keep using it. I saw Manny go 3-for-3 with one bat, then use another bat the fourth time up. I saw him hit a home run and then, in the very next at-bat, against the same pitcher, switch to another bat. Heck, one day in Oakland he hit three homers using two different bats.

Sandy Alomar got mad at him one time because he kept breaking Sandy's bats.

During the 1999 season, after Manny hit a homer on a half-swing, the Yankees accused him of corking his bat. Everybody on the Indians laughed hysterically. There isn't enough cork in the world to fill all the different bats he used. The guy is just so strong and so good that I think he could pull a branch off a tree and still hit the ball 400 feet.

The stuff in your locker was never safe when Manny was around. He'd wear other people's shoes. He'd put on other people's T-shirts, socks, and underwear. He used to steal bullpen catcher Dan Williams's pants. His favorite place in the clubhouse was the locker that had a tag reading, "NO NAME." It was where the clubhouse guys put stuff when they couldn't figure out whom it belonged to. Manny would root around in there and take caps and shirts and anything else that struck his fancy.

Manny would even put on other people's underwear. He didn't care if they were medium or extra-large. He'd just toss them on, then go out and get three hits.

After a while, Manny stopped talking to reporters. I think a big reason was that he wasn't very comfortable speaking English and was afraid he'd say the wrong thing.

ANOTHER GUY WHO WAS A HIT on the field but difficult for the public to figure out was Eddie Murray. He didn't talk much to reporters, and he could really intimidate people with that nasty look of his. But he's funny—a lot funnier than most people think. He didn't mind talking to anyone, even the media—as long as they weren't actually interviewing him. He didn't like to sign autographs, either. He was an old-school guy: "I'm just a baseball player; I want to play my game and be left alone." But when you got to know him, you found a truly funny man.

Kenny Lofton could be a bit surly around fans and reporters, but he was a great teammate. Early in 2000, I sensed a real change in him. I think it's just a matter of maturity. He had always been a little hard on people he didn't really want to deal with. And he really didn't want contact with the press. But he seemed to warm up that season. It was the year he came back from his shoulder surgery. I don't know if that had anything to do with it, but Kenny finally seemed to understand that journalists are just doing their job. They don't want to bother him; they just want a few minutes to get some information for whatever it is they're writing about. He was just a lot more open all of a sudden. And I think he began to appreciate how much goodwill he had built up in Cleveland.

ONE OF THE TEAM'S biggest stars is at the opposite end of the spectrum from Albert. Jim Thome is the nicest fellow you'd ever want to meet. He's a hard-working guy from Middle America who gets along with just about anybody. He'd do anything for you.

His teammates liked him so much that, on his birthday in 1997—August 27—we decided to honor him by wearing our uniforms the same way he does—in the 50-year-old style where you roll up your pant leg to just below the knee, exposing most of the colored sock. In his case, that's about five miles of socks.

I hate that look. I agreed to go along with it just for Jimmy's birthday. Unfortunately, we won the game, so we had to wear the Big Socks again the next night. Suddenly, everybody on the team started to get hot, we started a big winning streak, and we couldn't get rid of those damn socks. We wore them all through the season, into the playoffs, and right on through to the seventh game of the World Series.

Tony Fernandez hated that look, too. No wonder. With his thin legs and the long socks, he looked like a lizard. I didn't look much better. In a fashion sense, we were the ugliest double-play combination in baseball.

Around the league, the trend on pant lengths has gone in two different directions. A bunch of players, like Chad Curtis of the Rangers, Marquis Grissom of the Dodgers, and Orlando Hernandez of the Yankees, have gone to the Thome style. Some of them, including Grissom, say they're doing it as a tribute to Jackie Robinson and the old Negro League players, who all wore their pants that way.

The opposite extreme has also come into vogue. Some players are cutting the elastic in the bottom of their pant legs so that their pants hang over their spikes, almost like dress pants. Barry Bonds is among them.

During 2001, Russell Branyan was our unofficial team leader in this category. His uniform pants were so long you half expected him to trip.

That season, the long-pants guys won me over, too. I had worn my pants at ankle length for years. But they would creep up my leg and, with the elastic in there, they'd stay creeped up until I pulled them back down. I figured that if my pant leg was loose at the bottom, I wouldn't have to worry about pulling it back down all the time. So I borrowed some tape-cutting scissors from the trainers and cut the elastic out of the bottom of all my game pants. Then I poked two small holes in the front, right at the bottom; I run my shoelaces through there and tie them. That way, the pants aren't going anywhere.

For almost my entire pro career I have worn high-top rubber spikes, rather than the low-cut metal cleats worn by a lot of players. I decided to switch in the minor leagues after accidentally stepping on a bat that was lying on the ground. When I stomped on that bat, the impact forced the metal up against my foot and gave me a bruise that took about two months to heal. Even before that, I had worried that the metal cleats might catch in the dirt when I was sliding and I'd wreck my ankle. So I tried the rubber and, when I discovered that I still had good control and balance, and could steal bases just as well, I said, "Why bother with cleats?"

The rubber knobs on the bottom of my shoes aren't much

good on the rubberized warning track that goes all the way around our field, but metal cleats aren't any better. The track is dangerous for everybody, although I realize having a dirt track that long would cause a lot more problems with maintenance.

I like high-tops because they give your ankle a little extra support. I like the way they look, too. I tried them soon after I saw Bill Buckner wearing them in the 1986 World Series—not that I was trying to model myself after his World Series performance. But I tried them and liked them.

Players don't have many fashion options when it comes to uniforms. For a few years, our starting pitcher got to choose which color top we wore. Some guys, like Bartolo Colon and C. C. Sabathia, liked our blue top because dark colors make you look thinner. If I had been a pitcher—which, trust me, will not happen in your next three lifetimes—I would go with the traditional white at home and gray on the road. I think those look sharp. If I started losing, I'd probably change colors to try to change my luck.

Not that I spend a whole lot of time worrying about baseball fashion. The length of a player's pants and the color of his jersey is not exactly the key to a team's success. What *can* make a difference, believe it or not, is the seating arrangement in the clubhouse. That can affect team chemistry. And team chemistry can make a difference in wins and losses.

CLUBHOUSE SEATING is done mainly by seniority. If you're a veteran player, you can request a certain locker when it comes open after a trade. But if somebody is there before you, you're usually out of luck, even if you're Babe Ruth.

The initial assignments are made by the clubhouse manager. I got lucky in 1994 and was handed a corner locker, which is prime real estate. I've been in "the Hot Corner" ever since. For my first seven years, Sandy Alomar sat on one side of me. When Sandy signed with the White Sox after the 2000 season, Jim Thome moved to Sandy's old spot.

On the other side of me, for my first four years, was Jose Mesa.

After he was traded to San Francisco in the middle of 1998, that locker was open, off and on, for quite a while. In 2001, my buddy Jolbert Cabrera moved into the neighborhood.

That Cabrera would end up sitting next to me at a locker in Cleveland, Ohio, is beyond belief. Our relationship began, long-distance, when I was 18 years old and he was 12.

A Latin man came up to me while I was playing in the instructional league and said, "Hey, Omar, how about helping out a couple of kids who are playing baseball back in my hometown in Colombia? Could you give me one of your gloves?" By that time, I had a contract with Rawlings. The man seemed nice, and I had two new gloves, so I gave him one. He took it back to his kids in Cartagena, Colombia. And one of those kids was Jolbert Cabrera. The man's other son was Orlando Cabrera, who in 2001 won a Gold Glove at shortstop for the Montreal Expos. Both of the brothers grew up using my glove!

The first time Jolbert told me that story, I almost died. Eight billion people in this world . . . I give away one glove . . . and it ends up going to the person who would become my best friend on the 2001 team, a guy with his locker right next to mine.

The things that go on in the clubhouse can have a real impact on a player's peace of mind. Let me put it this way: when Albert left to play with the White Sox, he offered our longtime clubhouse attendant, Frank Mancini, $200,000 to go with him. Frank declined. And when Manny Ramirez went to Boston five years later, Manny upped the ante, offering Frank $250,000 to go with *him*. Frank declined again.

Which raises two big questions:

First, why would a guy who makes probably $30,000 or $40,000 turn down that kind of money? Because Frank Mancini isn't driven by money. He is driven by his heart. And his heart is in Cleveland. He's a Cleveland boy who loves his job and likes to hang out with the guys.

Second, how could a man whose main job is picking up dirty laundry be worth a quarter-million dollars to a ballplayer? This

one is easy, provided you know Frank Mancini. Frank is, quite
simply, an amazing guy in an ordinary job. He's intelligent and incredibly well-rounded. He can talk knowledgably about art, reli-
gion, or fine wine. You can talk to this guy about any subject
under the sun. He is far more experienced than you might imagine, too. He's married to an Asian woman, and they have a beautiful little daughter; in the off-season, they travel the world.

GENERALLY, the guy with the biggest impact on the mood of the
clubhouse is the manager.

Mike Hargrove, who was my manager longer than anyone else
in the big leagues, was really laid-back. He didn't initiate much.
But I never had any problem with him. He was a good guy toward
me. Whenever I was having a problem with my game, he'd come
to me and we'd talk face to face and solve the problem.

Our relationship changed during the six years we were together. It grew. We became less like boss and employee and more
like two friends. We talked a lot more. One of the biggest things he
did for me was give me a lot more confidence in my ability to steal
bases. But we didn't just talk about baseball. We talked quite a bit
about life outside of baseball, such as family matters.

Still, I didn't necessarily disagree with the decision to fire Hargrove after the 1999 season. It was probably time for him to go.
After a while, a manager loses his effectiveness. Players just get
tired of hearing him and tune him out. It's not like he did a bad
job managing that last year, but I think we probably needed a
change. He had ample opportunity to win it all in Cleveland, and
things just weren't going the way they were supposed to go. After
finishing the regular season 21 games ahead of second-place
Chicago and winning the first two games of the five-game Division Series against Boston, we never, ever should have been
bumped out in the first round.

Charlie Manuel is a completely different type of manager. He's
a lot more fun, a lot more like one of the players. Every time you
see him he's smiling and cracking jokes. It doesn't matter what the

situation is. If you're in a 2-1 game in the ninth inning and he's bringing in the closer, he'll crack a joke and relax you. He's great at keeping things relaxed. That's important, because there's enough pressure in this game as it is.

But Charlie isn't a pushover. During the middle of his first season as manager, 2000, Charlie thought the team was *too* relaxed. He took the ping-pong table out of the clubhouse and removed the big, comfortable leather sofas. He banned card games.

The ping-pong table had been the brainchild of Albert Belle. He had it delivered in 1995, and soon big tournaments were held. Belle, Paul Shuey, Eric Plunk, and Orel Hershiser were the ones who usually duked it out. Later, Kenny Lofton and Richie Sexson were among the regulars.

Charlie didn't like the way we had been performing, and he wanted us to work a little harder at getting on our game face. "This is not a country club," he declared.

Sometimes Charlie surprises us with the moves he makes during a game. He doesn't spend a whole lot of time analyzing a situation and pouring over statistics and thinking about what will be coming up four innings later. It's gut instinct. He just reacts. He does it fast and doesn't look back. You'll be ready to go on deck and he'll just say, "You're not going to hit. Get out of here. I want so-and-so."

In general, I think that's good. These days, managers have so many numbers and so many scouting reports that they drive themselves crazy.

Speaking of crazy . . . plenty of fans questioned whether General Manager John Hart had lost his marbles during the 2001 season when he traded for the controversial John Rocker.

It was a high price to pay. Both of the pitchers we sent to Atlanta—Steve Karsay and Steve Reed—were having good years, Karsay in particular. Karsay had the lowest earned run average on the staff, and had been spectacular as a setup man. His ERA was 1.28, and opponents were hitting only .187 against him. The problem, from management's perspective, was that he was going to be a free agent at the end of the 2001 season. And Steve had made no secret of the fact that he would rather be a starting pitcher or a stopper, not just another guy in the pen. Rocker, by contrast, could not become a free agent until 2004.

And Rocker could play. I batted against him twice during exhibition games and was highly impressed. He had good stuff. It was tough to pick up the ball coming out of his hand. That, combined with his upper-90s velocity, makes hitters uncomfortable.

But the trade involved more than just the issues of contracts and talent. Rocker's infamous *Sports Illustrated* quotes in December of 1999 had made him a pariah, both inside and outside of the game. In the story, he made a number of snide comments about blacks and "foreigners." The comments were so offensive that Major League Baseball suspended him for two weeks. When he returned, some of his former teammates in Atlanta called him a cancer in the clubhouse. So before Hart pulled the trigger on the trade, he decided he'd better poll the veterans on our team and ask them whether they would object to playing with Rocker.

Charlie Manuel came to me and said, "What would you think about bringing this guy to the team?" And I said, "Well, is he ready to pitch? Is he healthy? Is he still throwing hard? If so, I think he can help, because he's got a good arm. I think everybody can get over what he said. We're here on business, and if he can help the team, I think it's going to be a good addition."

All of the other veterans said roughly the same thing. So on June 24, 2001, Rocker pulled on a Cleveland Indians jersey.

Obviously, I wasn't thrilled with Rocker's derogatory quotes about "foreigners." But everybody says things they regret. I think people can learn from their mistakes. And I was willing to give him the benefit of a doubt.

Still, it's dangerous to risk team chemistry. I think it's a highly underrated factor in winning and losing. Even though the championship Oakland A's of the 1970s supposedly hated each other, I believe that, all else being equal, you're going to perform better if you enjoy the people you're working with.

You have to care about your teammates. If somebody gives up the winning run, you shouldn't stroll into the clubhouse laughing or playing music. Some guys do. They only care about their own performance. But I really feel for my teammates, especially if somebody makes an error. I don't know if I feel quite as bad for pitchers, because pitchers are in their own weird world. But I do try to show respect to people who just made a big error or are going through a tough streak. I don't play music and I don't smile.

During the first few weeks Rocker was on the team, I only talked to him once or twice. And we didn't get any closer as the season went on. When you encounter a guy like Rocker, who mostly keeps to himself, you don't want to break into his world. You wait for him to come to you. If he wants to talk or ask you a question, fine. But if you see a guy who is constantly off in a corner, the best thing to do is just leave him alone.

THE CLEVELAND INDIANS seem to be able to absorb almost any kind of character. We've had a lot of weird people come through during my years with the Indians, but the core of this team has been around so long that we just shrug and try to keep the same tone. When you are put in a position to deal with a person who is different from you, you can learn something. I look at it as an opportunity.

A lot of people in America seem to have a problem dealing with people who don't look exactly like they do. To me it seems very strange to be living in the 21st century and still see so many divisions between the colors.

In the major leagues, color is less of an issue than it is in the overall society. We literally live together for nine months a year, and you really find out what people are like. You naturally become closer. And the closer you get, the fewer significant differences you see.

I actually have fun with the race issue. I'm comfortable with it, because I've been around black people my whole life. Matter of fact, my dad is the same color as Jolbert Cabrera, really dark-skinned. So I grew up with it. And in Venezuela we just don't have much trouble with race.

On our team, at least, color is almost a nonissue. But occasionally there is friction between the Latinos and the Americans. Part of it, obviously, is the language problem. It's hard enough for two people to communicate when they speak the same language. If one of them has trouble with the other's language, things can get really awkward.

When Latin players first get to the States, they have some big cultural adjustments to make, too. They come from a different mentality. When a coach tells you to do something, he's telling you to do it to make you a better player. But some of the Latin guys don't see it that way. They are not used to people telling them what to do. They almost feel as if someone is trying to enslave them. So they rebel. They don't realize how important it is to follow directions. And the Americans don't realize what a big change the Latin players are going through. Americans sometimes think the Latin players are copping an attitude, when in many cases it's just a lack of understanding.

Of course, when you throw somebody like Albert into the equation, all bets are off. Nobody knows what makes him tick. Not even Albert.

But maybe we're being too harsh on old No. 8. Maybe we just need to put Albert into a broader perspective. After all, in 1898, I'm told, the Indians' Oliver "Patsy" Tebeau fired his *bat* at a heckler. In 1936, Johnny Allen trashed a hotel so badly that the entire team was thrown out on the street at 5 A.M. And during the 1960s, Sam McDowell got so drunk on an airplane that he was arrested when the plane touched down.

Compared to them, Albert seems—well, okay, Albert *still* seems pretty strange.

CHAPTER 11

You've Gotta Try Everything

A NEWSPAPER STORY published a few years ago listed my off-the-field resume. It read:

He is a serious painter.
He does stand-up comedy.
He plays the drums.
He collects art.
He has his own clothing line.
He has his own brand of salsa.
He has his own ice cream.
He designed his own house.
He has his own Web site.
He uses a digital camera and software to create art on his laptop computer.
He has his own interview program on the Internet.
He rides jet skis.
He plays paintball.
He races model cars.

Sounds like a brochure for a great summer camp, doesn't it? I had never added up all my hobbies, and the length of the list surprised me. But I have always made an effort try a lot of different things.

I also take advantage of the travel opportunities afforded by my baseball career. Why sit in a hotel room watching ESPN when you can be out roaming around in some of the most interesting cities in America. Some guys do. Maybe they want to save their energy for the game. Or maybe they're afraid. Or maybe they just don't know where to go. But I like to discover things. I like to learn about things just for the sake of learning. So I get out of my hotel room as much as I can.

During my first five years in the league, I went absolutely everywhere. Usually I'd start with the typical tourist haunts: In New York, the Statue of Liberty and the Empire State Building. In Anaheim, Disneyland. In Toronto, CN Tower. In Texas, Six Flags and Dealey Plaza. In St. Louis, the Arch.

When I first reached the majors, even my home city of Seattle was full of wonders to be explored. One day I went up in the Space Needle, the 605-foot-high structure that dominates Seattle's sky-line and has become the international symbol for the city. Built for the 1962 World's Fair, it has an observation deck near the top and a revolving restaurant at 500 feet. You hop into an elevator at street level and arrive at the top in about 45 seconds. The views are incredible. You can see Mount Rainier, Puget Sound, Elliott Bay, Lake Union, the entire downtown, and the Olympic and Cas-cade mountain ranges. Almost everybody who goes to Seattle eventually hits the Space Needle.

The day of my first visit, the line was long and things took longer than I expected. As a result, I showed up 15 minutes late for a 2:30 P.M. practice. My manager, Jim LeFebvre, read me the riot act. He was cussing and yelling at me like I had just hit into a double play on a 3-0 pitch. I felt like I was in boot camp. The gist of his message: You are here to play baseball, not to be a tourist.

He was right, of course. I couldn't argue. And his message wasn't lost on me: I haven't been late for a game or a practice since that day.

But that doesn't mean I sit around watching the clock.

I spend a lot of my free time in art museums. We're fortunate in Cleveland to have one of the best in the world. The Cleveland Museum of Art is one of my favorites. It has a little bit of everything and is so big that you can wander around in there for hours without getting bored. Plus, they change the exhibits all the time, so you always get to see something new.

Kansas City has a great art museum, too. It features paintings from the 1600s through the present and is divided by countries—German painters here, Italian painters over there, Dutch painters down the way.

Of course, I visit the Guggenheim Museum in New York. And I also like the museums in Baltimore and Minnesota. But every city has an art museum, and I visit almost all of them.

Cruising museums goes hand in hand with one of my true passions—painting.

As a boy, I loved to draw. But I never had any formal instruction, and I didn't really know anything about painting until I came to the States. When I got here, I bought some paints and started to experiment. And I kept my eyes open.

In the beginning, I drew all abstract stuff, trying to mix up the colors and see what would happen. Then I started to collect paintings and meet some real painters. I'd ask them for advice, then go home and try their tips.

My all-time favorite artist is Salvador Dali. I'm also a big fan of Peter Max. I like his use of color, the vibrancy he produces. And I actually own a large piece by Alexandra Nechita, the child prodigy from Romania. She's awesome. She is going to be the Picasso of this generation.

When I sit down in front of my own canvases, I'll try to imitate the various masters, copying one style one day, another style the next. People seem to like what I have done, but I know I can get much better. The toughest thing to master is the light that you create on your painting. Capturing a feeling of depth is difficult, too.

I use a wide variety of colors and have experimented with various textures, such as plastics and a special sandy substance that holds paint.

During the winter of 2000–2001, I took my first real lessons. I went to the Seattle Academy of Art and studied oil painting for two months. I had been working with acrylic paint, which is less expensive and easier for a beginner. Acrylic paints dry in a couple of hours, rather than a couple of days. So if I drew something I didn't like, I could just draw a whole new scene right on top of it.

I've been learning a lot about oils—how to apply them, how long it takes for various mixtures to dry. Much depends on what type of medium you use. The medium is another oil that you mix into the paint. The one I use most often has a base of linseed oil and dries in about two days. Because oil paint dries more slowly than acrylic, it is more forgiving. If you see something you don't like long after you have drawn it, you can just add paint and change the color or the shape.

In 2001, I began to wade into more traditional painting, concentrating on faces and bodies. I've done a number of nudes (from photos, not live models). Painting people presents a whole new set of challenges. But I love that form, too.

I've also done some off-the-wall stuff—literally. When Ryan Klesko was with the Braves, he heard about my artwork and asked me to draw him a design for a tattoo. I gave him several choices, and he went with one for his arm that looks like spikes going around a fence.

Almost everything else has been on canvas, on which I've completed well over 50 paintings. My main interest isn't selling them. I paint for fun. It's a great escape.

When I sit down to paint, I can leave baseball and everything else behind. I lose myself in the work. Sometimes it feels as if I'm crawling right inside the canvas. It's just me and that canvas—unless my son, Nico, decides to help out. Usually I paint in my garage, because I have plenty of room and I like the light coming in from outdoors, but Nico tends to run around when I'm painting and get paint on the cars. Which is not the type of painting I had in mind.

During the season, I sometimes get frustrated because I don't have big chunks of time to devote to a painting. With a game almost every day, I can only grab a half-hour here or there and can't give my art the attention it deserves. No wonder most of my best work has been done in Seattle in the off season, when I have all the time in the world and can stare at the canvas for hours on end.

MOST OF MY HOBBIES are more sociable. I love music and play the drums every chance I get. I have jammed with fellow Indians at places like Nautica in the Flats, and I even took the stage in Las Vegas one off season with players from around the league, some of them "real" musicians, people like the Yankees' Bernie Williams, who is an accomplished classical guitarist.

Compared to somebody like Bernie, I'm a raw rookie.

My drumming career began when I bought timbales. I love salsa music, and with the timbales I could follow along with the rhythm. But the timbales weren't loud enough. I needed something bigger and rowdier. *Rock 'n' roll, baby!* So I went out and bought a whole drum set. After a couple of years, I upgraded to a Ludwig set.

I'm learning the drums the same way I learned painting—by going out and watching people who are good at it, asking for tips, and just plain experimenting. Sometimes I'll see somebody at a club in Cleveland and ask him to come show me stuff on the drum set in my basement. That drives my wife crazy.

My musical debut with my teammates came in September 1999 when we drew 4,000 fans to the Nautica Stage. Joining me for the Tribe Jam were Jim Thome, Dave Burba, Richie Sexson, and Mark Langston. Langston is really talented. An actual professional musician was there, too—local legend Michael Stanley.

I love all kinds of music. But if I were stranded on a desert island and could only take one CD, I'd take one by salsa artist Oscar D'Leone. In the late '70s, he put out a CD with Dimension Latina that has 12 songs, every one of them a gem. He covers all the bases: family, parties, Christian living, sex, you name it. Every time I'm down on myself, I'll put in that disc and it will pump me right up again.

I've been lucky enough to join him onstage three times. He's a big baseball fan, so every time he sees me at a show he waves me up. I play the timbales for him, so I don't really get in the way.

Music has amazing powers. Sometimes I think I could write pretty good lyrics. Maybe that will be my next adventure. But I'm pretty sure I'll never be able to write melodies. I don't know how people can hear original music in their heads. I guess that's why we pay $50 to see them perform.

If I were good enough, my ultimate dream would be to play with Metallica or Van Halen. But I'm not in their league, and I haven't even met any of those guys. But another of my rock heroes, Sammy Hagar, threw out the first pitch at a game in 1998. I made the batboy get his autograph on a ball. I also have baseballs autographed by Gloria Estefan and Ted Nugent.

THE INDIANS' HEAD HONCHOS don't mind a little musical moonlighting by their employees. But they're probably not too wild about some of my other hobbies—like paintball.

When we play in Seattle, I'll usually invite a few teammates over to my house for a game. During a road trip in '98, Manny Ramirez, Enrique Wilson, Einar Diaz, and I spent an afternoon running around my property, blasting each other with paintball guns.

If you've never seen paintball, it's a war game where you dress up in camouflage, sneak around in the woods, and shoot other players with "bullets" containing paint. When the gelatin-coated ball hits you, the paint splatters on your clothes and you're "dead."

The balls really pack a wallop. A direct hit is guaranteed to leave a bruise. But that's what makes it fun. If you know you'll suffer a little when you get hit, you have plenty of incentive to play the game as hard as you can. And if you wear the right equipment—mainly, helmets with big plastic shields over your face—

you're probably not going to get maimed. All of this makes paintball much more exciting than a video game, where the only risk is being taunted by a bunch of microchips.

During the last decade, paintball clubs have sprung up around Seattle and Cleveland and lots of other parts of the country. People can rent equipment, buy a certain number of rounds, and go to war on special playing fields. The best places have a mix of woods and fields, with platforms and forts and other structures to hide behind.

I first tried paintball after seeing an advertisement for a place in Seattle. I took a buddy to see what it was all about, and we found 200 guys running around in camo gear, blasting away at each other. It looked like so much fun that we headed right to a store and bought some guns.

At that point, we weren't sure how much we would like playing, so we went with the lowest-priced guns, which set us back about $150. Those didn't work too well. The balls would get stuck and break in the chamber, and we'd have to take the whole thing apart and clean it. Meanwhile, the guys with the better guns were slaughtering us. So we went back and bought middle-of-the road guns. Those worked much better. They shot more accurately and were easier to clean. But we were still getting clobbered by the guys with the expensive guns.

Everybody wants to be king of the hill, right? Soon we were heading back to the store to get the best paintball guns money can buy. The ones I have now shoot something like five balls a second. Nobody can get close to us. We can advance at will. At last, we became a force to be reckoned with.

The rules at most public paintball fields say that once you're hit, you're finished for that game. Not at my house. When we play at home, the participants are given magical healing powers. If you can clean up your "wound" (get most of the paint off) you're allowed to jump right back into the fray.

Manny, Enrique, and Einar had a great time during our battle. When we got to the ballpark that day, we had all these purple marks on our bodies, and people were asking, "Where have you guys *been*?" We just laughed.

Some day I might combine two of my hobbies and shoot a paintball at a canvas. I've been thinking about that for a while. I want to buy a screen and put it about two feet in front of the canvas and see what kind of pattern I get. Dali did stuff like that. He'd take some balls and throw them into the canvas to get an explosion effect.

I've done some informal testing in that regard. In Seattle, we have a doghouse that was painted white and black, to look like a Dalmatian, with a red roof. But the dog doesn't use it, so I like to blast paintballs at it. The color scheme now includes blue, green, and yellow. It looks pretty cool, if I do say so myself.

Maniacal paintball games would not be warmly received in my Westlake subdivision, where the yards are relatively small and noise travels. But I can get a decent adrenaline rush in Cleveland by riding my jet skis.

During off-days, I'll head down to Lake Erie with my two jet skis and a pal and we'll go out and zoom around for a couple of hours. I love to jump the wakes of boats—especially the big ore freighters—and to do 360-degree spins, where you jerk the handlebars all the way to one side while going full speed, and the ski spins around while a wall of water rushes over you.

I bought my first jet skis in 1993, when I was still playing with Seattle. Every few years they come out with a better, faster model, and I'll trade in my old ones. I have a machine now that will hit 60 MPH. Which is, of course, absolutely crazy.

Speaking of crazy, my best experiences with jet skis came when we owned the house in Sarasota, Florida, during the mid-1990s. Every time a big storm was brewing, I'd fire up the jet ski and head out into the big rollers. One day, hurricane warnings were posted and the waves were running at least six feet. I went out and had a blast. The waves were so huge that I could get inside them and drive around in a complete loop, as if I were driving around the inside of a pipe.

Sure, these stunts are a little risky. In fact, the Indians could nullify my contract if I were to get hurt doing something stupid on a jet ski during the season. And I always think about the possible consequences. But I know my limits. I know what I'm capable of handling and what the machine is capable of handling. That's part of being an adult. I don't do stupid stuff. But I do believe in taking responsible risks. You can't live your life inside a bubble. If you do, you're going to miss out on a lot.

Nicole likes the jet skis, too, but she won't ride them in Cleveland until the water temperature gets over 70 degrees, even with a wet suit. She hates to be cold even more than I do.

When we first got the skis, we would sometimes take her dog along for the ride. He had a little jet ski vest and would sit right up on the handlebars, loving every minute of it. What could be better for a dog than wind in your face and water all around you?

I've also done plenty of waterskiing. I got good enough to do jumps and tricks, but I'm limited to using two skis. I'd like to slalom, but I can't seem to get up on one ski.

I've always loved the beach and the water. The only water sport I've tried that I don't particularly like is surfing. I think part of the reason is that I don't like the culture. Most of those surfer guys aren't the kind of people I want to hang around with.

PART OF MY SPARE TIME is taken up with a handful of side businesses. Because the Indians have played so well, and because I'm perceived as a decent guy, I've had good success with commercial products.

My first venture was salsa. In June of 1998, we introduced Omar Vizquel Salsa. I didn't think up the idea, I didn't create the recipe, and I have nothing to do with manufacturing it. But I did contribute the paintings for the labels. Bob Barlow of RBA Sports, a Cleveland marketing company, said at the kickoff news conference at Tower City that he saw one of my paintings—a real colorful one called *Fiesta*—and immediately thought it would make a great salsa label. So we got together and cut a deal. We sell the stuff in mild and medium intensities. Most people in Northeast Ohio aren't fond of really hot stuff.

Launching an ice cream venture at the start of the 2001 season was fun, too. Omar Vizquel Baseball Ice Cream came about after I took Nicole and Nico to a shop in Westlake—Mitchell's Homemade Ice Cream—during the summer of 2000. We liked their ice cream so much that I asked my marketing guy, Barlow, to contact the owners, Mike and Pete Mitchell, to see if they could develop a brand to carry my name.

In the off-season, they sent a bunch of shipments of ice cream to my house in Seattle, and we tested them to see what we liked. We settled on four flavors: Triple Play Berry Sorbet, Double Play Chocolate, Bases Loaded Mint Cookies & Cream, and Omar's Awesome Vanilla Bean.

The stuff was made by hand in three-gallon batches, and it was really good. I'm careful about what I put my name on. Nothing can mess up your good name faster than being associated with an inferior product.

My biggest off-the-field commercial venture has been my clothing line. Clothing is important to me. Sure, lots of times I'll hang around in grungy T-shirts and shorts, but when I go out I like to look good, even if the situation is relatively casual.

When we first came out with OV clothes, we offered T-shirts, hats, sweatshirts, and silk boxer shorts, all of which included my name. Then we added leather pants and shirts with collars. Then bathing suits. Now the foundation of the line is leather coats, ranging from cropped to knee length, in colors from black to metallic blue to a silvery mauve. We also use a lot of bright colors—greens, reds, yellows—and the style is kind of hip-hop. The clothes are tight-fitting and flashy.

We staged a fashion show in 1999 at Beachwood Place, and it turned out great. Several hundred people showed up at the mall's center court, and they cheered the whole time. I served as the narrator, and I recruited a few teammates to help model. Steve Karsay and his wife, Kori, took part, along with Dave Roberts and his wife, Trisha, and Sandy Alomar's wife, Christine. Nicole was up on the stage, too, although not necessarily of her own free will. She hates being gawked at, and she wouldn't even take off her sunglasses during the show.

The guys were really embarrassed, too. Even though we play ball in front of 44,000 people every night, we don't think twice about that because we've been playing ball our whole lives. Modeling is totally different. We felt ridiculous out there.

For the second show, in 2000, we used female models, along with some new Indian recruits: Justin Speier, Einar Diaz, and Jim Brower.

And, now, let's take time out for this commercial message: the clothing, salsa, and prints of some of my paintings can all be purchased online at my Web site, www.omarvizquel.com. The site was put together by an amazing young guy, Brad Koltas, who lives in Birmingham, Alabama. It's really sophisticated, with all kinds of video and audio bells and whistles.

During the 2000 season, *ESPN the Magazine* ran a reader contest to determine which athlete had the best Web site. It was a month-long competition involving 15 sites from a variety of sports. Two sites would square off at a time, and readers would check them out and vote for their favorite online.

In the end, we finished second behind Lance Armstrong, the Tour de France cycling champ. But the voting was a bit suspicious. As Brad watched the totals come in, he was convinced that Armstrong's camp was stuffing the ballot box. He was right. Armstrong's backers later admitted in the magazine that they had been "spamming" the site, voting over and over for Lance. Seems to me people should have known something was rotten when Armstrong won a preliminary round against tennis vixen Anna Kournikova. How could *that* be?

Still, we didn't feel too badly about finishing second. In the semifinals, we beat football player Warren Sapp—despite the fact that his site promised an autographed jersey to "any fan who cinched the nomination." In the tainted finals, we were neck and neck with Armstrong until the final day, when the spammers tilted the voting so much that the final margin was 62 percent to 38.

Every time I turn around, Brad is upgrading the Web site. In addition to the online store, it has a section called "audio updates," which are interviews with me that Brad conducts periodically; a "fan forum," where people can debate baseball topics; current statistics; links to other sites, like the Major League All-Star ballot (hint, hint); and a question-and-answer section where fans can send me e-mail. I take my Apple PowerBook with me on road trips, and when I'm in the hotel I can plug into the Internet and check out my mail. I admit I'm not very good about answering it, but I do enjoy reading it.

Some of my teammates are intimidated by computers. I enjoy them. I've been using one only since spring training of 2000, but I'm pretty good at zooming around on it. I not only use e-mail but play computer games, watch DVD movies, and mess around with sophisticated software programs like Adobe Photoshop and Corel Painter. I've actually created some decent artwork on the computer.

I LOVE GADGETS OF ALL KINDS. One hobby I started in Seattle was racing remote-control model cars. Mind you, I'm not talking about those little Radio Shack toys. I'm talking about nitro cars, real miniature racers with spark plugs, carburetors, and brakes. They're powered by nitro fuel, just like the thundering full-size machines at professional drag strips.

Years ago, I built my own cars from scratch. But it just took too long—about three weeks, by the time I made all the final adjustments. So now I go to the store and buy them already made. Even so, just working with them takes lots of patience, because the pieces are so small and all the tools are little and stuff always needs to be adjusted. It's not a hobby for everyone.

I helped get Sandy Alomar, Jr. interested in the cars, and he has turned into a fanatic. He keeps at least one of them in the trunk of his real car at all times, in case he finds a big, deserted parking lot and feels the need for speed.

The last few years he played in Cleveland, he kept a bright-red miniature Ford next to his locker in the Jacobs Field clubhouse. He sat right next to me, so I saw it every day. It had an Italian-made Novi Rossi engine and could hit 60 MPH. Occasionally, when there weren't many people around, he would take it outside and zoom it around the rubberized warning track that circles the playing field.

At 6-foot-5, Sandy is way too tall to be a catcher. But he looks even more out of place playing with his little toy cars. You should see him crouch down in his catcher's stance when he puts the little car on a starter and hooks up the glow plug.

After that you prime the engine, pumping up and down with a special tool, then fire up the car and let it idle for a while. You continue the warm-up process by weaving it around in small ovals. Finally, you're ready.

From a standing start, the cars scream off with a high-pitched whine, terrorizing everyone and everything within earshot. Some of the more expensive cars can do 70 MPH.

Unfortunately, the cars are a lot like catchers: they have lots of moving parts and they're constantly under repair.

All that maintenance can wear a person down. You have to know how to fix a car and you have to enjoy that kind of work. Otherwise, you'll be heading to the shop for every little thing, because almost every time you run a car, something happens to it. Either you have to adjust the carburetor so it burns better, or you have to change the spark plug or something.

Then you have to worry about the other bozos on the road. During spring training of 2000, Sandy was running one of his fastest cars around the Indians' complex in Winter Haven, Florida, when a UPS truck squashed it. Sandy was calibrating the carburetor and didn't have his foot in front of the car and it took off, right into the path of the truck. Sandy was upset because he had asked the guy earlier to move out of the way. But he made the best of a bad situation. He autographed the car's mangled body and gave it to the UPS driver.

During the off-season, when Sandy returns to his native Puerto Rico, he spends virtually every free hour running his cars. He lifts weights, then goes to race. The hobby is hugely popular in his homeland. Several other Puerto Rican ballplayers have the bug, too, including Carmelo Martinez, who, like Alomar, once played for the San Diego Padres, and Martinez's cousin, Edgar Martinez, of the Mariners.

Driving these cars is harder than you might think. The directional controls on the radio transmitter work one way when the car is heading away from you, and the opposite way when it's heading toward you. That makes things particularly interesting when you're racing around an oval, trying to pass other cars.

Like a lot of my hobbies, this one isn't awfully expensive. A decent model will set you back about $400. The faster cars sell for about $900—an amount you could easily drop on a good set of golf clubs.

OTHER GUYS ON THE TEAM have some really intriguing hobbies, too. Take Travis Fryman. Travis could afford any kind of high-tech gadget he wants, but his favorite thing to do is shoot an old-fashioned bow and arrow.

At one time, the soft-spoken third baseman hunted with guns. He grew up shooting small game with his grandfather. Then, after making it to the big leagues, he was introduced to archery by a friend of his father's. He was instantly captivated and became a deadeye with the compound bow. But that seemed too easy. Using those big, powerful contraptions, with their cables and pulleys, almost seemed like cheating. So Travis regressed once again, to the simple longbow. At this rate, he'll soon be living in a cave and hunting with stones.

Travis is a religious guy and a highly ethical hunter. He won't shoot at a deer from farther than 20 yards, because he's afraid he wouldn't be accurate enough to kill it instantly, and he doesn't want to just wound it and have it run around in pain.

A writer once asked me, "If you were walking through the darkest, scariest alley in America and you could chose only one teammate to accompany you, who would it be?" I said, "Travis Fryman. He has the heart of a warrior."

He really does. And I'm not just talking about his hunting. On the baseball field, nobody is grittier. He has played in a lot of pain over the years, but he never lets on. When you're in a tough situation out there, you know he's going to come through. He pushes himself so hard that it rubs off on the other players. It doesn't matter how big a person is; it's the size of his heart. Travis Fryman's is enormous.

With an average salary of about $3 million, most of the Indians could wade into any hobby they want, and some of them get pretty creative. But money isn't necessarily the key to off-the-field happiness. Some of the most popular hobbies are the classic ones, like fishing.

Although I'm not a big fisherman, plenty of guys on the team are. Paul Shuey, who lives right around the corner from me in Westlake, is a fanatic. He says he owns 30 rods and reels—and he doesn't consider that to be extravagant. He says he needs all that stuff to hook all the different species that are swimming around out there.

Often he'll invite along a teammate, like Fryman or Dave Burba. Two of his other fishing buddies were Steve Karsay and Steve Reed, who were traded to Atlanta during the 2001 season. But Shuey will rarely invite more than one other person. Too many people and you defeat the purpose, he says.

He likes the contrast between standing on the pitcher's mound in front of 44,000 screaming fans and sitting in complete isolation, thinking about life. We all need to stop thinking about baseball for a while, and his way to meditate is with a pole in his hand.

During baseball season, the Shue doesn't have time to do

much fishing from boats. Occasionally he'll head out on Lake Erie to go after smallmouth, but Lake Erie can be tough in terms of the weather.

So when the Indians are at home, Shuey usually heads for a nearby lake or pond and simply throws in a line from shore. Sometimes he'll take along his young daughter, Morgan.

As hobbies go, this one doesn't seem to make much sense. Whenever he catches something from a lake or pond, he throws it right back in. In salt water, he says, he'll eat what he catches. He once hauled in a 150-pound bluefin tuna and had sushi forever— which makes a lot more sense.

These fishermen are a strange breed. During our first road trip to New York in 2001, Burba and Reed spent most of an off-day fishing in the East River. From the looks of the East River, you'd think the best thing they could catch would be spare tires. But they reeled in 15 or 20 fish, and they claim fishing is the Big Apple's best-kept secret. Burbs had so much fun that he dragged Jaret Wright with him a couple of days later. Good thing they're catch-and-release guys, too.

I think I'll pass on that hobby. But, otherwise, I'm up for almost any adventure. The only way to find out what you really enjoy is to try everything.

CHAPTER 12

Glove of Gold

I N THE MIDDLE OF THE 1998 SEASON, *Sports Illustrated* published a small article in which two of the magazine's baseball writers argued about who was the best defensive shortstop in the game.

Stephen Cannella voted for Rey Ordonez of the New York Mets, writing that the

> Cuban defector [who] landed on American soil in 1993 has shown he can cover nearly every inch of that ground with his glove. No one since Ozzie [Smith] has ranged from the hole to shallow center as gracefully or as often as Ordonez, and his howitzer arm turns those dazzling stops into outs.

Veteran writer Tom Verducci argued in favor of me:

> Reliability is a shortstop's top priority, and no shortstop has been more reliable than the Cleveland Indian whose record .981 career-fielding percentage doesn't even reflect his 37 errorless postseason games. Vizquel didn't muff a single ground ball from August 1997 until he booted one last Saturday [July 1998]. *SportsCenter* loves the acrobatic Ordonez, but would you take Dominique (Human Highlight Film) Wilkins over Larry Bird?

Now, I don't claim to be the best shortstop in baseball. But I will say this: I have seen Ordonez in action. He makes some unbelievable plays. He has great hands. But I think he makes a lot of routine plays look really tough. He's in the dirt all the time. He seems to dive and slide on plays that don't require it. I can make that same play without getting fancy. I pride myself on making the hard plays look easy. I think that's the hallmark of a great shortstop. A routine play should always look like a routine play.

Rey is much flashier than I am, and I think that's exciting for the fans. But I'm not so sure it serves a player as well in the long run. I guess it's just a question of different styles.

I'm very proud of my fielding. After the 2001 season I collected my ninth consecutive Rawlings Gold Glove award, given annually to the best defensive player at each position. The honor is particularly gratifying because it's voted by the managers and coaches in your league—people who really know the game and have watched you all season long. The voters aren't allowed to choose anyone on their own team. So it's not a popularity contest like the All-Star balloting tends to be.

With the Indians, I have had plenty of Gold Glove company. Early in the 2001 season, the team handed out Gold Gloves to three-quarters of our infield. Third baseman Travis Fryman won his first. Second baseman Robbie Alomar his ninth. (He now has 10, moving him ahead of Ryne Sandberg for the all-time lead at his position.) Only Jim Thome was left out, and even he is above-average with the glove.

The awards themselves look really cool. They feature a big, open, metallic glove. I keep them on some shelves in my computer room at home in Seattle.

Your first Gold Glove is always the most exciting. Number two is great, too, because it tells you that the first one was no fluke. And then, with number three, you start to cop an attitude. You think to yourself, "I'm a Gold Glover, baby." After your third one, they all kind of blend together. But it will be a real thrill if I can get 10 or 11 or 12. A tenth would move me ahead of Luis Aparicio, the greatest shortstop ever to come out of Venezuela. Reaching that milestone would be important—not only for me, but for the people of my homeland. Aparicio is the only Venezuelan to be voted into the Hall of Fame. With 10 Gold Gloves, I might have a chance to follow him to Cooperstown.

But I don't go into each season saying, "I have to win a Gold Glove." You just can't do that. The award is not something you win over a period of two or three weeks. You have to go out and do your job consistently for the entire year. Plus, you have no real control over it. It's not based on fielding percentage or anything concrete. The judging is subjective. The good news is, at this point, if no other shortstop has a spectacular year and if I don't totally screw up, the voters might say to themselves, "Well, what the heck. Let's just give it to Omar again."

Sometimes I get the feeling that the baseball honchos aren't nearly as interested in defense as they used to be. In the old days, they'd hold a big ceremony in New York to hand out the Gold Gloves. Then they started just giving them out before a home game the season after you won. For my eighth Gold Glove, they didn't have any ceremony at all. They just handed it to me before batting practice.

The Tribe's infield was so steady during the 2000–2001 seasons, we didn't take formal infield practice before our games. Infield is a great part of baseball tradition; some fans come early just to see a team take infield. But with Gold Glove winners all over the place, the coaches figured we didn't need a formal drill. Plus, we took a lot of ground balls between batting-practice pitches, so we got enough work to stay sharp.

Whenever I'm fielding a grounder, even if it's off a fungo bat two hours before the game, I do it in a way that will help improve my defense. I don't fool around. I try to make my best throws to second or to first. Even when it looks like I'm goofing around between innings—like kicking a grounder with my foot and popping it up to my glove—it's an act that will help me in the field, because it's reinforcing the need to be ready for bad hops. I don't practice very much any more, but the practice I do is quality stuff. If you don't take practice seriously, you get into bad habits.

Some shortstops do unorthodox things to try to keep their fielding sharp. The great Cardinals shortstop Ozzie Smith used to practice by taking ground balls while kneeling. I see Alex Rodriguez and others doing the same thing. I'm not sure what they get out of that. I'd rather practice the way I'm going to do it in a game. But it comes down to personal preference. It certainly worked for Ozzie. Even though I saw him late in his career when he had lost a step, he was still incredibly talented. It's no wonder he owns a record 13 consecutive Gold Gloves.

DURING THE 1999–2001 SEASONS, I was fortunate enough to play next to one of the best second basemen in the history of the game.

On the field, Roberto Alomar and I are similar. We can read things that other people can't. Sometimes we had almost a psychic connection. I'd say to myself, "Oh, please don't throw that pitch." And then I'd go talk to Robbie between batters and he'd say, "I was telling myself the same thing."

We also liked to improvise a lot. We didn't worry about specific techniques, just getting the job done.

Our approach toward the game is different, though. Robbie spends a lot of time looking at videotape. He'll spend hours analyzing things like a pitcher's pickoff move. He'll watch what the pitcher does with the ball, with his hands, his head, his legs. He knows every pitcher's every move. He knows a pitcher's quirks so well that half the time he gets such a huge jump on a steal that the catcher doesn't even make a throw to second. Robbie knew from the ball-strike count and some little twitch in the pitcher's leg that he was going to throw home.

He approaches hitting the same way. If he goes 0-for-4, he'll come back into the clubhouse and watch the video to see why the guy got him out. And when he figures it out, he retains it. He's like a computer.

Robbie can do everything: field, hit, hit with power, throw, and steal bases. During the 2001 season, he and I were among three guys on our team who had a permanent "green light" on the bases. In other words, any time we thought we could steal a base, the manager let us try. The other guy was, of course, Kenny Lofton, the team's all-time leader in stolen bases. I moved into the fourth spot on the career list during 2001, passing Ray Chapman.

Lofton, Alomar, and I all are fast and have been around long enough to know when to take a chance and when not to. During 2001, another speedster, my buddy Jolbert Cabrera, had a conditional green light.

My stolen bases dropped to 13 that year, mostly because I didn't try to run as often. Why run the team out of an inning when Alomar and Juan Gonzalez are hitting right behind you?

I don't consider myself a great base stealer, and I don't break it down scientifically. But I certainly keep my eyes open. Sometimes I turn a little when I'm leading off and try to sneak in and look for the sign from the catcher. If you see the signal for a change-up or breaking ball, you know you have a better shot at swiping second.

Unlike Robbie, though, I steal almost completely on feel. I don't spend hours studying pitchers. I'm not a big fan of watching videotape. We have a whole video room at Jacobs Field where they can dig out any video you could possibly want to watch. The guy who puts the tapes together, Frank Velotta, is a good pal of mine. From 12 different angles, he can show you how your 1995 swing compared to your 2000 swing. But it just doesn't seem to help me much. I'll sit down after a game, thinking I had tried four totally different approaches during the four times I came to bat, and all the at-bats look exactly the same. I just can't tell the difference.

Robbie and I differ in another way, too: he wants to have a hand in every little thing that happens on the field. Robbie spends more time on the mound talking to the pitcher than the manager. I hardly ever go to the mound. I figure I ought to hang back and concentrate on what I need to do to help us out of a situation. But Robbie likes to offer his input because he's such a student of the game. Sometimes that put our catchers in a difficult position. Einar Diaz might be talking about a scouting report that says to pitch a guy outside, and Robbie would come to the mound and tell the pitcher to throw inside. The pitching coach had been quoting 10,000 scouting reports that say the guy can't hit an outside pitch. But maybe Robbie figures the hitter knows about the scouting reports, too, so the pitcher needs to buzz him inside to keep him honest. That's what baseball is all about—making adjustments. And Robbie has a great feel for it.

That's why he's the best second baseman in the game today—and maybe forever. I don't know how good Bill Mazeroski was, or Luke Appling, or Nellie Fox. People say they were the best. I never saw them, so I can't tell you. But there's no doubt in my mind that Robbie Alomar is the best second baseman in baseball right now. It's hard to believe anybody could play the position any better.

Robbie believes that God put him in this world to play baseball. That's why he works so hard at it. People who think baseball players get paid just for the three hours they're on the field haven't met Robbie Alomar.

Before Robbie came along, I worked with a cast of thousands at second base. Between the departure of Carlos Baerga in the middle of 1996 and Robbie's arrival in 1999, I played next to all of the following guys:

David Bell.

Jeff Branson.

Joey Cora.

Shawon Dunston.

Tony Fernandez.

Julio Franco.

Jeff Kent.

Torey Lovullo.

Bip Roberts.

Jose Vizcaino.

Enrique Wilson.

I think that's all of them. After a while, you sort of lose track.

I had to communicate more with some guys than others. Bip Roberts and I needed to work out a lot of things. Tony Fernandez was the opposite. He came to Cleveland later in his career and had already been a four-time Gold Glove–winner, so he knew exactly what he was doing. We clicked.

My first Indians partner, Carlos Baerga, wasn't a real solid defensive player, but I liked his attitude. He was always happy, always talking to you. It was easy to communicate with him.

Jeff Kent was not a guy you could talk with much. He kept completely to himself. It wasn't just me; he didn't socialize with any of his teammates, and I hear he doesn't in San Francisco, either. Kent really struggled at second base when he played in Cleveland in 1996. Although he's still not the world's best defensive player, maybe no other player has enjoyed a bigger turnaround after leaving the Indians. Kent went from hitting .265 in limited duty to becoming the National League's Most Valuable Player in 2000. I always knew the guy could hit. But when you're not playing every day, it's hard to get your timing down and your confidence up. Sometimes a team can have a tremendous talent sitting on the bench and nobody knows it, because maybe he got a bad rap with his previous team and he just doesn't get enough playing time. Then, all of a sudden, you stick him in full-time and say, "Wow! Where did that come from?"

When we were going through that two-year revolving door for second basemen, the media talked about how difficult it must be for me to adjust to all of their different fielding styles. But it really wasn't. You just need a little bit of communication. Some guys have a preference in terms of the way they want the ball delivered, but that's no problem for me. Whatever they want, that's what I'll do. I'm flexible.

The thing that wore me down a little was helping them get into the right place on the field. Half these guys weren't even real second basemen. We kept trying to turn shortstops and outfielders into second basemen, so they didn't have a great feel about where they should play. I'd have to move them around a lot.

MY OWN PREFERENCES? I don't have any. Sometimes I'd turn to the guy playing second and say, "All I want from you is a good throw. I don't care how you do it or which side it's on. Just give me a throw that I can handle and I can turn the double play."

I use the smallest glove size in baseball—10 inches. It's a Rawlings SXSC, custom-made for me. The only other person I've seen with a glove that small is Mike Bordick, the Baltimore shortstop who has the second-highest career fielding average of all time, right behind me. Bordick has great hands. Like me, he doesn't want a big glove, because that makes it harder to fish the ball out of the pocket. In fact, I don't so much catch the ball as stop it.

The biggest glove used by a shortstop is about 12 inches long. Alex Rodriguez uses a big one, as do Derek Jeter and Nomar Garciaparra.

You might be surprised to learn that I don't use an Omar Vizquel autograph model. Instead, I use a Torey Lovullo model.

Just kidding.

But my gloves don't have any extra writing on them. I know Rawlings makes an Omar Vizquel model, because people bring them to me to autograph. But I prefer my glove plain.

Each season I start with a new glove. I break it in during spring training, use it the whole season, and then put it away for safekeeping. I don't give away my old gloves to anyone. I save them so that some day I can give them to a place that will treasure them like I do—maybe a museum.

Okay, I did trash that one glove, the one I made three errors with at the beginning of the 1994 season. But otherwise, my gloves are my treasures.

Although I'm proud to be the all-time leader in fielding percentage among shortstops, that statistic can be misleading. Other guys with great fielding percentages don't have a lot of range, so they don't get to as many balls.

In 1965, the Indians' Rocky Colavito set the team record by playing an entire season in right field without making a single error. At the risk of knocking the Rock, I'm told he was very slow and just couldn't catch up to a lot of the balls other players could have reached.

Guys who don't have great range can sometimes compensate by knowing where to play the individual batters. Cal Ripken never had great range, but he was always in the right spot. Tony Fernandez didn't impress me with his range when I played with him, but maybe that was because he was in the later stages of his career. I don't think the Phillies' Larry Bowa had great range, either, but Larry got to a lot of balls simply because he did his homework and knew where individual batters tended to hit it.

When people ask me what makes a shortstop great, I say two things:

1. Making the hard plays look easy.
2. Making all the routine plays.

Some shortstops will make a spectacular play and then turn around and boot an easy one. You simply have to make the easy ones. The Orioles' Mark Belanger made the routine play 10 times out of 10. Because of that, they call him one of the game's greatest shortstops. He didn't turn in too many spectacular plays, but he was as steady as a treasury bond.

I said earlier in the book that quick feet are one of the keys to fielding, and that's a trait that is frequently overlooked. But soft hands are important, too. When you're watching a top shortstop, you can barely see the ball going into the glove and being transferred to the hand. Before you know it, the ball is heading to first base.

Not many people have soft hands. But plenty of people have a stronger arm than I do. I'm the first to admit that I don't exactly drill holes in Jim Thome's first baseman's mitt. However, I'll put my accuracy up against anyone's.

The only season I had trouble throwing was 1996, when I developed a bad shoulder. I'm still not sure how it came about. I first noticed it when I got to spring training, and it never got any better.

That March, on the eve of Opening Day, the pain was already so bad that the team sent me north to Lutheran Medical Center in Cleveland for an MRI. It showed no damage to the rotator cuff—my biggest fear—and only a slight fraying of the labrum, along with tendonitis.

I was determined to play through the pain. I reduced the number of practice throws I was making, from 50 a day to about 30. But that didn't help much. I was in constant pain that entire season. Some nights after a game, my arm hurt so badly that I couldn't sleep. Sometimes I'd wake up and my whole arm would be numb. Some mornings it hurt so much that I could barely brush my teeth. I was afraid I'd have to pull the plug. But I kept working with free weights and machines. And I ingested more drugs than you'd find at a typical Walgreen's. I think I took anti-inflammatories for six months straight.

Even with my body flooded with drugs, I could barely make the throw to first base. As a result, I committed 20 errors—five more than I made in any other season in the major leagues. Not all of the errors came on throws. Sometimes I'd try so hard to get my feet in a position to help my arm that I'd boot the grounder. But I was swinging the bat well—eventually recording what at that point was a career-high .297—and I was willing to put up with just about anything to stay on the field.

Immediately after that season I underwent arthroscopic surgery. While they were in there fixing the labrum, they took out a tiny bone from the shoulder socket.

I worked hard on the rehabilitation program, and my arm bounced right back. About six weeks after the surgery, I felt great. I started throwing then, and when I returned to spring training in 1997, my arm was stronger than ever.

Part of the credit for my comeback has to go to our strength and conditioning coach, Fernando Montes. Fernando, a big, friendly guy, came to the Indians in 1992 after three years at Stanford. He works wonders with the players. Mind you, he's not your favorite guy when you're coming back from an injury. He pushes you so hard that you begin to hate him. But he's doing it to make you better. He pumps you up mentally, too. Fernando is a guy who never gets any credit but deserves a ton of it.

DURING A GAME, I throw the ball only as hard as I absolutely have to. That's not because of any concerns about my arm. That's for better accuracy. Some guys like to show off their arm; they throw bullets to first even when the play isn't close. But easing up on your throw a little gives you a lot more accuracy. And because my transfer from glove to throwing hand is quick, I usually have plenty of time even when I lob the ball.

Actually, some of the infielders who rifle the ball to first do that because they don't have a choice: they're not in a position to throw when they first stop the ball. They stop it and *then* move into throwing position. When I catch the ball, I'm already in throwing position.

Players and coaches sometimes tell me, "I don't know how you do it, but you get me by one step every time. Just when I think I'm finally going to beat one out, the ball is there an instant before I am." That makes some people mad. In 1995, Cecil Fielder of the Detroit Tigers got riled up, and the benches emptied. Nobody threw any punches, but our teams exchanged plenty of angry words.

With two outs, Cecil hit me a hard one-hopper and didn't run hard to first. Travis Fryman, then playing for the Tigers, was on first base, and he busted his butt to get to second. It would have been a close play, because Baerga was pretty far from the bag. So I decided to go to first base. Cecil was taking so much time getting down the line that I threw almost a fly ball.

Cecil thought I was showing him up. Fryman did, too. I wasn't showing anybody up. That's just the style I play. I'm not going to throw the ball any harder than I have to to make the play.

THE BEST DEFENSIVE PLAY I've ever made, all things considered, was that stop in Game Six of the 1997 World Series, the one in which I dove to grab a shot by Charles Johnson and threw him out at first. We were ahead only 3-1 in the sixth inning, needing to win to force a seventh game. With two outs, the Marlins had runners on second and third. I knew that if that ball had gotten through, or if my throw was off-line, they'd have scored two runs, tied the game, and grabbed the momentum.

I may have made better plays, from a sheer physical stand-point, but when you add up everything that was involved in that one—the World Series pressure, the importance of that particular game, the importance of that particular situation—I think that was my best.

I'VE NEVER LIKED ASTROTURF. It's too easy. Ordinary fielders look really steady because nobody gets any bad hops. And now that I'm getting older, I like it even less because it's hard on my back and knees.

Fortunately, fewer and fewer fields use Astroturf. In the American League, only Minnesota and Toronto have fake fields—Tampa Bay, too, if you count their synthetic grass. But that stuff looks and feels more like real turf.

The Metrodome, home of the Twins, is the worst. Playing there is like playing with a baseball made of flubber. The game doesn't even seem like baseball.

The first time the Indians played the Twins during the 2001 season—53 games into the year—we felt as if we had to learn a whole new sport. The Twins got seven hits on balls that didn't even leave the infield. The winning hit came on a chopper that bounced so high into the air that Travis Fryman couldn't even get it in his glove before the runner scored from third. It was ridiculous. The small areas of dirt around home plate and around the bases are so hard that your spikes hardly even penetrate. It's like walking on ice. And because it's so hard, routine bouncers turn into hits. They should outlaw the place.

Of course, it works both ways. In that same game, I hit a hard ground ball that just made it past the second baseman . . . and it rolled all the way to the wall for a triple.

ALTHOUGH I'M KNOWN FOR MY FIELDING, I take lot of pride in having turned myself into a respectable hitter. In 1999, I hit .333—the fourth-highest season average for a shortstop in Cleveland Indians history. Only Lou Boudreau (.355 in 1948) and Joe Sewell (.353 and .336) did better during the team's first 100 years in business.

When it comes to hitting, I have the advantage of good eyesight. My parents didn't need glasses, and neither do I. The team tests the players each year in spring training; my right eye is 20/20 and my left eye—which is my dominant eye—is 20/15.

My disadvantage, as I've already mentioned, was learning to switch-hit at the age of 21. I had developed bad offensive habits by the time I arrived in the States. Although I have managed to work out most of those kinks, hitting has remained my biggest concern.

When I was working my way up the ladder, few of my teammates and coaches ever offered me advice on how to play shortstop. But on offense, it has been another story. The Mariners didn't have many batting instructors in the minor leagues, so I'd listen to any batting tips a teammate might offer. Even now, I'm vulnerable to advice. I'll consider tips from teammates or pitching coaches or family members or gas station attendants . . .

When you're hitting well, you're never quite sure why. Same when you're hitting poorly. For me, it's mostly timing and feeling comfortable up there. And it comes and goes.

The year I hit .333, I thought I owned the world. I was walking around with my chest all puffed out. I was sure I could get a base hit off Sandy Koufax during a hurricane. I was on a season-long roll.

Today I'll watch videotapes from that year, trying to recreate the feeling. I look at my stance, my feet, my shoulders, my bat, everything. I try to remember what I was thinking about. And every night when I go to the plate, I try to duplicate it. But that just doesn't seem to work, at least not as consistently as it did in 1999.

I guess '99 was just one of those years. That's the way it is for most major league players. You can have a great year or two at the plate, but you can't sustain a .333 average year after year. I'm amazed by the few guys who can. Robbie Alomar. Paul Molitor. Pete Rose.

It's not like I don't work hard on my hitting. I'm a slave to the batting cage. I have huge calluses on my hands from all the extra hitting I take. I used the cage so much during 2001 that I broke two pitching machines. I'm not going to turn into a mediocre hitter because of a lack of work. If I'm going down, I'm going down fighting.

The funny thing is this: had I been born a decade earlier, nobody would ever complain about my hitting. During my first six years as an Indian, my batting average was .290. That may not be high compared to big bombers like Alex Rodriguez and Nomar Garciaparra, but for most of baseball history a shortstop with a .290 average would be considered Ruthian.

I only hit about four homers per season. In the American League, in this era of the power-hitting shortstop, I get pretty frustrated. Believe me, I'd love to hit more homers. I've been trying to gain weight so I can hit the ball harder, but nothing works. I've tried everything. I lift weights in the off-season. I take lots of vitamins. A few years ago I even tried taking that stuff everybody was taking—creatine, a controversial supplement that is sold over the counter in health-food stores. But it didn't do much for me. I guess the only thing that would really help is steroids—and I'm not going to do that. I'm not willing to sacrifice my long-term health for a little more power.

Never underestimate the lengths to which a pro athlete will go to get better. I've tried all kinds of things—at least the ones I knew wouldn't hurt me—in hopes they might help just a little. For example, about half the guys on the 2001 Indians regularly had their necks and backs adjusted by chiropractors. One of them, Marty

Cordova, got yanked around about once a week. He says his back gets out of line because of all the twisting and turning he does when swinging the bat.

Well, I went to a couple of chiropractors, because I'm always looking for an edge. But today I don't believe in that stuff. I think they're phonies. They touch you and say, "Ooo, there it is! Do you feel that?" I didn't feel anything different.

I've also tried acupuncture. But that seemed like any other type of rehab method: It makes you feel good for a little while, but soon you're back to your original condition.

Still, those gimmicks are downright mainstream compared to one of my experiments.

A friend took me to see a guy on the outskirts of Caracas who practices black magic. Lots of people in Venezuela believe in it. The practitioner has a poisonous snake wrapped up inside a container with alcohol and whiskey, and he uses that as a lotion to massage your body. It's supposed to improve your muscle strength.

Now you know how much I would love to be a home-run threat, to have a legitimate chance to blast the ball out of the ballpark every time I go to the plate. But that just isn't going to happen. I could hit several more homers every year if I tried to hit homers, but that's not the way I'm going to stay in this game. I have to try to hit line drives.

Mind you, I'm not a 98-pound weakling. During the winter of 2001–02, I was bench pressing 300 pounds. But for the last 10 years I have weighed between 170 and 175. That's just about right for a guy 5-foot-9—although it's not exactly McGwire territory.

My main goal in the off season is to keep my legs strong. One day I'll bike for half an hour, the next day I'll do some kick-boxing. I have friends who are into that, and it's good exercise. I also play a lot of racquetball, which is even better exercise. I love racquetball. Other days I'll run on my own and do speed exercises. I have a workout in which I move from side to side, mirroring the movements I need to make as a shortstop.

My goal is just to stay fit. You can overdo your off-season training. Look what happened to Nomar Garciaparra. He's a fanatic about working out. Right before the 2001 season, he was pushing himself so hard that he split a tendon in his wrist and missed a huge chunk of the year. That's one of the reasons I quit playing winter ball in Venezuela after the 1995 season—I didn't want to get so worn down that I'd hurt myself.

I use a 33-inch bat that weighs 31 ounces. Sometimes, if I'm not hitting well or I'm feeling slow, I'll drop down one ounce. I did that early in the 2001 season, because I needed more balance and wanted to be quicker to the ball. During a typical season I might switch back and forth three times. It just depends how I feel. Sometimes you'll feel tired during the second week of the season or you'll feel as strong as ever in the season's final week.

People often wonder if it's frustrating to hit the ball hard all night and not get a hit. Sure. But I get just as frustrated when I'm making bad contact and I bloop in a couple of wimpy singles. Even though the singles look good in the box score and boost the old batting average, you are well aware that you're just not hitting the ball like you should.

Still, I'd gladly trade a hard out for a wimpy hit.

In Cleveland, I have developed a reputation as being a decent clutch hitter. I think I hit better in those situations because I focus more. During the late innings, you know how important every pitch is and your concentration is intense. And after a while, success in clutch situations feeds on itself. If you start to believe you're going to be successful at crunch time, you're more likely to succeed. Remember, 80 percent of this game is mental.

BY THE WAY, I'll have you know that I'm not only a shortstop. My resume also includes one inning at second base and one inning in—yep—right field.

Both occasions were emergencies. The manager had run out of players.

My outfield foray took place during one of the wildest games

I've ever seen. On the last day of August in 1999, we were playing the Angels at Jacobs Field. They got off to a 12-4 lead, and everybody figured the game was over. Manager Mike Hargrove began running in substitutes.

But then our offense erupted. In the eighth inning, we got five hits in a row. California brought in a new pitcher, who got two outs but gave up another single.

In came the Angels' ace reliever, Troy Percival.

Percival proceeded to give up a two-run single to Robbie, a two-run single to pinch-hitter Harold Baines, and a three-run homer to Richie Sexson. Up came David Justice. Frustrated, Percival drilled him in the ribs. Justice headed directly to the mound and, partway there, took off his batting helmet and fired it at Percival, hitting him in the shoulder. The benches emptied.

After the brawl, Percival and Justice were ejected. Justice's departure wiped out what remained of our bench. Carlos Baerga came in to play third, moving Enrique Wilson from third to short. Jim Thome went from DH to first, moving Sexson to left. Which meant we still needed a right fielder to replace Justice.

That would be me.

At first, Hargrove was going to send Robbie to right, but coach Clarence Jones pointed out that I shag fly balls in the outfield almost every day. So Hargrove wrote me into the "9" position for the first time in my career.

It was cool. Thanks to our 10-run eighth inning, we won the game, 14-12.

Unfortunately, nobody hit any balls in my direction. So I guess I won't be in line for any extra gold.

CHAPTER 13

All-Star

O N THE LAST DAY OF JUNE IN 1998, Mike Hargrove called me into his office for a meeting. Sometimes, a manager summoning you for a private conference means trouble. But this meeting couldn't have gone better.

Hargrove, who was about to serve as the manager for the American League All-Stars in Denver, sat me down and said, "You deserve to be in the All-Star Game. I think you have been playing great. You're coming with me."

I was thrilled. Finally, I had reached one of my last remaining individual goals. Though my Gold Glove collection continued to grow, one thing that kept escaping me was a spot in the Midsummer Classic. And I was dying to get there.

Obviously, my biggest baseball goal is winning a World Series. That would mean everything. But any player will tell you that being identified as one of the best in the game is a special honor.

That day I called my parents, who were as excited as I was.

My selection as a backup also helped my wallet. Like several other Indians players, I had a clause in my contract that said I would be paid an extra $50,000 if I made the All-Star team.

I was having a good year, but I hadn't planned for this. In fact, I had made reservations for a family outing at Cedar Point. It had become an early-July tradition. But bagging that plan was certainly okay with me.

I became the first Indians shortstop to make the team since Lou Boudreau in 1948.

The game was played in Colorado at Coors Field, which had opened just four years earlier. The atmosphere was great, because lots of my friends were at the game, including Manuel Ordonez, Andres Galarraga, Alex Rosaris, Fernando Vina, and Sammy Sosa.

Sammy was having a monster year. He was in the middle of that magical home-run race with Mark McGwire and had hit 19 bombs in June alone—the all-time major league record for homers in any month. I was lucky enough to play with Sammy in the minors, and we're still good friends.

The American League's clubhouse looked like Jacobs Field: six Indians were on hand. The others were Jim Thome and Kenny Lofton, who had been voted by the fans to start, and Bartolo Colon and Manny Ramirez. Manny and Bart were All-Star rookies, too.

I brought my video camera to the Monday workout. For some odd reason, I was not invited to participate in that evening's home-run contest, so I took the camera along to that, too, and did a running play-by-play commentary. I even conducted pregame interviews, talking to pitchers like Aaron Sele, Troy Percival, and John Wetteland about whom they expected to win. They all went with McGwire—who didn't survive the first round.

I picked Thome to win, based on the fact that he just kills balls in batting practice and was really pounding our batting-practice pitchers in the weeks leading up to the game. When I told the other All-Stars that Thome was my frontrunner, they gave me some strange looks. I told them: "Wait. Just wait."

Jimmy came close. He finished second only to Ken Griffey, Jr. (who originally said he wasn't going to participate because he was worried about messing up his swing).

I brought the video camera because I wasn't sure I'd ever make another All-Star game and wanted to capture all the memories I could.

My problem, of course, is that the American League has so many great shortstops, some of whom are major power hitters.

Alex Rodriguez and Nomar Garciaparra are the biggest offensive guns on their teams. Derek Jeter of the Yankees isn't a power hitter, but he hits a few homers and his average is usually well above .300. And every one of those guys is younger than I am.

A-Rod and Jeter were also on the 1998 team. Hargrove took a little bit of heat for leaving off Nomar, but I had finished third in the fan voting, only 24,868 behind Jeter. I was hitting close to .300, and in the entire first half of the season I had made only one error.

Hargrove defended his actions in a way that made me smile, telling reporters, "Omar Vizquel, I think, is the best shortstop ever to play the game of baseball."

In a runaway vote of the fans, A-Rod was the starter. I didn't see action until the eighth, but I made the most of it. On a 2-1 count and a runner on first base, Jeff Shaw from the Dodgers threw me a fastball down the gut and I smacked a line drive over the shortstop's head.

That was a huge moment in my baseball life. But, just as in the World Series, I wasn't particularly nervous. I prepare myself mentally to deal with big situations and, when the time comes, I am reasonably calm.

I came to the plate again in the ninth and grounded out. But that's okay. I'll take a .500 batting average in All-Star competition.

In front of 51,267 people, the good guys won, 13-8—the highest-scoring All-Star game ever. Colon, whose parents were watching back in the Dominican Republic, picked up the win despite giving up a three-run homer to Barry Bonds that may still be airborne.

I knew there would be a lot of people and a lot of pageantry in Denver. What surprised me the most was the autograph room set up by Major League Baseball. They had all this stuff the players were supposed to sign for each other and the public. I walked in and saw three tables full of dozens and dozens of balls, and all these bats and shirts and hats and other memorabilia. If you signed everything you were supposed to, it would have taken two hours. Obviously, nobody is going to do that. But if you're lucky, most guys sign most of the stuff and you'll wind up with a ball with all the other guys' names on it.

We also were given a dozen of our own team's caps, which we were encouraged to trade with other players. I came away with caps from most of the teams. I also kept my game jersey as a souvenir. It's in a frame on the wall at home in Seattle.

THE FOLLOWING SUMMER, 1999, I had to cancel another family vacation. Nicole had made all the arrangements for a three-day getaway to Miami. But once again, I wasn't complaining when they put me on the All-Star roster. She wasn't, either, because she knew how much it meant to me.

My selection in 1999 was a bigger surprise and, in a sense, a bigger honor. This time there were no charges of hometown favoritism, because the American League's manager was Joe Torre of the New York Yankees. He named his own shortstop, Jeter, along with me. At the time I was hitting .333 and was among the league leaders in steals.

This time, Garciaparra edged Jeter for the starting job. That seemed appropriate, with the game being played in Fenway Park, Nomar's home field. I placed third in the voting, only about 51,000 votes behind Garciaparra.

I really enjoyed getting to know Nomar better. He's one of the nicest guys you're ever going to find. He's really down to earth, talks to everybody, and loves discussing baseball. We chatted about other shortstops and the way they do things.

That 1999 game also provided an indication of the growing influence of Latin ballplayers: one-third of the 18 starters were Latino.

The Tribe again sent six players. And this time, four of them were starters, which is almost unheard of. Joining Lofton and Thome in the lineup were Ramirez and Roberto Alomar. Charles Nagy joined me as a reserve.

The Indians immediately set the tone. In the first inning, Lofton singled and stole second. Manny walked. Then Thome lined a single off Curt Schilling to score Lofton. Tribe 1, National League 0.

I made my entrance in the seventh inning and immediately made a big defensive contribution. Vladimir Guerrero was batting with two outs and a guy on first. He hit one up the middle. As soon as I saw the ball on the ground, I said to myself, "I have to do something good here, because I came to an All-Star game and I ought to look like an All-Star." If I screwed up, it wouldn't really matter, because it wouldn't affect the standings, so I figured I'd try something wild. Moving behind second base, I caught the ball in my glove and flipped it backward under my arm. It was a perfect flip to the second baseman, Boston's Jose Offerman, to end the inning. That play was shown on several highlight shows.

I also helped turn a double play that ended the game.

The American League won 4–1, and Indians played a role in all four runs.

WHEN I WASN'T SELECTED for the 2000 or 2001 All-Star game, we returned to our family tradition of visiting Cedar Point. In 2001, Nicole, Nico, and I were joined by Jolbert and Delbys Cabrera, Einar and Leslie Diaz, Ellis and Dory Burks, and all of our kids. Our mob numbered about 25 people.

We were treated like royalty. Baseball players only have a couple of days during the season when we can do something with our families for an entire day, so we want to make the most of it.

The park provided special escorts to make sure fans didn't keep coming up for autographs the whole time. Park officials also gave us special passes so we didn't have to stand in line to ride the rides. We could go right up front and hop on. Because of that, we were able to get through the entire park in about five hours. Normally, it takes that long just to catch three rides. Every time we go to Cedar Point they treat us well. And we always bring the employees baseballs and cards and stuff.

Still, our crew didn't exactly cut through the park at top speed.

I think we stopped every 10 feet. It was, "I wanna take a picture here!" "I want a cotton candy!" "I need a soda!"

But somehow we hit everything. In fact, we worked out a deal with the kids: we would stay in the kids' area for two hours, then move to the grownup rides—the Magnum 200, the Millennium Force, the Raptor, the Mantis . . . I love coasters. The bigger and faster and scarier, the better. We had a blast.

I think Cedar Point is the best amusement park I've ever been to—including Universal Studios and Disneyland and all the others I've visited on road trips. It has more of what adults want— namely, rides to go crazy on.

The next day, we gave in to the kids again and went to the wave park.

After playing baseball almost every day since February, it's nice to get away from the game for a couple of days—although having three days off at the All-Star break is certainly a mixed blessing.

So this year, do me a favor. As they say in Chicago, vote early and vote often.

MY ALL-STAR GAME SLUMP of the past few years is no real surprise, given the quality of American League shortstops. Many writers say that A.L. shortstop is the most competitive All-Star position in baseball.

However, another nice honor came my way during the summer of 2001.

Unlike the All-Star games, this one wasn't telecast internationally. In fact, it wasn't even telecast locally. Still, it was a day I won't forget.

Because the 2001 season was the 100th anniversary of the Indians becoming a charter member of the American League, much of the promotional activity that summer revolved around the anniversary. The main event was the selection of the top 100 Indians of all time.

I was elected to the team by a panel of sportswriters and team officials, and I was one of six active players chosen. The others were Robbie Alomar, Travis Fryman, Kenny Lofton, Charles Nagy, and Jim Thome.

All of the living members of the Top 100 were invited to attend the July 21 game between the Tribe and the Detroit Tigers and take part in a big pregame ceremony. Thirty-eight of us were able to attend.

When the former players walked into the locker room before the game, I felt like I was in the movie *Field of Dreams*, where the ghosts come out of the corn. Here were guys I had read about and heard about but only seen in photos on the walls outside the clubhouse. Suddenly, they had come to life, right in front of me, talking and laughing.

Rocky Colavito . . . Luis Tiant . . . Mudcat Grant . . . I was just in awe all day long.

Those 38 guys included probably the most popular player in Tribe history, Colavito, and ranged from the modern-day guys all the way back to Mel Harder, who pitched in old League Park and started the first game ever played at Cleveland Stadium. Mel, at age 91, was in a wheelchair but was still reasonably sharp and seemed to be enjoying himself.

The team staged events for the retired players all weekend, including a private brunch at Jacobs Field before the Saturday afternoon game. Suddenly, about 45 minutes before the first pitch, they all came pouring into the clubhouse, wearing all the different styles of jerseys the Indians have worn through the years. Each guy had been given a replica of his old uniform, with his name and number on the back.

Rick Manning and Duane Kuiper were in the flaming red tops of the mid-1970s (as Manning noted, those looked pretty cool—unless you were wearing the flaming red pants that used to be worn with them). Guys like Sonny Siebert and Joe Azcue were in the sleeveless jerseys of the 1960s. Colavito and Minnie Minoso were in the pinstriped white of the 1950s . . . all the way back to Harder's old flannel jersey with the big blue "C" from the 1920s.

I got a chance to talk with quite a few of the guys and loved every minute of it. Minoso, a Cuban who was a great ballplayer half a century ago, came right up to me and asked for an autograph. He said, "I just want to tell you one thing: You can *pick* it, man!"

What a great compliment.

I chatted with another Cuban legend, Tiant, who was wearing his old No. 33 sleeveless jersey, which he left unbuttoned to let his sizeable belly stick out. He was quite a sight, with a big gray goatee and a nearly bald head. I loved hearing him tell tales of old Latin ballplayers.

The only guy with a bigger belly than Tiant was Johnny Romano, the catcher from the early '60s. Many of the older players, like Tito Francona, were still trim. Gaylord Perry looked like a real estate developer or investment banker with his tanned face and long, silver hair.

My old buddy Orel Hershiser, now a broadcaster, was in his usual form, teasing me as we walked from the clubhouse to the dugout. He was harassing me about being one of the senior citizens on the current club. When I told him I was 34, he said, "Well, you've got eight more years. But you'll have to DH after 40."

Real funny. Me at DH.

The best compliment I got all day came from Max Alvis, the third baseman from Texas, who told me, "My nephew came to the third-base line before one game and you signed an autograph for him and were really nice. I just wanted to thank you, because not many people do that anymore." He was particularly impressed that I acted that way not knowing he was related to a ballplayer.

It would have been an honor to be named one of the top 100 players in the history of any franchise, much less one with as long a history as the Tribe's. During the team's first 100 years, 1,534 men put on a Cleveland uniform.

We all milled around in the dugout waiting for our pregame introductions. Radio announcer Tom Hamilton ran the show from a podium near third base, while career highlights for each guy played on the scoreboard. When a player was introduced, he ran out to his old position on the field, joining others who played that same position. Some jogged, some walked, some walked with assistance, and one, Harder, was wheeled out.

Perhaps the most impressive for his age was Minoso, who bounded up the dugout steps and jogged to his position with wonderfully light feet.

Somewhat surprisingly, the biggest ovation went not to the legendary Colavito, nor to star-turned-broadcaster Herb Score, still recovering from an auto accident, nor to the last man introduced, Bob Feller. It went to my buddy Hershiser. Because of his engaging personality and gritty play and the overall magic of the 1995 season, the sellout crowd gave Orel a thundering standing ovation.

Nagy was pitching that day and had one of his best outings of the season. As he was walking to the bullpen before the game to warm up, he stopped and chatted briefly with Harder, who was sitting under the scorching sun in his wheelchair. It was a nice moment.

The other shortstops named to the team were Lou Boudreau, Ray Chapman, Julio Franco, Woody Held, Joe Sewell, and Terry Turner. Chapman, Sewell, and Turner were dead. Boudreau was sick (he died a few weeks later). Franco was playing for the Atlanta Braves. The only other shortstop on hand was Held, who looked to be in great shape. Woodie played for the Tribe in the late '50s and early '60s after coming to Cleveland in a trade for future home-run king Roger Maris.

I loved hearing the old war stories, like Vic Power stealing home twice in one game. Two steals of home in the same game! I can't imagine doing that in the big leagues. I have only stolen home twice in my whole career—once with Seattle, once with Cleveland. (My Cleveland steal took place during a 2000 game in

Boston off Rheal Cormier—it was the team's first straight steal of home in eight years.) I was caught trying another three or four times.

We beat the Tigers, 8-4, putting the perfect touch on a memorable day. Too bad this was one of the only games all year that wasn't televised. It was originally supposed to be a national telecast, but Fox changed its mind at the last minute and neither of the regular broadcasters, WUAB or Fox Sports Ohio, had time to pick up the pieces. Because of that, an awful lot of Tribe fans missed the 42-minute pregame ceremony.

The next day's *Plain Dealer* ran a huge photo on the front page of the 38 guys who showed up. Small bleachers had been set up in short center field, and all 38 players posed. The oldest guys were in front and the current players were teetering on the top step, trying not to fall off and maim themselves.

Inspired by the ceremonies, I had a good game. I doubled in the bottom of the first. Robbie and I turned double plays in the second and third. I also reached on an error and scored, then cracked an important two-run double in the seventh.

But what I will remember the most from July 21, 2001, is the friendly ghosts who came to life before my eyes.

CHAPTER 14

A House in the Country

L IKE MOST PEOPLE, I have always fantasized about building my "dream house," a big, luxurious place with lots of amenities, surrounded by acres and acres of land. Unlike most people, my success as a professional ballplayer has enabled me to actually do it.

Nicole and I found 15 acres east of Seattle, in Issaquah, and built a 10,000-square-foot palace, with an indoor pool, a small theater, and a whole-house computer system that controls the lights and heat and music and security cameras and almost everything else.

I am particularly proud of our house because the basic design is mine.

I started designing it way back in 1996. Ground was broken October, 1999, and construction took 15 months. Even after we moved in, the workers had to come around and take care of tons of little details.

I had never designed anything before this, but I did have specific ideas about what I liked and what I didn't. My first step was to start collecting copies of *Architectural Digest* and a regional magazine devoted to contemporary designs. Every time I saw a house I liked, I'd tear out the page and put it in a folder. I even labeled the folder, "My Dream House." I didn't merely save big exterior shots; I'd cut out any little thing that caught my fancy—appliances, fixtures, door handles, you name it. I probably had 100 clippings in that folder.

Eventually I sat down and started to draw. After I had about 10 different designs, I showed them to Nicole. She went through them carefully and decided which parts she liked, and we re-worked them over and over until both of us were satisfied. Then we took our plan to an architect so he could check everything over and generate the actual blueprints and specifications.

The first time I met the architect, I showed him the plans and said, "This is what we want." He was excited. He said, "Wow, it's neat when somebody brings me their own design. It's so much easier when people know what they want. Most people come in with really vague ideas."

The architect transferred my drawings to a three-dimensional computer program. After he plugged in all the layouts, out popped the plan. We had to tweak some of the room measurements a little, but everything looked just about right from the very beginning.

Nicole and I agreed early on that we wanted an extremely contemporary look—real sparse, with clean lines, high ceilings, large windows, and big walls to emphasize our artwork. I have six paintings on display that I bought, including an Alexandra Nechita, a huge Peter Max, and three abstracts from an artist in Hawaii. We also display five that I did myself. One has a big mirror next to it that reflects the color and makes the room feel much bigger. That's a lot of paintings if you display them correctly. Fortunately, we have a lot of wall space.

Unfortunately, from my perspective, the interior of the house isn't as wild as I envisioned. Nicole said that because it's a family home we ought to tone things down a bit. We have navy blue couches with gold accents on them and relatively conservative red designs on the living room walls. Another big room features white couches and a lot of glass things with bronze supports. Every room has paintings and glass pieces we have collected through the years. I love to collect big pieces.

Both our Seattle and Westlake houses feature a lot of yellow stuff. I admit I have a thing about yellow. One of my Porsches is yellow. My four-wheelers are yellow. My jet skis are yellow—as is the life vest I wear when riding them. Even Nico's old stroller is yellow.

Although Nicole is less adventurous than I am in terms of color, our tastes are very similar. She does much of the interior decorating, and our furnishings are bright and contemporary with clean, dramatic lines. Artwork takes center stage.

The Seattle home is about three times larger than the one in Westlake, and it's really comfortable. People tell me it takes a person several tries to get his ideal house design, but I'm happy with our first try. I don't think the builder or the designer made many mistakes. We were meticulous, going over every detail before the construction began. I even figured out where I wanted the power outlets. (We put 'em just about everywhere.)

Our major overall goal was comfort. We didn't want to have to walk too far to the kitchen, and we wanted to make sure the rooms with the loudest activity were away from the sleeping areas. The movie theater is away from the main part of the house, as is the pool and the computer room. We also have two guest rooms set off from the main living area so everyone has enough privacy.

I was much more fired up about the theater than Nicole, and she was much more enthused about the pool. It's an indoor pool. In Seattle, that's the only way to go. You just don't get enough warm, sunny days to justify an outdoor pool. It's rectangular, about 20 by 50 feet, with a cover that slides off and on with the touch of a button. On the bottom of the pool is a big, inlaid baseball made of small ceramic tiles. To one side of the pool is a nice sitting area with a fireplace; on the other side is a raised whirlpool. On the rare occasions when the sun is out, sliding doors open outside to patios and a wide, undulating lawn. A wall near the changing room features a mural of a baseball. When I have guests over, I ask them to autograph it.

The master bedroom and two children's rooms are close together and near a playroom. The master suite is pretty cool. It has a fireplace between the bedroom and the bathtub, and there's a flat-screen TV above the tub. As in every other room in the house, we can pipe in music from a big CD changer downstairs.

One of the neatest features of the playroom is the carpet. We had a little baseball diamond cut into it, using the appropriate colors for home plate, the mound, and the base paths. Nico also has a pair of Mickey Mouse chairs with big ears, and fun cartoon murals that brighten up the walls.

The only minor inconvenience with the overall design is that the kitchen is downstairs, so if we want a glass of water or something we have to hike down. But we solved that problem just by buying a small refrigerator.

My movie theater seats 14 people. I have 10 seats that are real plush, velvet and leather. I call that my First Class section. The Coach section consists of four stools at the marble bar in the back. The system is state of the art. An overhead projector can show DVD, VHS, 8 mm—about any format you can name. Nicole doesn't use the theater much, but I'm in there all the time.

Another of my favorite features is a big, in-the-wall fish tank that's between the main hallway and the kitchen. It's a saltwater tank with exotic, brilliantly colored fish. They're pretty finicky, though—they have to be fed twice a day with special food that's kept in the freezer.

The whole house runs on a central computer. You can walk up to a touch pad and punch up a TV show, run the lights, change the temperature, or pump music into any area of the house. The system can be a pain sometimes, because it will lose its memory and you have to re-code it. But when it works, which is most of the time, it's awesome.

The exterior is white stucco. The house itself is on a five-acre parcel; across the street we own another 10 acres that are still wild. I built motocross trails over there, and that's also where we stage paintball games.

Nicole came up with a real-estate agent who found us the land before it even went on the market. It was perfect. It's in the middle of nowhere, with soaring pine and deciduous trees and hilly terrain. When you go to bed, you have complete silence. Deer and other critters roam around constantly. Nico loves to watch the deer eating the flowers. But sometimes, the wild animals are a little too wild. Cougars have been spotted near our house. They aren't quite as loveable as deer.

One of the coolest features inside the house is a chandelier about the size of the Queen Mary hanging in our entryway. It's unique. We hired a Seattle glass blower named Dale Chihuly, who is not only well-known in the Northwest but has gained a following internationally. He won a Fulbright Fellowship in 1968 to work in the Venini factory in Venice, Italy, then founded his own glass school a few years later.

Chihuly's work has appeared in nearly 200 museums around the globe. In the 1990s he got together with glass factories in Finland, Ireland, and Mexico to create sculptures over the canals and piazze of Venice. In 1999 he created 15 installations inside the stone walls of Jerusalem at the Tower of David Museum. And in 2001 he opened a large exhibition at the Victoria and Albert Museum in London.

Chihuly's own house is very cool. In a hole underneath his swimming pool, beneath a heavy piece of Fiberglas, he put big pieces of crystal that were left over from his work with chandeliers. When you turn on the lights of the pool, it looks like the big pieces of crystal are sticking up into the water. It's really, really beautiful.

Despite his heavy-duty resume, Chihuly wasn't pretentious at all. He was fun to be around. He's in his 60s, has a big, curly head of hair, and wears a patch over his left eye. He came over to our house and whipped out about 10 different designs in five minutes. He was amazing to watch.

The chandelier is about 7 feet by 4 feet. Once we agreed on the basic design, he disappeared for five months, then called us up one day and said, "Your lamp is ready. But we're going to need a crane to put it up." The thing weighs 1,300 pounds. We had to in-

stall a new support beam on the top of the ceiling capable of handling nearly triple that weight.

I wanted the piece to be red, orange, and yellow—like a ball of
fire. Nicole wanted white. We compromised, and ended up with a
really pretty blue. The light plays off it in different ways, depend-
ing on where you're standing, the time of day, the season of the
year, and the weather.

In the winter of 2001, when a 6.8 magnitude earthquake hit 60
miles southwest of Seattle, the big light started swinging all over
the place. My father-in-law was there and was afraid it was going
to fall and leave a crater the size of an asteroid. But the support
beam held and the house suffered only minor damage.

We had a few cracks in the walls and the ceiling of the swimming room, and we lost a little glass piece that fell from a table,
but nothing more than that. We were fortunate. A 6.8 quake is a
monster. One person was killed in that quake and 272 suffered injuries, mostly minor. At the Seattle-Tacoma Airport, the glass was
broken out of the control tower and controllers had to work from
a tent. Closer to the epicenter, Olympia, the state capital, was a
mess. Highways buckled, big buildings were heavily damaged,
and rubble was everywhere. People don't think of Seattle in the
same context as San Francisco or Los Angeles, but we get our
share of earthquakes, too. Each year, nearly 1,000 quakes are
recorded in western Washington. Most of them are too small to be
felt. But when you feel one, you really feel it.

I was in uniform when a small quake hit Seattle on May 2,
1996. The Indians were playing the Mariners, and I was standing
out at shortstop in the bottom of the seventh inning when a
quake, later announced as magnitude 5.3, rolled through the
Kingdome, halting the game.

I didn't even feel it. Right as the quake was about to hit, Mike
Hargrove came out and made a pitching change, bringing in Julian Tavarez to replace Orel Hershiser. Tavarez had finished his
warm-up tosses. I was standing on the mound and catcher Sandy
Alomar said, "The ground is moving." We looked up and saw that

the public address speakers were swaying back and forth. Some fans in the upper deck were hurrying to the ramps. The P.A. announcer said, "We have just experienced an earthquake. Please move slowly to the exits."

Some people weren't moving slowly at all. The Mariners' long-time play-by-play announcer, Dave Niehaus, fled the booth, telling listeners, "I'm getting out of here!"

Kenny Lofton, who had gone through the killer quake in Los Angeles in 1994, made it from centerfield to the dugout in about two seconds. Tavarez was pretty panicky, too. He was so upset after the game that he couldn't even eat.

Nico and Nicole were at the game, along with Nicole's whole family. I went over to where they were sitting and had them jump over the wall and stand with me in the middle of the field. I'm not sure they were safer in the middle of the field than in the stands, but at least we'd be together.

I don't spend much time worrying about earthquakes, though. Every place on the planet has its problems. The tornadoes that rip through Northeast Ohio can be just as deadly as any other kind of natural disaster. Although I haven't spent a lot of time up close and personal with blizzards—and don't plan to—I know they can shut down a whole city for days. In Florida, where we briefly owned a house, we had to contend with hurricanes. Other places have volcanoes. And the worst damage I have ever seen anywhere was caused by floods and mudslides in Venezuela in 1999. So I'll take my chances with Seattle's quakes.

ALTHOUGH I DESIGNED OUR HOUSE, I'm not too hot at working on it. I never managed to pick up any handyman expertise from my dad, the electrician, and I have no clue when it comes to wiring or plumbing or other household tasks. So we always have to call somebody. During the season, Nicole's dad keeps an eye on the place, and he's the one who does the calling.

My wife has become quite the expert on vacuum cleaners. I'm still not sure what that's all about. All I know is that she seems to have developed an obsession with them. Every time a new model is introduced, she has to go out and test it. We have enough vacuum cleaners to clean up half the state of Washington.

The house was a ton of work. I put in a lot of time on the project, and I worried about it. It's so huge that I thought it might turn into a royal pain. But I'm thrilled with the way it turned out.

The one thing I needed to add after it was completed was another garage, because we were soon running short on garage space. We have the cars, the lawn mower, the four-wheelers and, of course, all those vacuum cleaners. Plus, I had converted one of the existing garages into an art studio.

Believe me, I realize how lucky I am to be able to create a place like this.

Ballplayers who start to get decent money often run right out and buy fancy cars. I like fancy cars, too. But the first thing I did when I started making a little money was to buy good stuff for my apartment—nice furniture, a VCR, things like that. Living in a nice environment is important to me.

And these days, the livin' is easy.

CHAPTER 15

Cashing In

I N ALL MY YEARS AS AN INDIAN, the only time I got much negative publicity was during the winter before the 1999 season, when people found out I was dissatisfied with my contract.

Four years earlier, I had signed a six-year deal that paid me $3 million per year. The team could exercise a one-year option after that, tying me up through 2002.

When I signed that agreement, I was coming off the knee injury (the one from when Ivan Rodriguez steamrolled me) and I wasn't sure how my knee was going to respond. So I figured I'd better sign for more than one year. All of my previous contracts had been for only one year, and I worried that another one-year contract might not give me enough time to prove I could still play at a top level. I was looking for three or maybe even four years.

When my agent said the Indians were offering six years, I said, "Oh my god! That's awesome! Go ahead and sign!" I just didn't give much thought to how the market might change over that period of time. Who could imagine that salaries would escalate the way they did?

Even though less-talented players soon started passing me by in terms of salary, I never felt trapped until after the 1998 season. That winter, salaries exploded. Contracts went so high that mine began to look like a minor-league deal. I had all those Gold Gloves and a solid batting average and had shown I could come through in big games, and I'd see guys who had only been in the league for a couple of years making twice what I was making.

I was by far the lowest-paid infielder in Cleveland. Second baseman Robbie Alomar had just been signed for $8 million a year. First baseman Jim Thome was averaging about $7 million, and was considered a bargain. On the other side of me, at third, Travis Fryman was pulling down $5 million.

Those guys deserved that kind of money. But I did, too. I thought the team should at least tack a few more years onto my contract at a similar rate.

General Manager John Hart said flatly that he was philosophically opposed to reworking a guaranteed contract.

My dissatisfaction found its way into the newspapers. In spite of what was written, though, I never seriously thought about holding out in 1999. I showed up at spring training on time and worked hard.

I will say, though, that if I hadn't gotten an extension before the 2001 season, I would have seriously considered not reporting to camp.

Fortunately, the Indians were willing to talk by then, and things worked out beautifully. In February 2001, I signed a $15 million contract extension through 2004. There's also an option year in 2005. Unlike the last deal, where the Indians alone could exercise the option, this option is mutual; if either side wants out after the 2004 season, I get a $1 million buyout.

No, it wasn't an Alex Rodriguez deal, the 10-year, $252 million windfall that dropped jaws all over the country. It wasn't even close to a Derek Jeter deal, worth $189 million over 10 years. Writers from national magazines didn't swarm around my locker to do articles on my new contract. But it was important to me and really made me happy.

The best thing about the new deal was that it meant I'd probably stay a Cleveland Indian for the rest of my career. Although I don't have a no-trade provision (and you can never rule anything out completely)—a guy with 10 years in the major leagues and five years with the same team can veto any trade. Plus, I have a personal services contract that kicks in after I retire. I'll work with the front office, coach kids, do public relations . . . whatever they want me to do.

I'm really proud of how the contract negotiations were handled. This time, nothing was written in the papers until the deal was almost done. I was determined not to get into the same mess I got into before the 1999 season, when Sandy Alomar blew the whole thing apart.

Sandy told reporters that, because I had freely signed a contract, I should honor it no matter what. That is his philosophy, and that's fine—except he told reporters all about it before he said anything to me. That really bothered me.

Sandy had been a good friend of mine. He sat right next to me in the locker room for a long time, and we talked about everything. So when I read his comments, they really surprised me—and really upset me. I thought he owed it to me to talk to me about it in person.

Besides, I didn't want it to become a public issue. I never wanted to show signs that I was upset about the contract. I didn't want the fans to know. Heck, I didn't even want my teammates to know.

When we got to spring training that year, the first thing manager Mike Hargrove did was call Sandy and me into his office. He figured that if we hashed things out right away behind closed doors, we could put the matter behind us and get on with baseball.

We had a pretty good argument. Sandy said what he thought, and I said what I thought—and there was a big gap in between.

The disagreement hurt our friendship. I lost some respect for him. We continued to sit next to each other in the clubhouse, and we kept talking, but from my perspective things have never been quite the same.

When the Indians wouldn't budge on a contract that year, I decided to go out and play my usual game and see what developed down the road. Instead of pouting or loafing, I played every bit as hard as usual. As a matter of fact, I had my best year ever at the plate, hitting .333. I finished second in the American League in stolen bases, with 42. I had career highs in hits (191), runs (112), RBIs (66), and doubles (36).

The following year, still with the same contract, I set an all-time fielding record for Indian's shortstops with only three errors in 156 games. In fact, my .9954 fielding percentage was the second-best for all shortstops in major league history, behind only Cal Ripken's .9956 a decade earlier.

I was determined not to let the contract become an issue, either on or off the field. And it wasn't, not after that one public flap.

No matter what I did, I certainly wasn't going to make a scene like the one Frank Thomas made during the White Sox's training camp in 2001. He stomped out of camp with six years left on a contract that paid him $10 million per year. Thomas told reporters it just wasn't right that A-Rod could be paid $25 million a year when others were struggling along in the $7 million-to-$9 million range. Then, when he returned to camp a week later, he declared, "It's not about money."

Or how about the mess made by Gary Sheffield when he was with the Dodgers? Sheffield, who piped up about the same time as Thomas, had four years left on a contract that paid him a little over $10 million per season. Sheffield wasn't content to squawk about his own pay. He started comparing his salary to that of his teammates.

"They're paying Kevin Brown $15 million a year until he's 41," Sheffield moaned to reporters. "They just gave Darren Dreifort $55 million, and he's won only 39 big-league games and he's had arm surgery. They gave Shawn Green $13 million a year. That's an insult. I'm getting less than Dreifort? I'm getting just $3 million more than Carlos Perez? It's not my fault they signed Perez to that stupid contract. They give out all these dumb contracts and, when it comes to me, nothing."

Most baseball fans wouldn't agree that $10 million a year is "nothing." Beyond that, imagine the reaction of his teammates!

In March, Sheffield reportedly called a team meeting and

apologized to his teammates. Afterward, everybody had nice things to say about moving on with the business of winning. But players don't forget those kinds of insults. Trust me.

Sheffield's rants made Dodger fans so angry that they booed him even in spring training at Vero Beach, Florida, usually one of the most laid-back sites in baseball.

I'LL BE THE FIRST TO ADMIT that baseball salaries sound crazy in the overall scheme of life. Heck, the average salary for the Cleveland Indians on Opening Day of 2001 was $3,065,833. That's 30 times what many doctors make. And we don't save lives.

On the other hand, we are the best in the world at what we do. People are willing to pay a lot of money to watch us. And we work our butts off to get where we are.

When I was in the low minors, I would stay at the ballpark after games, hitting the ball off a tee all by myself. I would beg the guys who were cleaning the ballpark to leave the lights on longer so I could practice. Meanwhile, my teammates would be heading out to the bars and making fun of me. They'd say, "Man, this guy is crazy! What is he doing?" Now I'm the one who's laughing. None of those other guys even came close to making the major leagues.

And fans often don't know the other things you have to go through to emerge from the minors. They don't know about the 14-hour bus rides. They don't know about the times you'd get off that bus, take a 20-minute nap, and head right to the ballpark. They don't know about the times when you're playing Single-A ball in Billingham and you have an old bus and it keeps breaking down and the players have to get out and actually push the stupid bus. (That happened more than once.) It's not like somebody handed me my job on a silver platter.

Once you get to the majors, your work is just beginning. At this level, the talent is so good that you can't survive unless you eat, sleep, and breathe baseball seven days a week. If you look at my hands during the season, you'll see thick calluses I've built up from taking so much batting practice. I don't just take the usual batting practice before the game, or even the "extra" batting practice that is offered most days before the regular batting practice. I also spend hours and hours in the indoor cages, pounding the balls coming out of the pitching machines, over and over and over. During the season, you'll often see little pieces of athletic tape on my fingers. That's to cover up blisters.

Another thing fans don't realize is that being a star player doesn't mean your life is suddenly incredibly happy. We have problems just like everybody else. In fact, in a sense, we have more things to worry about, because big money complicates your life.

Mind you, I'm not complaining. I wouldn't trade places with anyone. I'm just trying to point out that big money doesn't fix everything.

It does ease a lot of the daily hassles. We ride on charter jets, big 737s or A320s, with plenty of room to spread out. A player can take an entire row of seats. Sometimes, on a long flight, I'll flip up the armrests and take a nap across three seats. Which is considerably more restful than riding in the luggage rack on a minor-league bus.

Usually we get a choice of three entrees, and we can eat any time during the trip. The flight attendants come around constantly with food and beverages.

After we land, we get an envelope stuffed with meal money — $73 in cash for each day we're on the road. (What you don't spend, you keep.) It's no wonder some guys fight a constant battle with their weight.

I always bring along my CD player on flights, so I can crank up my tunes, and my Apple laptop, so I can play video games, watch a DVD movie or mess around with digital photos.

When we travel, we don't even have to go into airport terminals. Our charter buses drive right out onto the runway and we climb up stairs to the plane. We hardly touch our luggage. Once we hand it over at the start of a trip, it is placed on the plane, unloaded onto a truck, driven to the hotel and delivered to our rooms.

Not exactly like my days in Butte.

A LOT OF PLAYERS AREN'T EQUIPPED to deal with huge amounts of money. When they start to cash those giant paychecks every 15 days, they sometimes think they no longer have to worry about money at all.

No matter how much money you make, you can end up broke. Look what happened to heavyweight boxer Mike Tyson. You say to yourself, "How in the world can that guy make $30 million per fight and be bankrupt?" But it happens. When guys start out with nothing and all of a sudden have almost everything, some of them start to think they can tap any amount of cash at any time, just like turning on a water faucet.

Some newly rich athletes squander their money on ridiculously lavish lifestyles. You probably read about Dennis Rodman's 40th birthday party. In May 2001, he threw a weekend-long bash at his house in Newport Beach, California, bringing in two rock bands (without a permit) and 300 guests. He made a dramatic entrance in a helicopter, circling his house twice before landing right on the beach (without permission). When 30 cops showed up—some in riot gear—Dennis simply moved his party to a nearby restaurant.

Some baseball players are almost as flamboyant. When you try to act like a king, all of a sudden you can turn around and see nothing but red ink in your checking account.

Some players also spend a ton of their money on a big entourage. They not only have agents and accountants and investment advisers, but psychologists and personal conditioning coaches and motivational gurus. Most of it is baloney. What is some motivational speaker going to tell me? The only thing I need is my agent and my financial guy.

Players also can get into trouble by wading into risky investments. You are constantly being approached by people pitching grand schemes. A lot of those people talk a very good game. You start to think you can turn your big money into even bigger money without much danger. But, like the old saying goes, if something sounds too good to be true, it usually is. I'm pretty careful and don't make a lot of wild investments. But even I have been burned a few times.

The worst investment I ever made was when I hooked up with a guy in the music business. He was going to come out with CDs that contained 20-second pieces of new songs that were about to break on the radio. We were going to sell those to baseball, basketball, and soccer teams to play during their games. It never got off the ground.

I also jumped into a scheme with my former teammate Dave Winfield that hasn't panned out so far. He launched a company to sell lighting to businesses. The lights would be whiter and consume less energy at a cheaper price. But that just hasn't gone the way we had hoped.

But I've gotten in to some traditional stuff that has gone just fine, like a Burger King franchise in Washington, D.C., which I co-own with Winfield, Paul Assenmacher, and Jim Poole.

Unlike Manny Ramirez, who has changed agents about 4,000 times now, I have been with the same guy for my entire career. I signed with Adam Katz way back in Double-A ball and never saw any good reason to change. When I first hooked up with him, he was working with the Davimos brothers in New York. Two years later, he split off from that firm, and I had to decide whether to stay with the Davimoses or go with Adam. Our relationship was working, so I followed Adam. Today he has about 50 clients, including Sammy Sosa, Mo Vaughn, and Tim Raines. He moved to Los Angeles after he got married, and I often see him when we play in Anaheim.

I'm glad we decided not to make a big stink about the contract. The day after the news conference to announce the new deal, the writers and broadcasters remarked on my patience and attitude. Columnist Terry Pluto wrote in the *Akron Beacon Journal* that "[Vizquel] handled a sticky contract situation with the same grace as he does a bad-hop grounder to short."

UNFORTUNATELY, ONE OF THE TRADE-OFFS with big money and the free-agency rules is that now people skip around from team to team. Sometimes you'd like to keep a team together forever, but you can't. One of the best things about the Indians during the last few years is that were all a little underpaid, compared to the big-market teams, but many of us stuck around longer than usual.

The problem with a mega-salary like A-Rod's is that your team might not have enough money to pay anyone else. Look what happened to the Rangers in 2001. When we played them in Texas in May, I talked to some of their players, and they said, "Even if we score 10 runs every game, we're still afraid the other team will score 11 or 12 because our pitching is so bad." The season was only six weeks old and the Texas papers were already filled with stories saying the Rangers should pull the plug on the season, start dumping players, and rebuild the whole team.

Which leads us to another drawback with this job: at a moment's notice, your employer can send you to another part of the country. And they give you about 24 hours to get there.

Sure, many business executives can be transferred, too. But they have the option of saying no. If they want, they can switch to another company in the same city and usually do similar work. For a baseball player, there's really only one employer in America. If you don't play by the rules of Major League Baseball, you either have to leave the country or find another profession.

Sometimes it really hurts when you lose a friend through a trade. But you can't be sentimental about it. You have no control over trades. I learned that in my very first year in baseball. One day you're here, the next day you're there. Coping with that reality is just another mental part of the game.

But I always believed this: if you work hard and you try to be consistent at your job, you will be less likely to get traded. I always think people get traded for a reason. Maybe you are trouble in the clubhouse, or there's something they see in you that they don't want to deal with.

I think that's one of the reasons the Indians gave me the new contract in 2001. At the news conference to announce the new agreement, Hart said, "Two years ago, he talked to us. It was a very pleasant conversation. We declined to do anything at that time, and Omar never said a word about it again. He went out and played, even though he had a very outdated contract."

That is a lesson worth remembering. Hard work and patience usually pay off.

On the other hand, it's not as if I was being handed $252 million, like A-Rod. In fact, now that I think about it, my dear agent negotiated a deal for $237 million *less* than A-Rod's. Hey—maybe I should fire that guy!

But seriously . . . there's no getting around the fact that A-Rod's contract is breathtaking. As if $252 million isn't enough, he has a clause that says nobody in baseball can make more than he does. So if somebody passes him, the Rangers have to ante up even more money.

To tell you the truth, I'm perfectly happy with my paychecks. On my salary, I can do just about anything I want, within reason.

Now, if I had A-Rod money, I could do about anything I wanted *without* reason. Man . . . just imagine what you could do with all that dough!

I have. And here's what I'd do: I would buy a helicopter. I probably wouldn't put Dennis Rodman in it and land on the beach, but I love those machines. I have ridden in choppers several times and think they're really cool.

So I'd learn how to fly one. Then I'd buy one.

And just write 'em a big ol' check.

CHAPTER 16

Natural Disaster

WHEN I FIRST SAW the news reports on CNN, I couldn't believe my eyes. My homeland was being devastated by floods and mudslides.

It was December 16, 1999. I was home in Seattle, getting ready for Christmas with my family. And on television, the rain kept coming and my people kept dying. The death toll seemed to grow by the hour. Within no time, the tragedy was identified as Venezuela's worst natural disaster ever.

Fortunately for me, none of my relatives was directly affected. My parents were living in my apartment on the outskirts of Caracas, the place I bought when I was still playing winter ball. Although they saw plenty of water, the worst damage, by far, was northwest of them, in the coastal state of Vargas. Unfortunately, I had a lot of friends there.

Estimates on the death toll range from 30,000 to 50,000. We will never get a more precise number, because the government hadn't conducted a census in the areas that were hardest hit. Many of the victims were poor, living in shantytowns in forbidden areas on the side of the mountains.

Remember, Caracas is not directly on the Caribbean. Between the city and the coast is the Avila mountain range. For years the region's poor people built shacks on the mountainsides north of the city. They weren't supposed to build there, because the ground is so unstable, but they were broke and the land was free and the government did little to try to chase them away.

In 1999, Venezuela was suffering through the worst economic recession in its history. Millions of people were living on the mountainside, many of them in slapped-together shacks made of tin, wood, and cinder block.

But the poor weren't the only ones affected. When the torrential rains arrived, whole chunks of mountain slid down to the sea. Businesses, resorts, and upscale condos were smashed, too, and one of the country's top tourist destinations was all but erased.

The beaches of the central coast are referred to as El Litoral. Both Venezuelans and foreign visitors frequented the peaceful, scenic area. But the beaches essentially vanished, filled with mud and debris.

The news reports coming back to Seattle were gruesome. They talked of dead bodies sticking out of the mud. Dead bodies bobbing in the water off the coast. Dead bodies buried under 15 feet of mud, and survivors digging frantically for family members with pickaxes.

One story said workers at a Caracas cemetery had dug 1,500 graves for corpses that hadn't even been identified. Photographs of the dead were posted at the cemetery's gates, so survivors could look for relatives. The faces in the pictures were mangled and, in some cases, still had pieces of vegetation hanging out of their mouths.

As these horrors unfolded, the rain kept coming. By Christmas Eve, the region had received 18 inches of rain in the month of December—nine times the usual.

An estimated 150,000 more people were left homeless. In some places, the landscape had changed so dramatically that people couldn't even tell where their houses had been. Even those whose homes escaped major damage were miserable, because the mudslides wiped out water and sewer lines, forcing them to contend with dehydration and disease.

Businesses disappeared. Livestock drowned and crops were ruined.

The government went into high gear, ferrying in supplies and ferrying out people. Citizens volunteered to help. (My brother and sister worked at tent shelters.) Soon, other countries, particularly the Unites States, joined in.

Whole towns were cut off from the rest of the nation, so food and water had to be flown in by helicopter. The people got up early every morning to wait for it. But sometimes the helicopters wouldn't return for two or three days, so they had to go all the way around the mountain—a half-hour drive—to stand in line for food and water, and then lug it all the way home.

People with less patience looted stores and robbed their fellow citizens.

Among the homeless was my old minor league buddy, Jorge Uribe. He had been living in La Guiara, where he was teaching physical education. The mudslides demolished his house, along with much of the rest of the town.

I had to do something.

Within a week, I hooked up with World Vision, a Christian organization that provides help to people around the world. An arm of the National Council of Churches, the group quickly raised $400,000.

I figure I brought in about $100,000 of that on my own, because we set up an account in Seattle and I was doing TV and radio shows almost every day, urging people to contribute. I also called my teammates and former teammates, and they sent donations. The first day alone, I phoned Harold Baines, Dave Burba, Travis Fryman, Dwight Gooden, Steve Karsay, Mark Langston, Kenny Lofton, Charlie Nagy, Steve Reed, Paul Shuey, Jim Thome, and Jaret Wright.

The Cleveland Indians' organization kicked in $10,000.

Then, the first week in January, I flew from Seattle to Caracas to survey the damage and see what else could be done.

Even though two weeks had passed, the situation was still horrendous. When I took a helicopter into the trouble zones, what I saw made me sick. You could see hands sticking out of the mud. Workers were still plucking out bodies as fast as they could. Others were spreading a white chemical powder all over everything to try to reduce the stench created by the decomposing remains.

Some of the houses that weren't buried had been pushed right down the mountains into the coves. In some places you could stand on the mud in the street and look into a second-story window. In others, all you could see was a roof sticking out of the mud.

The houses that remained in place were an absolute mess. All the beds and TVs and kitchens were covered in mud.

Some of the rocks I saw were literally as big as a school bus. A single rock! Imagine that thing roaring down at you. The noise must have been ferocious.

They said the first major mudslide took place at about 6 A.M. Another major slide occurred about 2 P.M., and a third came late in the evening. People were terrified of what would happen next.

For many of those in the path of the mud, the dangers were not exactly unknown. Six years earlier, mudslides killed 150 people, hurt 500 more, and left 11,000 homeless.

We talked to many people who were still living on the mountains. They didn't have much in life, but what little they had was there, and they simply refused to leave.

I got tears in my eyes more than once. I'd never seen anything like it. The people really touched my heart. You'd go to bed and all you could think about was the kids who had nothing.

I talked to my lifelong buddy, Carlos Lopez, to try to figure out what I could do. At first I was thinking maybe we should try to bring baseball players to the disaster areas to pitch in with the relief effort, maybe help distribute food and water. But Carlos thought we should stick with what we know: baseball.

Or, in this case, its lower-key cousin, softball.

We began to plan a charity softball game involving current and former major league stars. They would donate their time, we would sell tickets, and everything we made would be used to help the flood victims.

Something like this normally takes about six months to arrange. But we didn't have that kind of time. Not only did we need to generate money, we needed to stage an event that would boost the country's morale.

We put the whole thing together in 10 days. We worked from seven in the morning until 10 at night, contacting the players, arranging for visas, dealing with security and tickets and everything else that is involved in moving a huge crowd of people in and out of a public facility. I even had to track down bats, gloves, and balls.

And we couldn't expect the players to find the field on their own in a foreign country. We had to arrange for cars to take them in and out and make sure everything ran on time. If you don't treat people well, they probably won't come back.

The schedule was absolutely crazy. Fortunately, we got the support of the president of Venezuela.

Hugo Chavez has been a controversial figure. He was jailed for two years after participating in a failed coup attempt in 1992, only to emerge as a folk hero, perceived as a champion of the poor. He is a leftist who admires Fidel Castro. And in 1999, he pushed through a new constitution that eliminated the old congress and supreme court.

But he was certainly good to me.

When President Chavez heard about my efforts, he invited me to the Venezuelan White House to meet him. I had never been there before, so it was a real honor.

He is a serious baseball fan. The year before, in fact, he actually pitched batting practice to Sammy Sosa, who was in Venezuela for a home-run contest.

We waited about 20 minutes outside the president's office. While we were waiting, the vice-president came by and chatted with us. He gave me his phone number and told me that, if I needed anything to make the game work, I should just give him a call and he would send people over and take care of it.

Finally, we were led in to the president. He called me by name and gave me a big hug. Just to tease me, he was wearing a baseball cap from the team of my old archrival, the Navegantes de

Magallanes from Valencia. I, of course, had played for Caracas, and the Caracas-Valencia games were wars. The two cities are only about 100 miles apart, and they have developed an intense rivalry. There stood the president of the nation, wearing the cap of my archrival. I had to laugh.

We were in a big, beautiful salon with ornate chairs decorated with gold leaf and red velvet. On the walls were oil paintings of the previous presidents. It was just like in the movies. The president would look over to an aide and say, "Hey, bring me some sandwiches and juices for the kids," and the guy would hustle away and get them. To a person like me, who grew up as an ordinary citizen in middle-class Caracas, it felt like a dream.

The president volunteered to go to the phone and try to get his pal Sosa to come to the game. Unfortunately, Sammy couldn't make it. But we were able to attract several big-name players, including Dave Winfield, Dennis Martinez, Tony Fernandez, Andres Galarraga, Magglio Ordonez, Julio Franco, and Jose Rijo. We also had some well-known Venezuelan singers and TV personalities.

It was a huge event. Twenty thousand people showed up at the stadium in Caracas. For only the second time in history, all four of Venezuela's television networks showed the same program at the same time—our softball game. (The only other time that happened was a telethon to raise money for cancer patients.)

I bought and donated tickets to 500 kids in hopes of boosting their spirits. It seemed to work. The weather was typical Caracas—sunny and 85 degrees. It was a good, close, one-run game with a lot of humor, and it seemed to take everybody's mind off our troubles.

President Chavez pitched five innings—and was relieved by El Presidente, Dennis Martinez (he's had the nickname for a long time, because he's so popular in his native Nicaragua that people say he could become the president there).

The rules were flexible. We had about 13 people on the field at a time, and an announcer did live commentary over the P.A. system right in the middle of the action, interviewing the celebrities, sort of like one of MTV's rock-and-jock match-ups. We even gave some of the kids from disaster areas a chance to hit and pitch.

The game raised about $225,000. That money has been used to buy chairs, blackboards, and schoolbooks for the kids. It also has helped rebuild some of the schools. We've replaced fallen walls and cleaned out basements that were previously unusable.

The distribution of the money was well organized, which is not always the case in a relief effort. Specific people were assigned to help specific geographic areas. My attention was devoted to one nine-block neighborhood.

Even now, the battle continues. Full recovery will take years and years.

One thing that haunts me is the fact that many of the people who died shouldn't have been living where they were living. The areas are classified as "red zones," because the ground just isn't stable enough. But probably 30 or 40 percent of the population just doesn't care. They build wherever they can find a place. Nobody seems to be able to stop them. They simply move their stuff right in there. And they're still building! Some of them went right back to where they were and built right on top of the ruins.

Every time I go to Venezuela, I see the people moving deeper and deeper into the mountains. When is it going to stop? I think God was sending them a message: Don't do this. But when you talk to the people, they just don't care. They say, "There's no way I'm moving. If I'm going to die, I'm going to die under my own roof."

VENEZUELA IS A DIFFERENT COUNTRY from the one I left as a 17-year-old. Largely because of its economic problems, the crime rate is up. Even ordinary people don't always feel safe walking the streets.

The economy is still struggling. From time to time, I'll pack up boxes of clothes that I don't need and send them down to my cousins. Shoes are quite expensive back home, so every time I visit I bring about 10 pairs. They especially like the Nike stuff.

My heart will always be in Venezuela, though, despite the country's growing problems.

Nicole is somewhat less enthusiastic, especially since the 1993 coup attempt. When the planes were bombing, she was terrified. She wanted to leave and never come back. She has returned a few times, but she just isn't very comfortable there.

I, of course, thought the coup attempt was great entertainment. I was out taping the action on my video camera. They were bombing the freeway. I think they were trying to hit the police station. Nicole was just terrified. Some of the bombs were landing right near us. You could feel the heat from the explosions and see the shrapnel flying.

At one point, the rebels took over a couple of the national television stations.

The people were going a little nuts. Martial law was declared for three days because of looting. You couldn't even leave your house. If you were moving around the streets, you could be shot.

We were in my apartment, about 15 miles from where all the Americans were. The embassy was pulling them together to try to get them out. Dave Burba and his future wife, Star, happened to be in Caracas. They were pretty freaked out, too.

The whole thing was surreal. I never expected to see anything remotely like this in my own hometown. When we were growing up, Caracas was as stable as Cleveland.

In terms of the pace of life, though, Caracas is total chaos—even in the best of times. Like Manhattan, Caracas is limited by its geography. In the case of Caracas, it is largely surrounded by mountains. Because there's no space left to grow outward, it expands upward. More and more people have crowded into essentially the same amount of space.

But you get used to it. Nicole is actually more comfortable driving in Venezuela than in Cleveland. Drivers in Caracas seem to have fewer wrecks than the drivers in Cleveland, even though they drive more aggressively. I guess you just learn to go with the flow, like getting through a revolving door that's moving quickly.

Nicole does have a hard time coping with some of the cultural stuff, like the *Brujerias*. They practice black magic, which they call *Santeria*. They pray to spirits. They want somebody from the past to come and talk to them. There are different ways to do it—they pray with blood, they pray with animals, they light candles. It's similar to voodoo—if they have a picture of you, they think they can put a curse on you. There's a lot of stuff like that in Venezuela.

The *Brujerias* got a lot of publicity because they supposedly predicted the 1999 floods. So now they're saying that eventually the ocean is going to erode the mountains and wash away Caracas. They call that the "cleansing of the evil," which is not exactly the way most people would view the deaths of their fellow countrymen.

On the other hand, Caracas does have some unusual features that are quite attractive to outsiders. During the summer of 2001, for example, a gallon of gasoline there cost 39 cents.

Venezuela's second-biggest industry, after petroleum exports, has been tourism. But tourism has dropped because of the political instability. When people read about coup attempts, they tend to look elsewhere for a vacation site. But my country is still a wonderful place to go. If you hang around with the right people and you know where you're going, there's no better place. We have beautiful beaches and beautiful people, and they treat you well.

Drugs are not nearly as big a problem in Venezuela as they are in Colombia. Our biggest problem is the stealing. Because the economy is so bad, some of the people just go out to the street and rob the first person they see.

Checkpoints are set up all along the roads, and you need to carry documentation at all times. Even in the city, people are randomly checked. It takes Americans a while to get used to that. Not me. Even after living in the States for so long, I don't have any trouble making the adjustment to Venezuela. Actually, it's a tougher adjustment for me going from Venezuela to the States.

I wouldn't mind returning to Venezuela after my playing days, but that depends on Nico and Nicole. And I think it's going to be a tough sell.

ONE PROBLEM I HAVE IN VENEZUELA is that now I'm so well-known, I have a much harder time moving around freely.

I was reminded of that in the spring of 2001, when the Indians traveled to my homeland to play two exhibition games against the Houston Astros.

Major League Baseball has really made an effort to reach out to foreign countries, which only makes sense, given the makeup of big-league rosters. A quarter of all current major league players were born outside the United States.

The Indians-Astros games were part of a "Month of the Americas" celebration, which also included games in other Latin countries. In our case, the site was Valencia, one of the eight cities that are home to the Venezuelan pro league. Unlike Caracas, which is often a tourist destination because it is near the coast, Valencia is an industrial town, similar in size to Cleveland. And, like in Cleveland, the people who live there take their baseball seriously.

If you think Jacobs Field gets wild at times, you should see the ballparks in Valencia and Caracas, especially when those two teams square off. It looks less like a modern baseball game than an old-fashioned NFL game.

From the very beginning, the *fanaticos* are screaming and dancing and heckling. And then the beer kicks in.

Fans do the wave in Venezuela, too, but with a twist: when they stand and throw their hands into the air, their hands are frequently holding cups of beer. They let go of the cups and everybody gets a shower of *cerveza*.

The exhibition games were held on a Saturday and Sunday in mid-March. I flew in a day early so I could spend time with my family. On Saturday morning, we drove from Caracas to Valencia.

Normally that journey takes about two hours. On this day, we needed three hours, because we kept stopping along the way. We pulled over for breakfast and had some *cachapas*, which are like pancakes with cheese. We'd see a roadside stand with mangoes and pull over there. Then we'd stop for cookies or *arepas*. The roads are asphalt, but there's not much room on the sides, and we were lucky we didn't get sideswiped on one of our stops.

Finally we arrived in Valencia and checked into a nice resort hotel the team had reserved. We got two rooms, one for my mom and dad and sister and friends, and one for Nicole and me. Then I went to a luncheon, where I met with Luis Aparicio and Dave Concepcion. Luis was the honorary captain for our team, and Concepcion was serving in the same capacity for the bad guys.

Naturally, the talk turned to the long tradition of Venezuelan shortstops. They said they liked the way I play. That really meant something special coming from people like them. Concepcion said, "The only thing you need to be an Aparicio is No. 11 on your back."

Where I come from, that's the ultimate compliment.

When our team bus arrived at the ballpark, fans were standing 10 deep at the fence. All 18,000 tickets were sold out for both games, and scalpers were doing a brisk business.

It's almost impossible to sneak into major league games in America these days, but in Venezuela, the system for issuing credentials is not exactly watertight. In fact, when Nicole arrived at the gate, she was told that four other women had already shown up claiming to be my wife. My mom was with her, so the guards were really confused at that point. But they let them in.

The locker room had been completely refurbished for the major leaguers. That was nice, except for a sign that read: "Please do not drink or brush your teeth with this water." That bothered me. I had been drinking that water for all those years and never got sick once.

The scene must have looked bizarre to the American-born players. Police and military people were everywhere, walking around in bulletproof vests and riot gear. The players were taken everywhere they needed to go, and advised not to go anywhere by themselves. Fortunately, there were no incidents—other than owner Larry Dolan getting his pocket picked at one of the games. But that could happen anywhere.

What seemed to surprise the American players the most, though, was how well known they were. Venezuelans get regular broadcasts of major league games. They watch *SportsCenter* every night. So the fans know the American players at least as well as American fans do.

It wasn't just stars like Jim Thome who were recognized. Even our backup catcher, Eddie Taubensee, was asked for autographs by name, which floored him.

Most of the team couldn't believe that I was worried about the kind of reception I'd get. But they didn't realize the extent of the rivalry between my old team, Caracas Leones, and the Valencia team. To make matters worse, in my last season of winter ball, 1995, Caracas won the championship. So I honestly didn't know whether I would be cheered or booed.

But when they called my name that first night and I walked up the stairs of the dugout and trotted out to the foul line, the crowd went crazy. Our "captain," Aparicio, wearing glasses and a Chicago White Sox uniform with his No. 11 on the back, walked over and gave me a hug.

The fans embraced me, too, with a standing ovation that seemed to last forever. I literally got goose bumps. I showed the bumps to Kenny Lofton, who thought the whole scene was great. He told me to keep waving and tipping my hat. I did, but I couldn't wait until the next player was introduced so the attention would finally be off me.

Our radio play-by-play announcer, Tom Hamilton, said my appearance was like the return of a conquering hero. I don't know about that, but I was so happy with the ovation I got, and so caught up in the atmosphere, that when the Venezuelan national anthem began, I ran over to the singer, threw an arm around him and joined in.

Mind you, this wasn't just any singer. This was Ilan Chester, who is a hero in Venezuela. I have his CDs, as do millions of other fans. I surprised him, but he took it well.

The next day, Sunday, we were playing a day game, and I helped with the anthem again. This time, though, it had been planned in advance. After my impromptu performance, the officials asked me and Richard Hidalgo, a Venezuelan who plays for the Astros, to accompany another recording star, Mirla Castellano. We stood on either side of her as she belted out the song, watching our yellow, blue, and red flag wave above the field. Hidalgo and I were pretty far from the mike, so I'm not sure how much our voices could be heard. But it's the thought that counts.

Every pro baseball game in Venezuela is like a festival. You get flashing lights, wild music, dancing girls on the field . . . it's like a gigantic party. I love it.

I hadn't played in Venezuela for about six years, so I hadn't seen this stuff in a long time. It was exciting not only for the Latino players but for the Americans, too. Except for a few guys, like Lofton, who played winter ball there in 1991, the rest of the Indians had never experienced anything like this. Not even in Yankee Stadium.

But the level of pageantry at this event surprised me, too. It was like a World Series game—all the extracurricular activity was geared up a few notches. They had a DJ out past center field, and wild women dancing every song. Between innings, they had dancing all over the field, as well as men doing acrobatics.

In the middle of the second game, a woman wearing a white No. 13 Indians jersey ran onto the field to get my autograph. I signed quickly as a cop led her away. In the stands, there must have been 500 people wearing Omar Vizquel jerseys.

My dad was really getting into it. He had a couple of beers, and when the dancing girls started boogieing in the stands, he started dancing with them. My mom wasn't exactly thrilled with that scene. I think Dad heard about it later on. But he was just excited about the game. He hadn't seen me play in a while, and was as proud as he could be.

Every time I did anything, even fielding a routine grounder, the place went wild. Fortunately, I got a hit in both games. On both Saturday and Sunday, I went 1-for-4, with the hit coming in my first at-bat. After that first hit, the pressure was off.

I would have liked to have spent a lot more time visiting old friends, but we were on a tight schedule. Immediately after the second game, the team was on the plane for Florida. We arrived in Orlando a little before 9 P.M.

For some players, the weekend was essentially another episode in the middle of a long spring training season. But not for me. Having the chance to play in Venezuela as a major leaguer was one of the high points of my life.

It's a good thing I was wearing sunglasses when I said goodbye to my parents and climbed back on the bus. This time, I wasn't shedding tears of sadness about my homeland, but tears of joy.

I didn't want the visit to end.

CHAPTER 17

Life on the North Coast

HOME-FIELD ADVANTAGE can be overrated. During the 1994 game in which I made three errors, a guy sitting right behind Nicole yelled, "Omar, quit smoking crack!"

Having played in Venezuela, I'm used to all sorts of verbal abuse. But Nicole isn't. And sometimes she has a hard time sitting out there in the stands, listening to the criticism that inevitably breaks out when things aren't going well. It even hurts her when fans yell at the other players, because she has gotten to know many of them and their families.

Until the late '90s, Nicole went to every home game. But as I became increasingly well-known, more and more people recognized her, too. She is not a public person. She feels uncomfortable when people stare at her. Some of the fans figured out where the players' wives sit, and they come around during games just to gawk. She understands why people do it—they're just curious—and she doesn't hold it against them. But she's more at ease watching the games at home on TV.

Nico was a bit of a problem at games, too. Generally, games last three hours or more, and his attention span during the late '90s was about three minutes. Things changed by the middle of the 2001 season, when he had matured enough to start helping out occasionally as a batboy.

Fortunately, the fans don't heckle me very often. In fact, Nicole and I are constantly amazed at how the people of Northeast Ohio embraced me and so many other Indians over the years.

Far more typical is the reception we get during the Tribe Jam each summer at Nautica, the small outdoor concert stage on the west bank of the Flats.

For three years running, about half a dozen Indians have teamed up with local rock legend Michael Stanley to put on a benefit show. The money goes to Cleveland Indians Charities, which, since it was started in 1989, has donated nearly $3.5 million to area youth organizations.

The charity arm of the team also raises money from auctions of memorabilia, golf outings, tours of the stadium, and a party called Picnic in the Park with the Stars, which is thrown each summer right down on the diamond at Jacobs Field, where the fans can mingle with the team and get autographs. But one of the charity's biggest fundraising events, and the most enjoyable one for the players, is the Jam.

Here's a good example of the level of Indians fever that has existed since the opening of Jacobs Field. In July 2001, we were playing at Nautica in front of 4,000 people who had paid $20 per head, when the skies opened up near the end of the show. The performers on stage had a roof over them, but the crowd in the stands did not. And you know what? Not a single person left. They just kept bopping and clapping away, as if the rain were a normal part of the show.

Actually, nothing was normal about that show, or any of the others we've put on. I'm not sure why, but ballplayers always seem to think they are great singers and musicians and all they need is a chance. Actually, most of them sing and play about as well as Michael Stanley hits a 90 mile-per-hour slider.

Are you listening, Burba?

Dave Burba ambled onto the stage that year to sing *Sweet Emotion*, the funky Aerosmith tune. Let's say he could use a little more work on his timing. And his pitch. And remembering the lyrics. It wasn't pretty. Burbs didn't seem to be terribly aware of his musical shortcomings, though, and the crowd loved every moment of it.

At least Jim Thome knows his limitations. The electric guitar he strapped on wasn't actually plugged into anything. But Jimmy *looked* good. And when he sang the old Sonny and Cher duet *I Got You Babe*, most of the crowd was preoccupied with his singing partner, Jennifer Lee (who backs up Stanley regularly, has a marvelous voice, and wears black leather pants).

Like Thome, pitcher Bob Wickman got into the spirit visually, if not musically. When he spontaneously strapped on a guitar and duck-walked across the stage, the crowd went nuts.

Other guys were actually performing—or at least attempting to. Marty Cordova was halfway competent with an electric guitar, and Georgia native Russell Branyan took a pass at *Folsom Prison Blues*, the old Johnny Cash country classic.

I had a blast. In addition to playing drums on a bunch of songs alongside Stanley's drummer, Tommy Dobeck, I was the lead singer on *Crazy Train*, by rock psycho Ozzy Osbourne. Michael Stanley is not exactly a huge Ozzy fan. He said being on stage for an Osbourne song was the low point of his career. But what does Stanley know? Come on, man, this isn't a library. It's a rock show. So let's rock!

Near the end of the set, I was front and center for *American Woman*, a song that takes on some extra meaning when it's sung by a Venezuelan who married an American woman. I thought I pulled it off nicely. I sung it with passion and hit the notes. My concentration was good, and it needed to be: Thome and Jolbert Cabrera came out during the song and started bumping and grinding against me.

Then the rain started coming in sheets.

We all joined Stanley and his band for *My Town*, and returned with an encore of *Wild Thing*.

Considering the players got together for exactly one prac-tice—a 90-minute session at the Rock Hall the week before—things went about as well as could be expected.

The Tribe Jam helps a good cause and is a nice social event for the guys and their wives. And, having won that afternoon's game against St. Louis on a Thome homer in the bottom of the 10th, we were in a festive mood already.

However, I am still taking abuse for my choice of an on-stage outfit. I wore a pair of flaming red satin pants with fancy stitching on them. Don't spread it around, because I don't want to give anybody the wrong impression, but the pants were Nicole's. I can fit into all of her stuff, which really annoys her. And the red pants seemed perfect for a hard-drumming Ozzy Osborne clone.

GETTING ON STAGE in front of a crowd is totally different from playing baseball in front of a crowd. We've grown up playing ball and are not self-conscious one bit. But performing something other than baseball is an adventure. Because it's so different, it gives me a real surge of adrenaline.

I ventured into stand-up comedy a few times, too. During All-Star Week in 1997, when the game was played in Cleveland, I even did a routine at the Improv comedy club in the Flats. During the weeks leading up to the game, I'd think of something funny, jot down a note, and toss it in a folder. After a while I had about 20 minutes worth of material. I didn't try to memorize everything, but I didn't write it all out, either. I took about three pages of notes, put them on my stool, and only had to look down a few times.

The whole routine ended up on *Comedy Central.* And a couple of clips wound up on ESPN and Fox, including this joke:

"My wife asked me to take her to a place she'd never been before. So I grabbed her by the ear and took her to the kitchen."

Nicole didn't laugh nearly as much as the other people in the audience.

I also had fun with a series of TV commercials the Indians put together for the 1999 season. During spring training that year, various players were cast in clever, goofy skits that were turned into 15- and 30-second spots.

Stopper Mike Jackson was shown at a pottery wheel, carefully molding a lump of clay. "It's very relaxing," Jackson says. "I like the feel of it in my hands. But my favorite part," he says, standing up, yanking the wet clay off the wheel, "is throwing the pot." He heaves the dripping mass against the wall.

Jim Thome was shown going through his elaborate batting ritual. A fan interrupts, asking for the location of the nearest restroom. "Over there, ma'am," he responds, showing the way with his trademark pointing of the bat.

Robbie Alomar was in several spots, including two with his brother. In one of them, Sandy is wearing shades and a Hawaiian shirt while lounging in a chair at home plate. "When we were just kids, Robbie was cute," Sandy says. "He would always carry my glove and get me water." The camera pans over to Robbie, who is ironing out wrinkles in Sandy's jersey. "It's good to have him back."

In another spot, Sandy is shown in file footage hitting homers and throwing out runners. The voiceover says: "Watch Sandy protect the plate." Soon we see Sandy eating a plate of hot dogs as Robbie tries to edge his way in. "Get out of here," Sandy tells him. "Get your own plate!"

For one of the spots, Robbie teamed up with me. The writer was having fun with the concept that Robbie and I are so fluid on the field that people say we look like ballerinas. So we were shown, in uniform, prancing around second base, doing all these exaggerated ballet-type moves, flipping our gloves over our heads.

The producers actually brought in a ballet instructor to try to teach us some movements. She looked like she was about 15. I assume she knew her stuff, but what difference did that make? What were we going to learn about ballet in one morning? That was like grabbing a ballerina and trying to teach her how to field ground balls. It just wasn't going to work.

Besides, manager Mike Hargrove didn't want us to miss too much practice, and he set a one-hour deadline for shooting each commercial. So Robbie and I just kind of tiptoed around, doing these fake ballet moves and looking ridiculous. It was great fun.

Sometimes, though, promotions don't work out as well as you'd hoped.

During the 2001 season, the Indians jumped on the bobble-head doll bandwagon. Bobbleheads, the small figurines with oversized, bouncy heads that are a throwback to the 1960s, had been creating a frenzy at stadiums all over the country. During the 2000 season, when the Minnesota Twins offered Kirby Puckett dolls to the first 10,000 people in attendance, so many fans showed up early that people who lined up six hours early were shut out.

And when the Mariners offered an Ichiro Suzuki doll to the first 20,000 patrons of a game in July 2001, fans camped out all night at Safeco Field. The M's hired extra security officers and brought in portable toilets.

Not to be outdone, the Tribe ran seven bobblehead promotions during 2001, more than any other team.

The first two were previewed during the winter: a Thome and a Vizquel. At least they said it was Vizquel. I didn't think it looked like me at all. When they asked me what I thought, I told them. So they sent back the prototype and tried again. The second version looked even less like me. But at that point, I just shrugged and gave up.

To tell you the truth, I think my doll looks more like Dave Burba.

But fans seem to love the thing. A story about the bobblehead craze in the *St. Petersburg* (Florida) *Times* said that on one evening in June 2001, on the Web site eBay, a Jim Edmonds doll went for $34.50, a Frank Thomas for $43, and an Omar Vizquel for $131. I guess it's nice to lead the league in something besides fielding percentage.

Most of my promotional efforts have had a bit more substance. Before each Saturday home game, we do a television show called *Omar y Amigos* in the press interview room near the clubhouse. I am the host, and we stage a question-and-answer session with another teammate and a roomful of schoolkids. The show is taped and shown at Sunday's game on the Jumbotron and the TVs throughout Jacobs Field. It is also sometimes shown as part of the pregame show of Fox Sports Net.

We did *Omar y Amigos* 11 times during 2001. For the first show, in April, we offered a special invitation to 14 Mexican exchange students who were visiting the area for two weeks. We also invited their host families, from Shaker Heights High School, and a local Girl Scout troop and Cub Scout pack. Typically we will choose kids from groups like the Boys & Girls Clubs, Cleveland Recreation Centers, Cuyahoga Metropolitan Housing Authority, and the Center for Families and Children. I buy tickets for the kids so they can watch the game after our session.

The program was originally Kenny Lofton's and was known as *Kenny's Kids*. But when he was traded to Atlanta during the 1997 season, I inherited it. I'm glad I did, because I love being around kids. And when we do *Omar y Amigos*, they really seem to appreciate the fact that a big-league ballplayer is taking the time to talk with them.

I ENJOY MOST ENCOUNTERS with the public, but sometimes the recognition just overwhelms me.

People will come right up to me any time, any place, even when I'm out with my family. It's really uncomfortable for Nicole and Nico when somebody approaches and acts like my wife and kids are invisible. Some fans are absolutely fearless. You'll be in the middle of a meal or trying to have a good time with your wife and they'll zoom right in on you, as if they had known you for years. I'll be trying to relax in a movie theater and inevitably somebody will say, "Hey, Omar, what happened on that play in the game today?" Hey, I'm just trying to watch a movie!

I guess that's to be expected. When you are all over the TV and in the newspapers, people start to think of you as their pal, even if they've never even met you.

But sometimes I'm just not in the mood to talk. Fans seem to forget that just because I'm a baseball player, I'm not deliriously happy all the time. We have just as many problems as most fans do.

Disguises don't work very well. As soon as I open my mouth, a lot of people recognize my accent and figure it out.

The good side to this is that, ironically, multimillionaire players are far less likely to have to pay for things than normal folks. For some reason, fans insist on showering us with freebies. You get into movies for free. You play golf for free. You go bowling for free. People open their arms to you. Of course, the favors usually come with strings attached. They'll buy you an ice cream cone and then want you to sign 35 autographs and visit their son's first-grade class in Wayne County.

But I can't get too upset with any of this, because I know how it feels to be on the other side.

When I got a chance to meet Michael Jordan, I was absolutely thrilled. Kenny Lofton is a friend of his, and Kenny took me to the locker room one time when the Dream Team was playing. Michael walked right up and said, "Hey, Omar, how are you doing?" I thought to myself, "Wow! I can't believe Michael Jordan knows who we are!"

MJ is a huge baseball fan. He knows all the players and a lot of the stats. Later, I asked my agent to try to get me a Michael Jordan autographed jersey. He did, and it hangs on the wall in my Seattle house.

I also got to meet basketball stars Karl Malone and John Stockton. I've admired both of those guys for years.

The Dream Teamers were great to me. But that hasn't always been my experience with superstars.

In Venezuela, when I was younger, I met some ballplayers and musicians who either said weird things or just acted cold, like I was beneath them. It ruined my image of them. One brief encounter becomes your overriding memory, and you lose a hero. That's why I don't go out of my way to meet celebrities today; I'm afraid I'll be disappointed.

That's also why I try so hard to be accommodating to the fans.

I don't want someone to think Omar is a bum just because I'm having a bad day the one time he or she encounters me.

Sometimes I'll find myself in a setting with nationally known celebrities. When I do, I'll usually just hang back. If someone introduces us, fine. If not, that's fine, too. Part of that is my fear of disappointment. Part of it is a fear that we'll have nothing to talk about. But I think a lot of that is an attitude passed down from my dad.

In Venezuela, I would give him special passes so he could sit right behind home plate or sit in the dugout, but he would never take advantage of them. He didn't want to look like a big shot. He would always sit back from the third-base line, way up where he could watch every move the shortstops made. That's the same place we'd sit when I was a kid.

On the other hand, I don't think I'll be able to hang back if I ever get anywhere near Muhammad Ali. He's one of my biggest idols. I always thought Ali saw life in a different way than most of us. Through all his pain and all his problems and all his fame, he kept himself low to the ground. He seems like a guy who has fun wherever he goes. I think he'd even be fun at a funeral.

ANOTHER PROBLEM WITH FAME, even regional fame, is that you start to think you're a god because of the way people treat you. I know players who sincerely believe they walk on water. I can understand how that happens. Everywhere you go, people tell you how wonderful you are. You have to work at keeping your feet on the ground. I constantly remind myself that I'm not really who the public thinks I am. I'm just another guy wandering around in the world for a little while. I sin as much as anybody else. I make as many mistakes as anybody else. Just because I'm in the public eye doesn't mean I'm a marvelous human being.

Even though I grew up in a very different culture, Cleveland has been a good fit for me, and I feel I have lived there long enough to know what makes the city tick. I've had experiences in Cleveland that simply would not have happened anywhere else.

But that doesn't necessarily mean I play better baseball at home. Unlike football and basketball, the home field advantage in baseball is relatively small. Actually, I often feel better playing on the road.

When you're in another city, you don't have to worry about anything but playing the game. You don't know anybody in town, so you don't have nearly as many distractions. I think a lot of the players feel the same way.

And, unless you're somebody like Alex Rodriguez, you can walk around most American cities without being recognized everywhere you go.

Not that we don't encounter hassles on the road. Most of the guys on the team use fake names to register at the team hotels. Otherwise, we'd spend all of our free time fielding phone calls from people who claim they're somebody's cousin and they were just wondering whether we can give them free tickets to tonight's game. Or we'd be fending off calls from morning radio DJs who would wake us up and harass us for the amusement of their local listeners.

Most of the Indians began using aliases in 1995, when we first became a baseball power. Albert Belle was "B. Euclid" for a while before turning into "B. Creek." Carlos Baerga, clotheshorse that he was, went by "C. Klein." Kenny Lofton was "P. Whitaker." My pal Alvaro Espinoza was "James Bond." Cynics said that was because his batting average was about .007.

I change my alias every two or three months, because word gets around so quickly. I have been Tony Banderas, Jean-Claude von Damme, Nicholas Cage, and O. Zorro.

Having traveled all over the country, I have a pretty good picture of where Cleveland stacks up. Sometimes, that can make me a little more jaded than I should be. For instance, I really liked Cleveland's Great Lakes Science Center—until I visited the science center in Pittsburgh.

During our road trip to Pittsburgh in 2001, I went to the Carnegie Science Center, right on the Ohio River near the ballpark. I took Nico, who was only 5 at the time. We were there for four hours, and even then he didn't want to leave. Remember, this is a kid who doesn't have the longest attention span in the world. But he loved the place. They have all kinds of mazes, movies, water games, sound games . . . all kinds of interactive stuff. It's the best science center I've ever seen.

Cleveland's Rock and Roll Hall of Fame and Museum is impressive. I love the architecture, the design by I.M. Pei. But the exhibits seem kind of weak. If you have a place like that, you should have a lot more exciting exhibits. Heck, the Hard Rock Café has almost as much memorabilia as the Rock Hall. If I were running the place, I'd spend more money to get more guitars and stuff.

THE REGULAR SEASON can be a long haul, especially if your team is struggling. During the playoffs, though, every little movement is so important, and you're concentrating so hard, that sometimes you totally forget the fans are there. You don't see them, you don't hear them, you don't worry about them. But during the regular season, that's a different matter. We play 162 regular season games, and some of them are a snore. Sometimes the pitchers are throwing a lot of balls and taking a lot of time, and batters are stepping in and out of the batters box, and you just want to grab people and shake them to get going. On the other hand, slow games give you an opportunity to check out the people in the stands.

Any player who says he never notices the people in the stands is fibbing. You can't help but notice. Fortunately, as a veteran player who has made countless trips to all the American League cities, I believe I'm qualified to issue some judgments about what I see.

The best-looking women—inside the ballpark—are in Texas. If we're voting on the hottest women citywide, I'd probably go with Toronto. In Toronto, you see a real mix of nationalities. Sometimes you find a blonde girl with blue eyes, and you expect her to be from Canada, and she'll say, "No, I'm from Africa."

Toronto may be the only place in the world where you'll find a Japanese girl with an Afro.

There's nothing wrong with looking, is there?

I've never had any big fantasies about movie stars, but I generally like larger women, like Anna Nicole Smith. I also like Charlize Theron. She's my type, too.

But this is all just theoretical, and I'm beginning to digress.

Sometimes, the between-innings entertainment is right on the field. One year we were playing the Royals in Kansas City. During the seventh-inning stretch, they would play a limbo game on the scoreboard. First, they'd pan the crowd with the camera and zoom in on a spectator. Then they'd superimpose an electronic bar on the picture, and the fan was supposed to do the limbo under the line.

Well, one day we were way ahead of the Royals, and Alvaro Espinoza told the cameraman to aim the camera on me out at shortstop. I looked up on the scoreboard and there I am on camera. The fans are screaming and cheering. So I start doing the limbo. The place goes nuts.

Same thing happened the second day of the series. We were winning, so I did another limbo dance. The place went nuts again.

Then, in the third game of the series, we were losing 5-1. The cameraman came after me again, but I wagged my finger in a "no way" sign.

When I came into the dugout after that inning, Mike Hargrove told me, "I knew you were a smart man. You weren't going to dance on a losing score. It would have cost you some money."

I love playing in Boston. It's a challenge. The people really get on you there. Some of them can be pretty creative. I enjoy that kind of atmosphere. That's why I love Yankee Stadium, too. Yankee fans are great at screaming nasty stuff at you. Ballparks like that remind me of my hometown.

The public address announcer in New York is a bummer, though. He makes me sad. Same with the one in Boston. He looks like he's 140 years old. And they play that horrible organ music. I can't stand that stupid organ!

My favorite announcer is the one in Oakland. He's got a really big voice. "NOW BATTING … OOOOOMMMAAAAAARRRR." The guy, Roy Steele, looks like he has a potato in his throat. But what a voice.

They play great music in Oakland, too. That franchise does a marvelous job with its music and between-innings contests. It really tries to get the fans involved. Too bad people just don't turn out for the games. During a big series there in late August of 2001, when we were in first place and the A's were streaking toward a wild-card berth, having won 16 of their last 18 games, only 18,133 people turned out for the first game of our series. The second night, only 19,434 showed up. On the third night, tickets were sold for $1 apiece—and they still drew only 40,992, less than our nightly average at Jacobs Field.

Of course, Oakland isn't the greatest city in the world. When we play the A's, we actually stay across the bay, in San Francisco. If I lived in Oakland, maybe I wouldn't want to venture out, either.

The Kingdome held so many great memories for me that I was sad when it was blown up in March 2000. By then I was starting my seventh season with the Indians. We were at spring training in Winter Haven, and I was in the clubhouse, watching the implosion live, at about 7:30 A.M. The wrecking company used 22 miles of detonation cord and 5,800 charges of dynamite to bring down the big toadstool. The whole thing took about 20 seconds.

Obviously, playing in Seattle is fun for me. Seattle's new park, Safeco Field, which opened a few hundred feet to the west in the middle of the 1999 season, is a nice structure. For $517 million, it ought to be. It has a retractable roof that can be opened or closed in 10 to 20 minutes, depending on the winds. But I like Jacobs Field much better. Although Safeco only seats about 3,000 more fans than Jacobs Field, the fans kind of get lost. Maybe the stadium is too spread out. I can't really pinpoint it. All I know is that, at Jacobs Field, the people are right on top of you and it feels much more intimate. I don't feel quite right at Safeco. Of course, I only play there a few games per year.

NO MATTER WHAT KIND OF ADVENTURES we have on the road, the best vibes are at Jacobs Field.

In Cleveland, the batters get to choose the song that is played as they walk to the batter's box. I change my selection fairly often. Sometimes I go with hard rock, sometimes salsa, whatever strikes my fancy at the time. You can even change your tune in the middle of a game by calling the music guy from a telephone in the clubhouse.

Cleveland has one "musical" tradition that I have begun to find annoying, though. The guy out in the bleachers, John Adams, has been pounding that drum for 20 years, at both the old park and the new one. At first I thought it was kind of cool. But he plays so much now that it's starting to get on my nerves. I wish he'd pick his spots.

And, although that *Cleveland Rocks* song by Ian Hunter always seems to get the crowd going, it's just another song for me. Mind you, I understand why it's so popular. It was written back in the days when Cleveland—both the city and the team—was down and out. And after the tune became the theme for the *Drew Carey Show* on TV, and the Tribe was in contention every year, and the city was finally getting a better reputation, longtime Clevelanders felt vindicated. The song reminds them how far they've come. But, musically speaking, it's just not a great song.

The tune that does fire me up is *What a Wonderful World,* by David Lee Roth. It's a slow, emotional number, and at Jacobs Field it is accompanied by slow-motion close-ups of the players on the big screen. That song makes me think about where I am and what I have and how much I love the game of baseball.

The best sound, of course, is the roar of the crowd when we do something right in a big game. I will never forget the volume level at some of those playoff and World Series games. Cleveland's fans are the best. All you have to do is look at their major league record for consecutive sellouts.

I was a bit surprised when we didn't sell out the 2001 season, too. I guess that had to do with the departure of Manny Ramirez and Sandy Alomar, who were both really popular with the fans, and the fact that we didn't make the playoffs in 2000. But as soon as we showed we were in the hunt for the 2001 division title, the place started selling out again. It's so much more fun to play in a packed stadium than a place that's half full.

What gives me the most pride about living and working in Northeast Ohio is the way we have been able to change the image of the baseball team. When I arrived, the Indians were best known nationally as the inspiration for the movie *Major League*, a fictional tale about a horrible baseball team making an improbable run at the pennant.

When I first headed to Cleveland, the movie didn't seem all that fictional. Now we can look at it and laugh.

CHAPTER 18

Instant Classic

SEA: 048 020 000 00—14 17 0
CLE: 000 200 345 01—15 23 1

WHEN YOU PLAY 162 regular season games a year, they all start to blend together into one big, unidentifiable blob of baseball. It gets to the point where, when you wake up in the morning, sometimes you need a minute to figure out what city you're in. Half of the time you don't even know what day it is. Every day looks the same. Every day is Monday, because you always have a whole workweek ahead of you.

But every once in a while you play in a game so incredible that you know you're going to remember it until your dying breath.

August 5, 2001, was one of those games.

It was a sunny summer Sunday. And for me it was noteworthy from the very beginning, because for the first time in his life my son was going to join me down on the field during a big-league game.

Now, I don't think they keep records on such things, even though they seem to keep records on just about everything else in baseball, but I have a feeling Nico was the youngest batboy in the history of the Cleveland Indians.

Compared to Nico—who was making his debut at 5 years, 10 months, and 24 days—Ellis Burks's son, Christopher, was a wily veteran. Christopher Ellis Burks was nearly seven when his dad first arranged to suit him up in an Indians uniform and have him pick up bats for the home team. Little Ellis made his debut early in 2001.

Nico got the job almost by accident. His mom was planning to go to a concert at Gund Arena with my sister and some neighbors. But we couldn't find a babysitter. So I offered to take Nico to the ballpark and let him run around in the clubhouse, maybe even put him in a little uniform and let him sit in the dugout during the game.

When we got to the park, we found out the concert had been postponed; Nicole would be able to watch Nico after all. But at that point, Nico was excited about being at the game and I didn't have the heart to change the plan.

I hooked Nico up with Brian Romanini, a longtime batboy who has become a friend of mine. I asked Brian to keep an eye on Nico and maybe let him fetch a bat once in a while. Next thing you know, the game is under way and little Nico has essentially become the home team's batboy.

When Brian gave him the green light, Nico would zoom out to home plate and gather up the used lumber. He looked a bit over-matched; instead of picking up a bat, he just dragged it along be-hind him, like a big person dragging a telephone pole.

I wasn't worried about his safety, because not many foul balls end up where he was sitting—on the home-plate side of the dugout—and because Brian was right there, watching him like a hawk.

I don't think Nico understood much of what he was seeing, be-cause every time the fans started cheering, he'd ask me, "Daddy, what happened? Daddy, what's going on?"

I knew that regardless of what took place between the lines, this was going to be a memorable night. But then the action on the field made it absolutely unforgettable.

First of all, playing against Seattle is always special, for reasons that should be obvious if you've read this far. And, this game was on national TV, which always adds a little juice to a contest. ESPN was on hand for *Sunday Night Baseball,* hosted by Jon Miller and Rick Sutcliffe.

It was our second time on national TV in as many days. Television follows what's hot, and Seattle was the hottest team in baseball—by a mile. The Mariners were playing incredibly well, winning 73 percent of their games. They were an amazing 50 games over .500 with two full months left in the season. Not even our 1995 team set that kind of pace. The M's were dominating on both offense and defense, leading the league in runs scored and earned-run average. Their bullpen was considered the best in baseball.

Because the TV networks can dictate almost everything, the starting times for both weekend games had been changed. Originally, we were playing Saturday night and Sunday afternoon. But because Fox scheduled Saturday afternoon games and ESPN aired Sunday evening games, that's when the fans were told to show up.

I was looking forward to the game, because I was tired of losing. Seattle had beaten us Friday in a 2-1 heartbreaker, then spanked us Saturday, 8-5. We were playing horrendous baseball, losing six of our last seven, and many of those weren't even close. The previous week, we had gotten blown out twice by Oakland, 17-4 one night and 11-2 another.

Dave Burba was on the mound for us, and he had been struggling for weeks. All of a sudden he had gone from a pitcher who was worth an automatic 15 victories to a guy who had a hard time getting through the fourth inning. When he started getting shelled early, I said to myself, "Here we go again."

We were down four-zip after only two innings. At the beginning of the third, Burba was ripped for three straight singles. Manager Charlie Manuel yanked him out and, probably figuring he had nothing to lose, inserted a raw rookie, Mike Bacsik. The poor guy wasn't just a first-year player; he was a first-*game* player. Bacsik had just been called up from Triple-A Buffalo, and here he was making his major league debut with the bases loaded and nobody out against the hottest team in baseball.

First batter: double. Second batter: single. Third batter: hit by pitch. Fourth batter: sacrifice fly. Fifth batter: Vizquel boots a grounder (only my fifth error of the year). Sixth batter: single. Welcome to the big leagues, Mike.

Eventually he retired the side. But we went to bat in the third trailing 12-0.

Things didn't get a whole lot better. We were still down 12-2 after four, and Charlie yanked out starter Ellis Burks. After five, we had regressed to 14-2, and Charlie threw in the towel. Out came three more starters, all of whom were nursing minor injuries. Our two best hitters, Robbie Alomar and Juan Gonzalez, were now gone, along with Travis Fryman.

In the other dugout, the M's manager, Lou Pinella, was thinking along the same lines. Out came Ichiro Suzuki, the rookie sensation from Japan, who was batting .322 and terrorizing teams on the bases. Edgar Martinez and John Olerud were given the remainder of the night off, too.

The fans began to leave in droves. The producers at ESPN were no doubt cursing their luck, realizing that most of the viewers who tuned in would take one look at the score and start channel-hopping.

Either the Seattle batters were totally exhausted or our rookie pitcher really settled down, because the M's offense suddenly got quiet. The score remained stuck at 14-2 until the bottom of the seventh inning. And then, ever so slowly, things began to get more interesting.

Russell Branyan led off with a homer. After two outs, we loaded the bases and Jolbert Cabrera singled home two runs. Now it was 14-5.

In the eighth, Jim Thome led off with a homer. With Branyan on first after being hit by a pitch, Marty Cordova homered. Score: 14-8. Two more runners reached, and the M's brought in lefty Norm Charlton to face me. He threw a fastball on the outside corner, and I went the other way with it, doubling down the right-field line. The score was 14-9.

This was the first time I truly thought we might have a chance. When I looked at the scoreboard, I realized a grand slam would bring us within one. What are the odds of a grand slam? Tiny. But you have to stay positive.

Our manager was certainly positive. In the eighth inning, Charlie told me that in my next at-bat I would get a triple into the right-field corner. He was sure of it. I just rolled my eyes.

Apparently, the M's manager was feeling positive, too, because Lou Pinella kept Charlton in the game rather than burn another one of his relievers.

The stage was set for the most amazing inning I have ever seen.

The first batter, Eddie Taubensee singles up the middle. But Charlton gets the next two guys, Thome and Branyan, and we're still behind *five runs* with *two outs* in the bottom of the ninth.

Cordova doubles.

Pinella gets serious, bringing in Jeff Nelson.

Wil Cordero walks. Diaz singles.

Pinella gets *really* serious, bringing in Japanese hotshot Kazuhiro Sasaki.

Lofton singles. The bases are loaded, and the tying run comes to the plate.

That would be me.

Imagine the drama. Imagine the tension. Imagine Nico walking up to me as I'm digging into the batter's box to slap me five. He does exactly that, oblivious to the situation.

I am facing one of the most dominant pitchers in the game. Sasaki has a brutal split-fingered fastball that starts about waist high then plunges toward the dirt. If you're not patient, he'll eat you alive.

I'm not having my best season at the plate. Early in the year, I stunk. I'm surprised Charlie kept hitting me in the second spot, because for the first few months of the season my batting average was slumming around in the .240 range. But I kept practicing and practicing, and eventually my bat came around.

As I dig into the left-hand batter's box to face Sasaki, it is nearing midnight and the crowd of 42,494 has dwindled to about 20,000. But they sound like 60,000. They seem to sense that they're witnessing something special.

Sasaki is throwing me nasty stuff, and I fall behind in the count. But I'm patient, taking some close pitches for balls, and I work the count to 3-and-2. He heaves another of those nasty splitters, and I foul it off. Finally he winds and throws a fastball.

It's a good pitch, on the inside corner at the knees. But I turn and rip it down the first base line, just past Ed Sprague, who dives but can't touch it. It rolls all the way into the corner as right fielder Charles Gipson races over. Cordero scores. Diaz scores. Lofton scores. I beat the throw to third, and Jacobs Field goes absolutely wild. The fans are roaring, and the guys in our dugout are jumping all over the place. I slap hands with third base coach Joel Skinner, unable to keep a big grin off my face.

Tie game.

In the Indians' radio booth, announcer Tom Hamilton is going wild. "Unbelievable!" he exclaims. "Unbelievable!"

Think of the odds: ninth inning, down five, two outs. I was the third batter that inning to have two strikes with two outs. If you made a movie like that, they'd laugh you out of the theater.

Most amazing of all: Charlie Manuel called the shot.

We had been down 12 runs. We were facing a bullpen that had given up only three runs in the previous two weeks. Half of our fans had gone. But we kept fighting back and fighting back, the drama kept building and building . . . and at just the right moment, I was able to come through.

Given the circumstances—a tough pennant race, the game on national TV, Seattle on a killer winning streak while we were on a big losing streak—that was the biggest hit I've ever had.

When I watched that hit later on video, I realized that the first baseman was out of position. In that situation, he should have been guarding the line against an extra-base hit. And the right fielder was playing too shallow. What's more, I was lucky the ball just missed the wall that juts out in foul territory about midway out to right field. Had it hit the wall and bounced back onto the field, rather than rolling all the way to the corner, the result could have been much different.

It was an amazing at-bat for me, and it actually changed the tone of my season. I had been losing confidence at the plate. That one at-bat reminded me of the value of being patient and really trying to see the ball.

After all that excitement, though, we still hadn't won the game.

With me standing just 90 feet from a victory, my pal Jolbert Cabrera comes up and grounds out to third.

Extra innings.

In the tenth, Bob Wickman comes on and holds the Mariners. In the 11th, John Rocker does the same thing.

We enter the bottom of the 11th. Jose Paniagua comes to the mound and gets Diaz to pop out. Then Lofton rips a shot up the middle. My turn. Paniagua throws me a fastball and I drill it to right field, moving Kenny into scoring position.

Cabrera digs in with his second chance to win the game. This time he comes through, hitting a broken-bat line drive to left field. Lofton sprints home, dives into the plate, and Jacobs Field rocks to the rafters.

Taubensee, who would have been the next hitter, reaches down, picks up Kenny and throws him onto his shoulder in delight. Players swarmed onto the field, pounding on Lofton and each other. Poor Nico almost gets crushed.

The fans just don't want to leave. It feels like a World Series victory. They keep standing and cheering as the P.A. system blares Kiss's *Rock and Roll All Night* and *Cleveland Rocks.* Horns honk throughout the downtown.

We are the first team to come back from a 12-run deficit in 76 years. It ties the biggest comeback in major league history. In 1911, the Chicago White Sox did it. In 1925, the Philadelphia Athletics scored 13 runs in the eighth to win a game 17-15. The Philly comeback took place against—you guessed it—the Cleveland Indians. So I'd say our win over the M's was poetic justice.

After the game, I was interviewed on ESPN. I was so excited that I was jabbering away like crazy. It wasn't the first time I had been interviewed live on national TV, but I couldn't have been happier.

Nico loved it, too. Right after the game he told me he wanted to be a batboy every night. So the next night I brought him back and let him alternate with Christopher Burks. One inning Christopher was the batboy, the next inning it was Nico.

That next night, I went 3-for-4, putting my average with Nico in uniform at exactly .700.

Unfortunately, the next day we left on a road trip.

The honchos at ESPN were so impressed by our comeback that two weeks later they rebroadcast the game over ESPN Classic as an "Instant Classic." We were playing in Oakland that night and couldn't watch the replay. But I don't really need to see the tape. I've got every minute of that game socked away in my memory banks.

ONLY A FEW DAYS LATER, we played a series in Seattle. And just when you thought things couldn't get any wackier between the Indians and the M's, they did.

During the second game of the series, I was at the plate when Mariners reliever Arthur Rhodes came into the game. He would be ejected before throwing a single pitch.

I had faced Rhodes maybe 10 times before. I knew about his pitching. In fact, I knew him well enough to say hi when our paths crossed.

I also knew he wore earrings, even when he was pitching. I had seen them before. But those were little ones. The earrings he was wearing now were huge—maybe 2.5 karats. Obviously, he was having a good year.

It was late in the afternoon and the sun was hitting those big diamonds and turning them into light bulbs. I told home-plate umpire Tim McClelland that the earrings were distracting. He immediately told Rhodes to take them off.

Rhodes went crazy. He started ranting at me and making threats. He kept pointing at my head, saying he was going to bean me. You'd have thought I slapped his wife or something. His reaction was totally uncalled for, and it made me mad. I figured I'd head out and pay him a visit.

We never had a chance to discuss things. The benches emptied and people got between us. Coaches Dick Pole and Grady Little and some other guys grabbed me. Rhodes just kept barking away and was soon ejected by McClelland.

I guess Rhodes considered the earrings to be his lucky charms. But he didn't have a right to react the way he did. This is a baseball game, not a fashion show. You can wear whatever you want away from the field, but Major League Baseball has a rule that says you can't wear jewelry or silver or any other shiny stuff on the mound. I had every right to complain. And the umpire immediately agreed with me.

I wasn't thrown out. I hadn't done anything wrong. Of course, if I had made it to the mound, I probably would have been ejected and later suspended, because I was really fired up.

When you're in the middle of something like that, the prospect of a suspension is no deterrent, because you don't even think about it. What did flash through my mind was that we didn't have many guys left on the bench. The only position player available that late in the game was Russell Branyan. And that's probably why I finally let things pass.

I didn't care that Rhodes is 6-foot-2 and 205 pounds. If you're in a street fight, you don't even notice how big a guy is. If you know you're right, like I did, and you're going to be a man, you're going to defend whatever is yours. He should have just taken off his earrings and then hit me with the ball or whatever he had to do. But he acted like a fool standing there yelling stuff.

Rhodes didn't learn anything from the incident. The very next day, he came in from the bullpen wearing the same big earrings, with the same umpiring crew. Did he think nobody would notice? He didn't even get to the infield before the crew chief stopped him and made him take off the diamonds.

He didn't throw at me, but he struck me out. My teammates told me he said something after the strikeout, but I didn't hear anything, because I was the third out of the inning and was in the middle of dropping my bat and helmet. I stood there for a second to see whether he would say anything as he walked to the dugout, but he didn't.

The only other time I got anywhere near that mad was in September of 1998, when we were playing the White Sox at home.

In the first inning, Chicago's Ray Durham hit a homer off Jaret Wright. When Durham came up in the third, Wright hit him. In the bottom of the third, Chicago's pitcher, Jim Parque, threw a ball four feet over my head. It was obvious what he had in mind, and it wasn't throwing a strike. The pitch landed on the track on a fly and bounced in front of the dugout suites.

Umpire Larry Young knew exactly what was going on, too. He started toward the mound, apparently to warn Parque or throw him out. Parque started strutting toward the plate, acting like a tough guy. So I started following the umpire. When Parque kept coming, glaring at me, I started to run at him. I was tackled by their catcher, Robert Machado, and both benches cleared.

Kenny Lofton was wolfing at Parque. Sandy Alomar was yelling at James Baldwin. Nobody landed any real blows.

I was thrown out for "charging the mound." Except I wasn't anywhere near the mound. Parque should have been thrown out for charging the plate. He was the one who initiated everything. That's what manager Mike Hargrove was arguing when he got thrown out, too.

I don't like it when a baseball game deteriorates like that. But I'm not going to back down when I'm right.

As for the earring trend, I guess I still haven't quite figured it all out. Right after the Arthur Rhodes affair, we returned home to play Boston and my old friend Manny Ramirez. Manny likes to wear earrings, too; unfortunately for him, the Red Sox have a rule against wearing them on the field. But instead of taking them out for the game, Manny takes a piece of tape and wraps it over his earlobes so the earrings don't show. How stupid is that?

I guess that's part of what makes baseball such a great game. You never know what you're going to see next.

CHAPTER 19

Instant Horror

On the morning of September 11, 2001, I was in a deep sleep in my room at the Fairmount, the team's hotel in Kansas City. We had flown in late the previous night after playing the White Sox at home, and I was taking full advantage of my cushy bed.

At about 8:30 A.M. central time, Einar Diaz woke me with a phone call.

He said, "Hey, they're bombing the United States!"

I thought he was kidding. I said, "What the hell are you talking about, man?"

"They just bombed New York!"

"You're crazy. Go back to sleep."

"Turn on CNN."

I did. And I couldn't believe my eyes.

Both of the twin towers of the World Trade Center were on fire. Soon, the Pentagon was on fire. I thought I was watching a movie.

Only four months earlier, my wife had visited both places. She went on a sightseeing trip with friends to New York and Washington and checked out the twin towers, the Empire State Building, the White House, and the Pentagon.

Now, right before my eyes, the twin towers were dropping. And an entire side of the Pentagon was crushed.

Slowly, the magnitude of the attack began to sink it. I knew life in the United States would never again be the same.

Nothing could have dragged me away from that television set.

I must have watched CNN for six hours straight. I ate all my meals in my room and sat there trying to get a grip on what was happening.

For the next week or so, baseball seemed much less important. I was thinking the same things everybody else was thinking: What's the future of the United States? What's the future of the world? Are we going to have a war? What's going to happen? The Russians and other countries have been selling weapons all over the world; do the terrorists have nuclear capability? Are they crazy enough to use it? Will this be the end of the world?

I thought it was critical for the United States to gain the support of the other Middle East countries and make sure they attacked the right people. If they just stormed in there and started dropping bombs and killing innocent civilians, the terrorists would come back even stronger.

Nobody I knew was hurt in the attacks. But one of our team psychologists, Ray Negron, had a sister working a block from the World Trade Center. He was really worried because she was gone that day and nobody knew where she was. Late in the evening, he found out she was okay.

But it could have been any of us in those buildings, or any of our families. The attack really shook us up.

All baseball games were called off that night, and the night after. We didn't know when the airports would reopen. So our traveling secretary, Mike Seghi, chartered three buses and we took off Wednesday evening after working out at Kauffman Stadium.

The clubhouse guys packed sandwiches for us, and we rented a bunch of movies to watch during the long ride. Seghi hired two drivers for each bus, so we were able to make pretty good time.

Bob Wickman was in my bus, which explains why we took a bit of a detour. It's hard not to like Wickman. He's really funny. He's always saying nice things to people, especially kids. And he acts like he's 12 years old.

Anyway, about four hours into the trip, we ran out of food, and Wick—who does enjoy his food—pleaded for us to stop at a Jack in the Box. For those of you who haven't had the pleasure, a Jack in the Box is a regional fast food joint, much like any other. You give Jack your order, drive up to the window, and collect your grub.

Well, the buses were too big to fit under the drive-up window's canopy. And because it was really late, the inside seating area was closed. So a bunch of us got out of the bus, walked up to the window, and ordered 25 hamburgers.

Kenny Lofton was with me, along with Ellis Burks and Jim Thome—maybe 10 guys in all. At first, the employees wouldn't serve us. They said they weren't allowed to serve people on foot. Finally somebody yelled at Thome to tell the guy at the window who he was.

Jimmy says, "We're a baseball team going to Cleveland on a bus." The guy says, "No way." Finally, Jimmy pulls out his driver's license.

The guy's eyes popped out. He not only took our order, but told his coworkers to unlock the doors so we could wait inside.

Even after we got their attention, though, they just weren't geared up to produce 25 hamburgers right away. After a long wait, Charlie Manuel ordered us to get back on the bus. At that point, we had collected maybe five burgers, which we ended up sharing among 15 guys.

The ride to Cleveland took about 14 hours. It gave me a flashback to the 1980s, when I was riding minor league buses all over the country. But I certainly wasn't complaining. Nobody else was, either. We knew what thousands of people were going through in New York and Washington, and we felt lucky just to be safe.

We talked a lot about what had happened, and what might still happen. We discussed the possibility of chemical and biological weapons being used by terrorists—a horrifying possibility.

THE BASEBALL HIATUS caused by the terrible events of September 11 produced one small benefit: after eight days off, my body felt completely rejuvenated.

Granted, baseball doesn't inflict the physical beating that football does. But instead of playing once a week, you play close to seven days a week. And after seven months of that, your body just starts to wear down, even if you reported to training camp in great condition. By September 2001, I was to the point where I desperately needed a day off.

Since 1994, I have averaged 151 games per season. Every manager wants to give his regulars periodic breaks, but some managers worry about it more than others. Sometimes you get the feeling the manager just forgets that you haven't had a rest for a month and keeps penciling your name in the lineup, day after day after day.

With Charlie, there's a lot more give and take than with most managers. Occasionally I'll show up at the park and be surprised to find I'm not in the lineup. But sometimes I'll swing by his office and say, "Man, I could really use a day off." He says he wants his players to communicate with him, because otherwise he won't know about nagging injuries or deep fatigue.

The unexpected break resulting from the terrorist attacks also enabled me to spend time with my family, which is rare during the season. I took Nico to school in the morning and went to one of his soccer games.

Not that I sat on my butt all week. After returning to Cleveland, we played intrasquad games to try to stay sharp. Although it felt a little like we had regressed to spring training, I took the games seriously. You can lose your edge quickly if you go a week without playing at full speed.

When we finally restarted the season September 18, at home against the Royals, nobody knew quite what to expect. Some people weren't sure we should even be playing that soon. After all, thousands of people were still missing in New York, and rescue crews were still working around the clock.

But I thought it was time. The terrorists had accomplished their goal—getting the attention of the whole world. Even though we knew there were more terrorists out there, we knew their job would be a lot harder with all the security in place. Besides, people needed something to distract them after a week of gloom. I knew the mood at the ballpark wouldn't be the same, on or off the field, but we needed to push forward.

THE FIRST GAME BACK was emotional—and strange.

Tighter security was obvious not only to the fans, whose belongings were searched on the way into the park, but to the players. A new sign was posted on the door of our locker room: "Players only. No family, friends, agents, or business associates."

Inside the park, it looked like the Fourth of July. Fans waved cardboard American flags that were given out at the gates. They wore red, white, and blue bandannas, sweatshirts, T-shirts, and jackets.

The players lined up on the baselines, something normally reserved for Opening Day and postseason games, and the crowd sang the *Star Spangled Banner,* accompanied by an awesome brass quintet from the Cleveland Orchestra. During the seventh-inning stretch, *Take Me Out to the Ballgame* was replaced by *God Bless America.* From time to time, the fans broke into chants of "USA . . . USA . . ."

Leadoff hitter Kenny Lofton got us off on the right foot with a homer in his first at-bat. He drilled another one his second time up. Travis Fryman hit a grand slam, and we cruised to an 11-2 win.

With all those homers, a lot of fireworks were shot off behind the scoreboard. And I'm sure I'm not the only one whose mind flashed to New York as the smoke wafted over the field.

The next night, we won again, 11-3.

Minnesota, which had been so hot early in the season, was continuing to struggle, and after the first two games we were on top of the division by seven with only 16 left to play.

We cruised home with the Central Division title, our sixth in seven years. When we clinched on September 30, at home, the postgame ceremony showed what kind of class our team has:

Kenny Lofton, Travis Fryman, and others insisted that Charles Nagy run the pennant up the flagpole in center field.

Charlie at first resisted, saying he hadn't contributed enough. But the veterans insisted, because they wanted to honor Charlie for being so selfless during the final month of the season.

With his pitching elbow in tatters, Charlie had told the front office in August that he had nothing left to contribute and was heading home for the rest of the season. A week later, though, he returned—and started throwing batting practice. Many people with Charlie's credentials would be too proud to throw BP. But Charlie is such a team player that he wanted to do anything he could to help.

HEADING INTO THE POSTSEASON I was excited, because I really thought we had a chance to make some noise. And I was determined to be ready.

Having hit only .255 during the regular season, I knew I needed to contribute more at the plate if we were going to go all the way. So I watched tons and tons of videotape and took hours and hours of batting practice. My work paid off. I hit .409 during the five games against Seattle, tops among the starters—and second only to Vic Wertz in Indians playoff history.

In Game Three of the series, our first game at home, in front of 45,069 screaming fans basking in unseasonably warm weather, I uncorked the biggest offensive game of my life. I singled, tripled, singled, and doubled, driving in six runs.

That was the most RBIs of any Cleveland Indian in playoff history. The previous record of five was set by a guy named Elmer Smith in 1920. No, I had never heard of Elmer Smith. I hope that 80 years from now people don't say the same thing about Omar Vizquel.

Anyway, the most important numbers that day were 17-2, the final score. We absolutely crushed the Mariners to go up two games to one in a five-game series. We had incredible momentum, with another game at home.

Unfortunately, we squandered it the very next day, when Bartolo Colon ran out of steam late in the game. Then we returned to Seattle a day later to face our worst 2001 nemesis, Jamie Moyer. Once again, he shut us down completely. End of season.

I was really disappointed, because we had the M's on the ropes. But losing the division series didn't ruin the whole season. It didn't feel like 1999, when we won our division by 21 games and lost in the first round to a far inferior Boston team.

I considered 2001 to be a decent year. We faced down a strong Minnesota team to win our division, and extended a record-setting, 116-win Seattle team to five games.

But I must admit I'm getting awfully tired of losing the last game of the season.

CHAPTER 20

Looking Ahead

THE MOST IMPORTANT THING in my whole life showed up on September 12, 1995. That was the day Nicole gave birth to seven-pound Nicholas Enrique Vizquel at Fairview Hospital in Cleveland.

Although I was right there with Nicole at the hospital, my timing was lousy. I slipped out to grab some breakfast and baby Nico arrived while I was gone.

We knew we were having a boy from the ultrasound pictures taken five months earlier. Unlike some fathers, I wanted to know the baby's gender. I don't like surprises.

Choosing a name was a little more complicated.

I wanted to name him Manuel and call him Manny. But Nicole thought he would get teased too much.

Nicole's favorite uncle was named Nick. At least she *thought* he was named Nick. Nicole's dad later informed her that her uncle's name is actually Wesley, which nobody ever calls him. Nick is a nickname that dates all the way back to when her uncle was a little boy. Apparently, Uncle Wesley used to enjoy taking off all his clothes and running around naked, so the family started calling him "Nakey." That evolved into Nicky, which turned into Nick.

Nick—or Nicolas—was the only name Nicole and I could agree on.

Today, everybody calls our son Nico. I like it. It has a nice, unique ring.

Laying your eyes on your own child is an absolute miracle, the most beautiful sight you'll ever see. I look into Nico's eyes and say to myself, "Wow! How could we have made something like this?" Our boy is just so full of happiness.

One thing that worries me, now that he's getting older, is that Nico might turn into a spoiled kid because he is being brought up with money. I think one of my main jobs is to help him grow up like a normal human being, to be humble. I don't want him walking around talking about all the stuff we have. I want him to be laid-back and try to help the other kids.

So far, I like what I see.

A couple of years ago, in Seattle, his school held a little party and Nico invited me to go. They were handing out bags of candy to all the kids, but somebody miscalculated and three kids didn't get any. When Nico saw that, he took his own bag and gave it to one of the kids. He said, "Hey, I want to share it with you. Reach in and get some candy to take home."

When he did that, I got the chills. He did it completely on his own. You can't teach something like that to a toddler. That comes from deep inside. That showed me Nico has a great heart.

I'm trying to keep Nico on the right path using the Bible as a guide. I believe in the Bible, and I believe all the events in the Bible actually happened. It is the greatest book in the world. You can read about any subject under the sun and get something out of it that pertains to your daily life.

I certainly don't live my life exactly like the Bible tells me to. But I'm trying. I guess everybody is trying. It's not easy.

I hope my beliefs will carry through to my son. He has been baptized, and we try to get to church fairly often. I can't go during the baseball season, because we play almost every day, but the team holds a 15- or 20-minute chapel service on Sundays, and I try to attend.

As Nico gets older, I hope to show him that you get the best feelings in life when you are doing things for other people. Over the years I have worked with the United Way; with Young Audiences, an arts education program in Cleveland; with Schools Now, which helps raise funds for local schools; with the Children's Miracle Network for Rainbow Babies & Children's Hospital in Cleveland; and, of course, with World Vision and *Omar y Amigos*.

I'm gratified that people have noticed my attitude toward life. After the 1996 season, I was given the Hutch Award, named after former pitcher Fred Hutchinson and given each year to the one big-league player who "best exemplifies character, desire and fighting spirit." In 1998, I was the Tribe's nominee for the Roberto Clemente Award, given to the player who combines outstanding skills on the field with solid community service.

I want Nico to realize that it's important to give back to your community.

Whether he follows me in baseball, though, is entirely up to him.

Nico started playing soccer at age five, and I can see he has athletic talent and is very competitive. But I certainly won't push him to excel in sports. My dad and mom didn't push me hard. I think you have to let the child pick and choose. You need to be there to support and encourage him, but you shouldn't force him to play a game.

Some of the fathers of kids on my childhood teams would constantly tell their kids what to do and how to do it. And at the end of the game, those fathers would tell anyone who would listen, "My kid is great." I hated that. I told my mom and dad, "Please don't ever talk like that about me. That's really embarrassing."

When it comes to youth sports, some parents are out of control. It's worse today than ever, because so many parents seem to think their kid is going to grow up and play professional sports. In most cases, that's simply not going to happen. The odds are just too great.

Parents were pushy when I was a kid, too. I remember in particular one of the dads on my youth team. They lived in a house about 40 minutes outside the city, and the dad was a baseball fanatic. He had a batting tee and a net you could hit balls into. He

ran us through a bunch of baseball exercises, as well as other ac-
tivities. It was very regimented, almost like military training. Here
we were, only 12, 13, 14 years old, and this guy would make us do
all this baseball stuff and then put us in a room and tell us to read
books. We certainly weren't going to read any books if nobody
was watching. We'd just sit in there and tell jokes to each other.

But I loved going to his house, because I couldn't do much on
the busy streets outside my home. These trips were like a vacation for me. I'd spend most of my weekends at his house, trying to
improve my game. The father helped me a lot. But I wasn't his kid,
and I could leave if I wanted to. He didn't really help his own kid,
because his kid was totally intimidated. The poor boy was scared
to death when his dad was watching, terrified of making an error.

The man meant well, but he didn't understand the impact he
was having on his own boy.

YOU CERTAINLY LOOK AT THINGS differently when you become a
parent. A baby changes your whole life. You even start acting different. You try to be more serious. Well, at least in the beginning.
After a while, I realized that I can't be too serious because basically I'm just another kid.

I enjoy playing Nintendo as much as Nico does. Heck, sometimes *I* invite *him* to play.

I saw a bumper sticker on the back of a car once that said, "I
refuse to grow up." I think that's my unofficial slogan, too. My
mom says, "When are you going to grow up? You have a kid now,
and you can't be doing all that kind of stuff!" And I say, "Mom,
that's the only way I know how to have fun in this life!"

Even at the ballpark I'll do things other players wouldn't
dream of doing. Late in the 1999 season, Manny Ramirez was on
the brink of breaking the Indians' all-time record for RBIs in one
year. Midway through the game, we had a big lead, and Manny
came to the plate with Sandy Alomar and me on base. He crushed
a 440-foot homer to break the record, and the crowd went crazy.
They kept applauding long after he reached the dugout, trying to

bring him out for a curtain call. At first, he didn't respond, so, as a joke, I ran up the steps and tipped my cap.

Another fun moment happened earlier that same season, when I hit a grand slam in the bottom of the ninth inning to give the Indians a comeback win over Detroit. It was the first homer I had ever hit to win a game, even going back to Little League. As I jogged around third and saw a big group of players waiting to congratulate me, I slid across the plate like a happy Little Leaguer.

Baseball is, at its heart, a kid's game, and to play it well you need a kid's enthusiasm and sense of fun. I try to remember that.

The summer Nico was born was a summer for baseball babies. Carlos Giovanni Baerga was born 10 days before Nico, and Hayden Mackenzie Poole (son of pitcher Jim) was born eight days after.

Neither of those players is on my team now, which points out something else I have learned. In major league baseball, nothing stays the same. From 1994, my first year with the Indians, to 1998, only 13 percent of the players in the big leagues stayed with the same team. Heck, by the 2001 season, my seventh with the Indians, only two people had been with the team longer—Charles Nagy and Jim Thome.

EVENTUALLY, the calendar catches up with every baseball player. I will start to slow down a step and start to miss balls I used to grab. Eventually it will be obvious I should hang up my glove. But I want to play for as long as I possibly can. My contract runs through 2005, including the mutual option year. At the end of that season, I will be 39.

How long can a shortstop play? I'm not sure, but probably not much past 37. After that, I think I'll be able to move over to second base, a position that's a little less physically demanding.

And when I'm too old to play at all, I want to become a manager.

That may surprise some people, given all of my off-the-field interests. But baseball is in my blood. I love everything about the game of baseball. I even like the tempo, which some people find too slow. In baseball you can watch a pitch and have another 20 seconds before the next one. As a fan, you can look around a little, talk a bit to your friends, and then come right back to the game without missing a thing. It's an enjoyable way to pass the time.

In basketball, you have to watch the entire game intensely. As the players sprint up and down the court, you've got almost no time to reflect on what just happened. In soccer, the teams score only one or two goals per game, so you better not look away or you might miss the only thing worth seeing.

But in baseball, things are happening constantly. Every pitch has meaning. A baseball game is a long, complex chain of events that builds up for hours to the final pitch.

Baseball is also about adjusting. I love the fact that a pitcher can get you out three straight times, but then you can come up in the ninth inning and still have a chance to be the hero of the game.

UNLIKE SOME MODERN PLAYERS, who have barely heard of Babe Ruth, I appreciate the history of baseball. Although I don't sit down and read books about old-time players, I pay attention. I check out the pictures on the wall when I go to another team's ballpark. And when they show old highlights on the big video screens at the various ballparks, I watch. I like to know what happened before I arrived.

I really enjoyed the HBO movie about Ruth that came out in 2001. I already knew all the amazing things he did on the field, but this was about the kinds of things he did off the field, how well he treated people.

I'm not sure how the Babe would react to all the attention he would get today, when ballplayers are suffocated by the media. I would certainly never want to come back in another lifetime as Babe Ruth or Michael Jordan or any other athlete who is a household name. Given a choice, I'd return as a regular, average person. I have seen the side of the coin that involves fame, and it's not as rewarding as you might think. Yes, it's nice to have the money and the cars and all that, but it can also wear you down.

People are always saying athletes are different these days, and in many ways that's true. But it seems to me the key to being a good baseball manager is the same: your relationship with the players and the way they respond to you out on the field.

I've been in the big leagues for more than a decade now, and I've played under a lot of different managers and alongside many different players, each of whom has taught me something. I think I have developed a real good feel for the game.

Most big league managers didn't play at this level for more than a few years. I think that's why Joe Torre is such a great manager for the Yankees—he played in the bigs for a long time, played the game well, and spent a lot of time around great baseball minds. He knows how to treat people. He knows how to communicate. He knows what to say in a pressure situation. The reason he knows all those things is because he has been there.

The toughest aspect of being a manager is releasing a guy or sending him down to the minors. You can really shoot down a guy's confidence if you do it the wrong way. But if you say it in a nice way, it can change the player's whole perspective on how to get back to the big leagues.

I've seen a lot of cruel people in this game. When they don't like a player, they just put him in the doghouse and won't even talk to him. They completely bury the guy. There has to be a better way to deal with those situations.

I've seen all different styles, and I think I know what works and what doesn't.

I'm happy I was able to play for Lou Pinella in Seattle. He had been a star in the major leagues and was an incredibly intense person. He seems to have changed a lot since the days I played for him. In talking to some of the guys on the Seattle team today, they say he has really mellowed. Instead of screaming in their faces, he'll sit them down and talk to them calmly.

My first manager in the bigs, Jim LeFebvre, was another intense guy. The guy who followed him, Bill Plummer, was the opposite side of the coin. He was never a regular in the big leagues and was really distant.

My manager for six years in Cleveland, Mike Hargrove, had been a major league star and had a pretty good managerial temperament. He was laid-back in a lot of ways, but very structured in other ways. In spring training, for example, he had specific ideas on how he wanted things to run, and you had to go by the book.

Hargrove's successor, Charlie Manuel, is much looser in training camp. That's great for the veterans, who know what it takes to prepare themselves. But there's a fine line. If the veterans get too casual and don't show respect for the game, they set a bad example for the younger players.

Unfortunately, aspiring managers usually have to start in the minor leagues and work their way up to the majors, and I'm not sure I could go back to those long minor league bus trips. What I hope to do is start out in the bigs as a coach and eventually progress to manager.

NO MATTER WHAT my baseball future holds, I want to make sure I carve out the time to travel. I love seeing new places and learning about culture and history.

Some day I want to go to the Vatican to see the pope and look at those historic churches. I want to tour Europe and look at the museums and the artwork. I want to go to Egypt. I want to go to the Serengeti to look at wild animals.

People sometimes ask if I think one of my journeys will be an all-expenses-paid trip to Cooperstown, home of the Baseball Hall of Fame. Man, I hope so.

How many Gold Gloves does it take to make the Hall? I don't know. That worries me a bit, because people don't seem to value the defensive part of the game as much as they once did. On the other hand, slick-fielding second baseman Bill Mazeroski, who was inducted in 2001, had a lifetime batting average of only .260.

My countryman Luis Aparicio made the Hall, too, and he only hit .262—exactly the same as defensive wizard Ozzie Smith, who was voted into the Hall in 2002—the first year he was eligible. Compared to those guys, my career average—.274—looks pretty decent.

The vote may come down to how many years I am able to play. Longevity is definitely part of the equation.

I've been to Cooperstown briefly. We played an exhibition game there a few years ago. You drive along for miles and miles and, just when you begin to think all of central New York State is one big farm, up pops the town in the middle of nowhere. Unfortunately, we didn't have enough time to tour the museum itself, but the town is just beautiful. I love the way the baseball theme is carried all through the place.

Even if I don't make the Hall of Fame, I won't have any regrets. If somebody gave me the chance to go back and change something in my life, I think I'd pass. Life has treated me well. I come from a great family; my mom and dad are still together; I've never been in any serious trouble; I've had a great baseball career; and, with Nico and Nicole, I have a great family of my own.

I don't regret a thing.

Well, okay, I regret not having more hair on my head. I always liked long hair. I miss my hair. It just won't grow anymore.

Even with a golden glove, nobody fields 1.000.

Acknowledgments

Special thanks to colleague Terry Pluto, who helped me understand the ground rules and lent his moral support; Tribe media relations manager Curtis Danburg, who responded to even the most ridiculous requests with a perpetual smile; Akron Beacon Journal executives Thom Fladung and Jan Leach, who sprung me from professional lockup long enough to write a book; Tribe vice-president Bob DiBiasio, who was just as helpful after six division titles as he was during the 100-loss seasons of the 1980s; manager Charlie Manuel, who granted me full access; and the talented staff at Gray & Co.

Nor would this book have been possible without the generous assistance of the following people: Bob Barlow, Kimberly Barth, Chris Bosio, Jolbert Cabrera, Tony Chiricosta, F. W. Cropp, Steve Darlington, Mark Dawidziak, Juan Escalante, Dick Feagler, Susie Giuliano, Dick Goddard, Jeff Gravley, Tom Hamilton, Mike Harrington, Mike Hegan, Marilyn Holley, Ed Kemp, Susan Kirkman, Brad Koltas, Carlos Lopez, Rick Manning, Phil Masturzo, Joe McGee, John "Face" McMillen, Manuel Mejias, John Murphy, Bill Needle, Jeff Nelson, Ray Negron, Sheldon Ocker, Steve Owendoff, Larry Pantages, Don Rosenberg, Kevin Salyer, Mike Seghi, Richard Spotz, Jr., Michael Stanley, Bart Swain, John Telich, Matt Underwood, and Nicole Vizquel.

— Bob Dyer

About the Authors

OMAR VIZQUEL is the starting shortstop for the Cleveland Indians. He has played in the major leagues since 1989 and has won nine consecutive Gold Glove awards for fielding excellence (an American League record). He has twice been selected for the American League All-Star team, and he has appeared in two World Series.

BOB DYER has won 17 regional and national writing awards since joining the *Akron Beacon Journal* in 1984. In 1993, he was one of the lead writers for a yearlong series that won a Pulitzer Prize. He has served as a feature writer, radio and TV writer, and columnist. A life-long resident of Northeast Ohio, he is a graduate of West Geauga High School and the College of Wooster. He lives in Copley, Ohio, with his wife and two daughters.